on track ...

J. Geils Band

every album, every song

James Romag

sonicbondpublishing.com

Sonicbond Publishing Limited
www.sonicbondpublishing.co.uk
Email: info@sonicbondpublishing.co.uk

First Published in the United Kingdom 2024
First Published in the United States 2024

British Library Cataloguing in Publication Data:
A Catalogue record for this book is available from the British Library

Copyright James Romag 2024

ISBN 978-1-78952-332-4

The right of James Romag to be identified
as the author of this work has been asserted by him
in accordance with the Copyright, Designs and Patents Act 1988.
All rights reserved. No part of this publication may be reproduced, stored in a
retrieval system or transmitted in any form or by any means, electronic, mechanical,
photocopying, recording or otherwise, without prior permission in writing from
Sonicbond Publishing Limited

Typeset in ITC Garamond Std & ITC Avant Garde Gothic
Printed and bound in England

Graphic design and typesetting: Full Moon Media

Follow us on social media:
Twitter: https://twitter.com/SonicbondP
Instagram: www.instagram.com/sonicbondpublishing_/
Facebook: www.facebook.com/SonicbondPublishing/

Linktree QR code:

Special thanks to
Sara Romag, Bruce Arnold, Crispin Cioe, Peter Corriston,
Susie Cullen, J. Douglas, Patrica Glennon, Bob Hinkle, Daniel Klein,
Lance Kovar, Stephen Lambe, Paul Lanning, Alen MacWeeney, Jim Mazza,
Mario Medious (The Big M), Steve Nelson, Stephen Paley, Raymond Paret,
Deborah Konczal Pastor, David Plastik, Francis Robinson, Richard Salwitz,
Dominic Sanderson, Speedy Schexnayder, Paul Shapiro, Derek Szabo,
Bill Szymczyk, David Thoener, Steve Tomlinson,
UMass Amherst Libraries Tom Benedek Collection,
Thomas Weschler and everyone who's ever been part
of the J. Geils family.

This book is dedicated to the memory of John W. Geils, Jr.

Would you like to write for Sonicbond Publishing?
At Sonicbond Publishing we are always on the look-out for authors, particularly for our two main series:

On Track. Mixing fact with in depth analysis, the On Track series examines the work of a particular musical artist or group. All genres are considered from easy listening and jazz to 60s soul to 90s pop, via rock and metal.

On Screen. This series looks at the world of film and television. Subjects considered include directors, actors and writers, as well as entire television and film series. As with the On Track series, we balance fact with analysis.

While professional writing experience would, of course, be an advantage the most important qualification is to have real enthusiasm and knowledge of your subject. First-time authors are welcomed, but the ability to write well in English is essential.

Sonicbond Publishing has distribution throughout Europe and North America, and all books are also published in E-book form. Authors will be paid a royalty based on sales of their book.

Further details are available from www.sonicbondpublishing.co.uk. To contact us, complete the contact form there or email info@sonicbondpublishing.co.uk

on track ...
J. Geils Band

Contents

Author's Note 7
Introduction: It's Got To Come Out – Early Days 8
The J. Geils Band (1970) 19
The Morning After (1971) 27
'Live' Full House (1972) 36
Bloodshot (1973) 41
Ladies Invited (1973) 48
Nightmares ...And Other Tales From The Vinyl Jungle (1974) 56
Hotline (1975) 63
Live – Blow Your Face Out (1976) 71
Monkey Island (1977) 76
Sanctuary. (1978) 85
House Party Live In Germany (1979) 93
Love Stinks (1980) 96
Freeze-Frame (1981) 103
Showtime! (1982) 112
You're Gettin' Even While I'm Gettin' Odd (1984) 117
Start All Over Again – Latter Days 123
Official Compilations 137
Bibliography 140

Author's Note

No fewer than five times have The J. Geils Band been nominated for the Rock And Roll Hall Of Fame in Cincinnati, yet in defiance of all logic, they've never been inducted. It's inconceivable how a band who brought honest, authentic blues and r&b to a wider audience while experimenting and creating original rock tunes from those roots – eventually climbing to the top of the album and single charts – doesn't get the recognition it deserves. Shooting their shot and blowing your face out, The J. Geils Band were one of the hardest working bands in the business and turned every show into a house party. While the band's work ethic meant live performances were a guaranteed success night after night, it took record sales a while to catch up, but when it happened, it happened bigger than anyone imagined possible.

The J. Geils Band On Track is not an attempt to identify the best Geils album or song or the best era of the band. It's merely a celebration of Those Bad Boys from Boston and a comprehensive guide and companion to their incredible music.

Note: For the sake of clarity, John Geils (the man) is referred to as Jay, the legal name he used for his later recordings and appearances. The group is referred to as The J. Geils Band, J. Geils, or Geils.

Introduction: It's Got To Come Out – Early Days

After well over a decade of nonstop touring and recording, even when at the top of the music charts around the world, casual fans still often assumed The J. Geils Band's frontman was Jay himself. That was not the case, of course, as Jay was the band's guitarist (and sometime mandolinist and saxophonist) who was content in the background burning it up with greasy licks and raunchy riffs, while it was the jive-talking, kinetic, rail-thin, microphone stand-vaulting Peter Wolf – 'Woofa Goofa' – who served as the Boston, Massachusetts-based group's singer and lead crowd instigator.

The band's namesake, John W. Geils, Jr., was clear on what he wanted to do in life by the time he was in his teens. In a February 2013 interview on Public Broadcasting Station WGBH's *Greater Boston* show, John said that when he sat down with a guidance counsellor to chart his future beyond school, he told the counsellor he wanted to spend his life as a race car driver or a jazz musician. John managed to do both, but not before finding fame and eventual fortune, cranking out unforgettable blues, r&b, funk, soul, rock, and pop music along the way.

John, known from a young age as Jay or simply J, was born in New York City and grew up in New Jersey. His father, an engineer and sports car enthusiast, took him to his first sportscar race at age ten, to a Louis Armstrong concert about the same time and to a Miles Davis show not long after. Both racing and music left an indelible mark and became life-long passions. His parents listened to jazz music around the house, introducing Jay to Benny Goodman, Duke Ellington, Count Basie, and Artie Shaw, and it was inevitable that Jay learned trumpet (and briefly tried drums) at an early age. In high school, Jay was in the marching band, as well as the school's physics, mathematics, and car clubs. He also found time to date schoolmate Meryl Streep, who later gained fame as an Academy Award-winning actress. By the early 1960s, Jay was learning guitar and soaking up blues artists like Muddy Waters and Howlin' Wolf.

In 1964, after graduating high school, Jay attended Boston's Northeastern University (where he played trumpet in the marching band) intending to study mechanical engineering. Within a year, he transferred to Worcester Polytechnic Institute, about 45 miles outside of Boston. At Worcester, almost immediately, he met Daniel Klein.

Danny Klein was born in the Bronx, New York, and his family moved to New Jersey when he was around six years old. Unlike Jay, his musical background consisted mainly of listening to rhythm and blues and other music on AM radio. Following high school, Klein arrived at Worcester Polytechnic Institute in the autumn of 1964 to pursue chemical engineering. At the start of his sophomore year, he met newly transferred Jay Geils. By this point, Jay was focused on guitar rather than trumpet, and when Klein and Jay decided to make some music together, Klein asked Jay what he should play, and Jay recommended bass. Klein then crafted his own washtub bass with a broomstick and a single string and he and Jay were soon playing jug band-style folk music. Unlike other members of The J. Geils Band, Klein didn't start playing an instrument until he was about 21 years old – save for a few grammar school lessons in clarinet – when he and Jay began working together.

Richard Salwitz (aka Pittsfield Slim and later Magic Dick) was born in Connecticut and was studying physics at Worcester when he happened upon Klein and Jay jamming in the student quadrangle. In a 2023 YouTube interview with fellow harpist Mark Hummel, Salwitz said he had a marine harmonica (or two) in his pocket at the time and asked if he could sit in with the two other musicians. At that, the three-piece jug band known as Snoopy and the Sopwith Camels (not to be confused with the San Francisco band Sopwith Camel) came into being. Performing publicly by late 1966, the jug band played acoustic, folk-leaning blues and was influenced by The Paul Butterfield Blues Band, among others. Jay sometimes played a manda-banj – a small banjo – and Dick had his own hyrdazoo invention, a kazoo inserted into a beer can filled with water, which produced a bubbling kazoo sound. Vocals in Snoopy and the Sopwith Camels were handled by both Klein and Dick. Dick recalled, 'We tried with a fourth guy (whose name is lost to time), a second guitarist for a brief period', but it didn't last.

Dick's first harp was given to him when he was three years old, sick in bed with a fever of about 104 degrees (40 Celsius). His mother gave him a Marine band harmonica in an attempt to cheer him up and certainly succeeded. 'I remember my mother giving me that marine band harmonica', said Dick. 'I remember it almost photographically' – but surprisingly, Dick didn't pursue the harp at the time. He picked up the trumpet when he was in the third grade, at age nine, and in the early 1970s, while in The J. Geils Band, he took trumpet lessons for about five years at Berklee College of Music in Boston. It wasn't until 1966 that Dick started to get serious about the harp, not long before he serendipitously happened upon Klein and Jay in the student quad.

The band's name, Snoopy and The Sopwith Camels, was likely a reference to the character of Snoopy in Charles Schulz's daily newspaper comic strip *Peanuts*, which often featured the imaginative beagle Snoopy as a World War I ace pilot flying atop his doghouse, named the Sopwith Camel (a British biplane). In late 1966/early 1967, The Royal Guardsmen had a huge hit with their song 'Snoopy Vs. The Red Baron', which may also have wedged itself in Jay's subconscious and influenced the group's name. The band lasted no more than six months, playing sorority houses and similar venues around the Boston area. Jay was the one more inclined to take a leadership role and it wasn't long before the three musicians were performing under the banner of The J. Geils Blues Band. When the band's sound shifted from acoustic jug band to blues, and Jay made the move from acoustic to electric guitar, Klein gave up the washtub and rented an electric bass. Although Klein is left-handed, he used a right-hand instrument because it was easier to find and less expensive than renting a left-hand bass and taught himself to play right-handed. Years later, Klein, known as The Ace on Bass and Dr. Funk, took lessons at Berklee for a short while.

Eventually, the band members did some soul-searching and had to decide whether to pursue music or focus on their studies. It was clear it wouldn't be possible to chase after both with success, but academics were a sure thing, while music was a great uncertainty. They made the difficult decision to drop out of college and move to Boston around late 1967, soon playing gigs at places like the Unicorn Coffee House. Influencing Klein's decision to focus on music was a university field trip to New Jersey, where he took a side jaunt to New York to see blues great Muddy Waters. The core of The J. Geils Blues Band remained Jay, Danny Klein and Magic Dick, but other musicians came and went, including Al Couchon on vocals, guitar and mandolin, followed by Tom Rand on drums and possibly vocals and Harold Stone handling keyboards and possibly mandolin. By the autumn of 1967, Stone was at Navy basic training and Rand was headed to the Army Reserves.

Along the way, in late 1967 or early 1968, The J. Geils Blues Band came under David Jenks and Ray Paret's Amphion Management, although any contracts that have surfaced from that period show Jay's signature on the agreements (using his full name of John W. Geils, Jr.). Paret was the one who had the contacts and started getting the band booked at venues like The Boston Tea Party and The Catacombs. Paret was key in bringing in Keith Lahteinen (from the Boston group Ultimate Spinach) on drums and vocals since Amphion Management was already handling Ultimate Spinach and had secured Spinach's contract with MGM Records. Lahteinen 'was a big blues fan', said Paret, 'and that's how (Geils) started to become a real blues band.'

After all this time, the exact roster and timeline of band members are difficult to pin down. Dick remembered someone named Joel (whose last name is lost to history) in the drum seat either before or after Lahteinen. Some accounts mention George Leh on vocals, but it's probable he was never in Geils, just a musician friend of the band. A March 1971 *Creem* article reflected on the beginnings of the band, a hazy matter even by then. Jay recalled some of the early members, even if he couldn't remember all their names, and mentioned 'a tall dude with an extravagant moustache... on drums and vocals', who was likely Lahteinen. During Lahteinen's tenure in Geils, Paret ushered the band into Petrucci & Atwell Studios (renamed Intermedia Sound studios in 1971 and by then partially owned by Paret) in Boston to cut some recordings. There's no record of what was recorded, and the demos have never been released.

Sometime in 1964, parallel to Jay and the others assembling Snoopy and the Sopwith Camels and then The J. Geils Blues Band, artist and musician Paul Shapiro was running a frame shop on Newbury Street in Boston, next door to radio station WBCN. Boston native Stephen Jo Bladd, another artist, worked a few doors down in another frame shop. 'We used to talk about music', said Shapiro. 'One day (Bladd) said, 'I've always wanted to play the drums.' I said,

'Buy some.' And he did. It's funny; he could play them immediately.' Initially, the two would jam together with no real plans. As Shapiro explained, 'We used to fool around, nothing serious.' Then, one day, Shapiro asked Bladd if he had any musician friends. Bladd mentioned a fellow art student named Doug Slade, who played guitar, but it still wasn't a proper band. One evening, Shapiro, Bladd, and Slade went to a party in Brookline Village (in the Boston metropolitan area) to perform, but nothing was rehearsed and nothing was official.

'We started playing Sonny Boy Williamson's 'One Way Out',' said Shapiro, 'and this guy walks up and it was Peter Wolf (then Peter Blankfield). He said, 'Let me try singing with you guys.' So he starts singing and pulls out a harmonica.' Like Dick stumbling upon Jay and Klein in the student quadrangle at Worcester, it was a serendipitous meeting.

Growing up in the Bronx, New York, Peter Wolf developed a love of music, absorbing everything from country and folk to doo-wop, r&b, jazz, and blues. His grandmother was an actress, his father a musician, and his older sister briefly a dancer on *The Big Beat*, a rock and roll show on New York television hosted by disc jockey Alan Freed. Wolf attended the High School of Music and Art in Harlem, which gave him the opportunity to attend shows at the Apollo Theater on an almost weekly basis. It was at the Apollo where Wolf saw acts like James Brown, Jackie Wilson, Don Covay (whose song 'The Usual Place' would be recorded on Geils' second album and with whom Wolf would later write several songs), and Dyke and the Blazers (Dyke's 'So Sharp' would be covered on Geils' second album). Soaking up those acts at the Apollo, Wolf learned the importance of real showmanship, of dressing for the stage, of creating an event, of working the crowd all the way to the very back row, of leaving everything he had on that stage.

Wolf has said he's afflicted with dyslexia and never officially graduated, but after leaving high school, he did some travelling and then procured a scholarship to Boston's School of the Museum of Fine Arts. The school had no student dormitories and Wolf has mentioned in several interviews that upon arrival in Boston, he spent his first night at a YMCA and his second night sleeping outdoors near the river. By chance, the following day, he met another art student who was looking for a roommate. That student was David Lynch, later a film and television writer and director (*The Elephant Man*, *Twin Peaks*) and the two shared an apartment for about a year. In Boston, it wasn't long before Wolf met Shapiro, Bladd, and Slade at that fateful party in Brookline Village and joined them for 'One Way Out'.

Reflecting on the four of them, Shapiro said, 'It was all very primitive.' Even so, that was the point where Shapiro told the others, 'Let's form a band.' He added, 'I had been masterminding forming a band for a while. I was heavily into blues… especially Chicago blues.' Doug Slade brought in his friend Joe Clark on bass, and things started happening quickly. Slade and Clark had been in other bands, but for Bladd, Shapiro, and Wolf, it was their first band (not counting when Wolf's The Three Imps made their one and only

appearance at a talent show when he was 11 years old). It was Bladd who came up with the band's name. Shapiro said, 'We went through this day trying to come up with a name and Stephen came up with The Hallucinations.'
As things started to get more serious, Blankfield changed his name to Wolf. There are differing stories as to how that came to be. One version claimed it was after his actress grandmother's surname, but it was also likely a nod to Howlin' Wolf. In a July 2023 interview with the *Boston Globe*, Wolf said it was a nickname he'd already had from his younger days in the Bronx.

Wolf knew Boston musician Barry Tashian, whose band The Remains had a regional hit covering Bo Diddley's 'Diddy Wah Diddy' and had toured for three weeks with The Beatles on their final US tour. When Tashian heard The Hallucinations, he proclaimed they were 'America's answer to The Rolling Stones', a label which carried over to The J. Geils Band and is often mentioned in reviews from Geils' early days. Tashian provided the band with his music manager and booking agent and that autumn, around October 1965, 'suddenly, this thing becomes official', said Shapiro. 'Before that, it was just fun. And instantly we start getting booked into these amazing gigs.' The Hallucinations began performing with acts like John Lee Hooker ('Serves You Right To Suffer', 'Boom Boom') and backing groups like the Shirelles ('Will You Love Me Tomorrow', 'Dedicated To The One I Love') and the Chiffons ('He's So Fine'). As the band became more successful, they started practising five days a week in Slade's loft and getting more professional. Though the band was young and learning, already 'Wolf was a great frontman', said Shapiro.

The band's repertoire included blues and r&b numbers like Junior Wells' 'Messin' With The Kid' and Howlin' Wolf's 'Smokestack Lightning.' Though Wolf was the lead singer, Shapiro handled vocals on songs like Willie Dixon's 'Wang Dang Doodle' and Bo Diddley's 'You Can't Judge A Book By The Cover.' With their growing reputation, The Hallucinations became the de facto house band at Ray Riepen and David Hahn's Boston Tea Party, a club venue that had started hosting rock bands in early 1967. Steve Nelson managed the place from late August 1967 through June 1968 (after Riepen bought out Hahn), and as he wrote in his book *Gettin' Home*, The Hallucinations played more shows at the Tea Party than any other band. Nelson wrote that Wolf 'really knew how to work an audience and had the charisma to do it.'

In early 1968, Riepen worked his way into Boston radio station WBCN. WBCN had recently switched from a dying classical music format to easy listening, which fared no better. It was Riepen who advocated for a freeform, rock music format on the growing FM scene and one of the first DJs Riepen hired was Wolf. On 15 March 1968, following fellow DJ Joe Rogers, Wolf was on the air as WBCN's second disc jockey when it transitioned to its counter-culture format. Wolf's show, 'The All-Night House Party', allowed him to play music from his own considerable collection of blues, soul, and r&b records and interview musicians like Muddy Waters, Van Morrison, and Howlin' Wolf, setting a pattern for bringing lesser-known musicians and songs to a greater audience. It also helped Wolf develop his jive-talking style as the Woofa Goofa Mama Toofa.

Charles Daniels, known as Big Charles or The Master Blaster (and not be confused with country music star Charlie Daniels), served as unofficial emcee at The Boston Tea Party and was friends with The Hallucinations and later The J. Geils Band. When Wolf started his overnight shifts at WBCN, Daniels was often on air with him, sometimes filling in when Wolf was performing late night Hallucinations gigs and not available. In the documentary *WBCN And The American Revolution*, Daniels said he was the one who christened Wolf 'Woofa Goofa.' As all of this was happening, The J. Geils Blues Band made the move from Worcester to the Boston area. And when Shapiro saw Geils, he said, 'they were very good. I was impressed.'

Eventually, Ray Riepen took over management of The Hallucinations, but with the band's gigs rapidly dropping off and Shapiro wanting to get back to painting, Shapiro made the decision to dissolve The Hallucinations. As The Hallucinations were disbanding, The J. Geils Blues Band were looking for a new drummer and singer. Wolf was already somewhat familiar with the musicians and talked to Jay, Klein, and Dick one night after they performed as a trio at a coffeehouse. Manager Ray Paret facilitated the arrangement and shortly afterward, Wolf and Bladd were officially in The J. Geils Blues Band. In 1968, the five-piece band were playing regularly in the Boston area and soon found themselves in Montreal, Canada, performing what were essentially short residencies at The New Penelope Club in May and September. Taking a cue from the shows Wolf had experienced at the Apollo, the band were developing their act, wearing stage clothes, working on choreography, dropping down on their knees, riling up the crowd and striving to put on a visual show to match the music. Dick borrowed a move from blues great James Cotton and would perform a somersault in the middle of a harp solo (while using a corded microphone, no less). In the early days, the band would open their sets by playing a couple of instrumentals to get the audience primed; then Wolf would come out and stir up the crowd even more.

By mid-1968, the five-man band had dropped 'Blues' from their name so as not to restrict their repertoire and became The J. Geils Band (though as late as 1971, some shows were still promoted as The J. Geils Blues Band). They kept the J. Geils name because they were under contract with Amphion Management and felt they could always change the name later. But it was obvious they'd already built a reputation and a following and rather than start all over again with something new, they retained the Geils name. In addition to dropping 'Blues' from the band name, Dick was looking to change his name from Pittsfield Slim. Sitting around brainstorming, it was Klein who suggested 'Magic Dick', in the tradition of blues artists with stage names like Chicago Slim or Magic Sam.

Around 1968, the music industry – MGM Records in particular – had started trying to hype music coming out of Boston as the 'Bosstown Sound.' Though it was contrived and there was no real 'Bosstown Sound', the intent was to create east coast competition with the counterculture San Francisco Sound. MGM Records, part of the Metro-Goldwyn-Mayer movie complex, signed several Boston-area bands, including Ultimate Spinach, in the late 1960s. In the book *The Sound Of Our Town*, Brett Milano claimed that in late 1968 MGM offered Geils a recording contract, which they nearly signed. According to Jay, the deal was similar to what they later were offered with Atlantic Records. He said the contract was for 'something ridiculous like $25,000 to make six albums. But it sounded good when we were lucky to make $600 a gig.' Jay stated it was Wolf who recommended they should pass on the contract because it 'doesn't feel right, it doesn't ring true.' Ray Paret, whose Amphion Management had signed several other bands to MGM, disputed that account and said Geils were never offered a contract with MGM. It's possible Jay was simply aware of what MGM was offering other bands at the time and knew that if they were made the same offer, it wouldn't be worth pursuing.

On 6 November 1968, The J. Geils Band performed for WGBH's *Mixed Bag* series. The band was still a five-piece and performed (in the studio) a 30-minute set consisting of 'Dust My Broom' (as recorded by Elmore James), Sam and Dave's 'When Something Is Wrong With My Baby', Sonny Boy Williamson's 'One Way Out', Chuck Willis' 'Too Late', John Lee Hooker's 'It's My Own Fault' and Wilson Pickett's 'Something You Got.' Not long after, in March 1969, they played their first shows at Steve Nelson's Woodrose Ballroom in South Deerfield, Massachusetts (immortalised on the debut album's 'Hard Drivin' Man').

Also in March of 1969, student Paul Lanning brought together five musicians – dubbed The Boston Blues All-Stars – for a one-off live performance which he recorded. The All-Stars were Jay, Danny Klein and Dick, with Barry Tashian and William (Bill) Briggs from The Remains. 'It was my final project in a TV production class at Boston University', said Lanning. 'The performers were all friends of mine who had occasionally been jamming together and were pleased to be taped doing what they loved to do.' Unfortunately, the four-song set was never broadcast as intended, but Lanning's video showcased the musicians' already considerable skills. Tashian sings two songs; one ('Chicken Shack') is an instrumental and Dick sings John Brim's 'Be Careful (What You Do)', which Geils would later record for 1975's *Hotline* album, with Wolf on vocals. Lanning said that both Jay and Tashian mentored him, and 'it was Jay who told me, 'When you don't feel good, you always still give the audience 100% of what they came for. When you *do* feel good, you give *200%*.' The entire band shared that ethos.' Years later, Lanning worked again with Geils when he was part of EMI America, Geils' record label after leaving Atlantic.

Sometime in 1969, the five-man band signed to Atlantic Records, thanks to the persistent efforts of Mario 'The Big M' Medious. Medious, an FM promotions director for Atlantic, was backstage at The Boston Tea Party with musician Dr. John and heard Geils performing 'Serves You Right To Suffer.'

'By the time I got out to the stage to see who they were', said Medious, 'they were off the stage. So I went back to the dressing room and asked, 'Where are the brothers who were just playing that blues set?' and Peter Wolf said, 'That was us, man.' It freaked me right out. I thought they were some brothers from Chicago.' Returning to Atlantic's offices in New York, Medious recommended to label president Ahmet Ertegun and partner Jerry Wexler that they sign Geils, but the two weren't interested.

Medious was undeterred. Among other efforts, he booked Geils a gig at a club in New York 'up on 71st street, a small place', he said. 'I invited Bill Graham, Ahmet Ertegun', and some others. Everyone was impressed, yet Ertegun still had no interest in signing Geils. However, after enduring several more weeks of badgering from Medious, Ertegun and Wexler finally relented. It helped that Wexler knew Wolf's friend Jon Landau (whom Wolf had met through manager Ray Paret), and when Wexler called Landau to inquire about the band, Landau echoed Medious' enthusiasm.

When it was time to sign a contract, Wolf went with Landau to Atlantic's New York offices. By this time, Paret was no longer managing the band. Fred Lewis, aka Freddie Blue, the band's road manager, along with Dee Anthony, had taken over management. But no management was present at the contract signing. Despite advice from Medious on negotiating the contract, Geils were more focused on the art, rather than the business, of music. Jerry Wexler intended to put Geils on the Atco label, the more suitable pop-oriented subsidiary of Atlantic. The band, fans of Atlantic's r&b and blues artists, insisted on getting their music issued on Atlantic Records – home to Ray Charles, Wilson Pickett, and Aretha Franklin – and Wexler agreed. It wasn't unusual at the time for the big record labels to structure contracts in ways that didn't benefit the musicians, and without any lawyers or managers present (and ignoring Medious' advice), a less-than-favourable contract was signed with no regard to the band for things like the length of the contract or royalties. Manager Anthony was later able to secure a slightly better contract, but it still favoured the record company over the group.

Landau, soon to gain recognition as a music critic, producer, and Bruce Springsteen's manager, had just finished producing Detroit band MC5's *Back In The USA*. When it came time for Geils' first album, Wexler sent Landau with the band to GM recording studios in Detroit – not necessarily to produce it, but to get a feel for what the band might accomplish. After a short time, everyone involved felt the essence of the band was missing. With no one satisfied with the results, the band returned to Boston and nothing from those original sessions has been released. Klein stated that the band's time in Detroit never progressed beyond basic drum and bass work and no songs were ever completed. It wasn't long after that session in Detroit that keyboard player Seth Justman joined the band.

Justman was born in Washington, DC, lived briefly in Boston, and grew up in Atlantic City, New Jersey, before moving back to the Washington, DC, area in 1967. Of all Geils members, Justman had the most experience performing in bands. He'd been playing keyboards since about age five, studying classical music as a child in Boston before moving to Atlantic City, and in bands by the time he was 12 or 13 years old, playing dances, bar mitzvahs, sweet sixteen parties, and even a nudist colony dance. Like the rest of The J. Geils Band, he was a blues and r&b fan, influenced by keyboard players like Jimmy Smith and Ray Charles. By 1968, he was in the band Open Road (later called Sky Cobb) but left to move to Boston to attend school in 1969. On his first night in Boston, his new roommate recommended they check out some live music, specifically Geils, who were performing at The Catacombs. Justman, 18 at the time, was immediately impressed and asked if he could sit in with Wolf, Jay, Klein, Dick, and Bladd. They turned him down. Justman kept showing up at their gigs, doggedly making his case to join them. Still, they said no. Biding his time, Justman worked with other musicians, even sitting in with George Leh's band Swallow at least once. Eventually, after several months, Geils relented.

Justman proved to be the magical missing piece and was possibly in the band by late 1969, yet the timeline is murky. Although Geils hadn't recorded yet as a six-piece and had no records, a promotional poster advertising three shows at the Stonehenge Club in Ipswich, Massachusetts, from 31 December 1969 to 2 January 1970 declared, 'Atlantic record stars the J. GEILS BAND', accompanied by a photo of the six-piece band. Yet, a contract signed on 5 February 1970 for a one-hour show (to be performed on 15 February) at Assumption College in Worcester, Massachusetts, lists the band as 'five musicians.' Days later, on 8 February, another contract (for a 27 February show) with the Rhode Island School of Design shows 'six musicians' in the band. Paul Lanning, who had videotaped Jay, Dick and Klein for his All-Stars student project, recalled being a guest of the band for a show at The Boston Tea Party in early 1970 and Justman wasn't yet in the band.

Steve Nelson, part of the promotion team putting on shows at The Paramount Theater in Springfield, said in his book *Gettin' Home* that he made a black and white videotape of Geils on stage at The Paramount the last weekend of April 1970. He captured performances of 'First I Look At The Purse' and 'Serves You Right To Suffer', but that video has never been released. In June of that same year, before their debut album had been released, Mario Medious managed to get Geils on the bill (along with Atlantic acts Dr. John, Cactus and Eugene McDaniels) at The Alternative Media Conference, an invitation-only event. Reports of the event said it was held at Goddard College in Plainfield, Vermont, though Medious stated the true location was Bangor, Maine. Medious donated over $3,000 to the event and provided the mostly unknown bands. There, Geils performed on an outdoor stage in front of record company promotors, DJs from FM freeform radio stations across the US, and underground newspaper reporters, providing extensive exposure for this band who didn't yet have a record in the shops (a recording of their set was allegedly later broadcast on WBCN). It would be only a matter of time and more hard work before the rest of the country and the world discovered Those Bad Boys from Boston.

As great as the music was, for Geils, it was never about just the music. It was about putting on a show and bringing a house party to the fans – rattling the rafters and reaching even those ticket holders in the balcony or way, way in the back ('there ya go, darlin'') – night after night, and turning those fans on to the greats like Albert Collins and John Lee Hooker and, of course, The J. Geils Band themselves. The college of musical knowledge was in session at every performance, and they educated their audiences on the performers and songwriters they revered while also creating their own unique sound. The audience wasn't there to watch the show; they were there to be a part of it. Through it all, Geils never took their audiences for granted and played each show as if their lives depended on it.

Related Tracks
'Messin' With The Kid' By The Hallucinations (Mel London) (2:53) (1968) [Unreleased]
The Hallucinations never officially released any recordings, but their slightly ramped-up version of the 1960 Junior Wells up-tempo blues tune 'Messin' With The Kid' surfaced in the 2010s. The lineup of Paul Shapiro, Bladd, Wolf, Doug Slade and Joe Clark handles the song with conviction and, apart from the saxophones, remains true to Wells' version. Guitar, drums, and bass start the tune and settle into a groove, with Bladd proving to be a powerhouse even then. Wolf's vocals are suitably gruff as he comes in with, 'Yeah, what's this you hear goin' around town.' Midway through, he lays down a harmonica solo and after another verse, Shapiro takes the spotlight with a guitar break before another verse. The track winds down with more harmonica and a big finish. From this one recording, it's easy to see how the Hallucinations became the house band at the Boston Tea Party. The Hallucinations possibly also recorded Howlin' Wolf's 'Smokestack Lightning' around the same time, but it has never surfaced.

The Bathroom Tapes (circa 1968) [Unreleased]
At the Kempton Street apartment shared by Jay, Klein and Magic Dick, the band regularly rehearsed and worked out songs. It was there that the legendary *Bathroom Tapes* were born. The name came about because Wolf recorded his vocals in the bathroom for the echo it provided while the others played in the front of the apartment. Although the recordings were alleged to have been played on Wolf's overnight WBCN radio program, they have never been released and the contents are mostly a mystery. Dick recalled that one of the tracks on *The Bathroom Tapes* might've been an original named 'Banana Blues.' Wolf has mentioned that their cover of 'Homework' was also part of it.

The New Penelope Club Live Recordings WBCN Broadcast (1968)
In September 1968, Boston's WBCN broadcast a show recorded at Montreal, Canada's New Penelope Club on Sherbrooke Street, where the five-man J. Geils Blues Band was working its second week-long booking following a similar stint in May. The club had a capacity of about 155 but could, and often did, hold more. The radio broadcast consisted of two sets of gritty blues and r&b numbers, the band beginning each set as a four-piece, with Wolf hitting the stage to join in after a few songs.

The first set starts with Pittsfield Slim (as Magic Dick was known then) handling vocals on 'Dust My Broom' and 'Look Over Yonder', followed by an instrumental before Wolf arrives for 'You Don't Love Me.' The second set follows a similar pattern, with Pittsfield Slim singing 'Somebody's Gotta Go' and 'Help Me' before Wolf enters for 'Everything's Gonna Be Alright.' The setlist included Eddie Burns' 'Orange Driver', which would be recorded for 1975's *Hotline*, and 'Funky Broadway', a holdover from The Hallucinations days, originally by funk band Dyke (Arlester Christian) and the Blazers. Geils would later cover Dyke's 'So Sharp' on their 1971 *The Morning After* LP and their 1976 live album.

The J. Geils Band (1970)

Personnel:
Peter Wolf: vocals
Seth Justman: piano, organ
Magic Dick: harp
J. Geils: guitar
Danny Klein: bass
Stephen Bladd: drums, vocals
Producers: Dave Crawford, Brad Shapiro
Engineers: Jay Messina, Geoffrey Haslam (remix)
Record label: Atlantic Records
Released: 16 November 1970
Running time: 33:22
Highest chart place: US: 195, CA: –, UK: –

With Seth Justman in place handling keyboards, the six-man J. Geils Band headed to New York's A&R Studios to lay down tracks for their debut album. Having honed the tunes through endless live shows, they recorded the entire set in about 18 hours in just over three days, even though, as Wolf explained in a May 1972 *Hit Parader* interview, the recording studio was booked for two full weeks. Many of the songs that made it to the final record were first takes, a testament to the band's tightness. The 11 tracks that made up *The J. Geils Band* consisted of five cover tunes and six originals, presenting a hard-driving mix of blues, r&b, rock, and soul. The original songs meshed perfectly with the covers, and the covers were authentic and true, being as much about showcasing the band's talents as they were about bringing the sometimes-obscure tunes, songwriters, and original performers to a wider audience.

Production on the album, handled by Atlantic staffers Dave Crawford and Brad Shapiro (no relation to Paul Shapiro from Bladd and Wolf's Hallucinations band), was solid but didn't capture the energy of the band in its live environment. When compared to later Geils albums, especially the live recordings, the sound here could sound flat and the performances reserved. Wolf was interviewed for a May 2016 *Stereophile* article and said although Crawford and Shapiro were very good at their jobs, the producers often just pressed the record button and told the band to play. At times the band might not have even been aware they were being recorded. Nonetheless, those songs let the world know what a J. Geils party was all about and the tracks have held up well even after 50-plus years. The whole process, from recording to mixing and mastering, was completed over about 70 working hours and the album was released less than a month later.

The black and white cover photograph of the band was courtesy of Stephen Paley. Paley has served as a television and radio producer, worked for Warner Brothers studios and Epic Records, published photos in *Rolling Stone, Vanity Fair, Life*, and other magazines and has photographed album covers for the likes of Aretha Franklin, The Allman Brothers, and Wilson Pickett. By the time of the photoshoot for *The J. Geils Band*, he was working at Columbia Records but knew Jerry Wexler and Ahmet Ertegun from his previous work with Atlantic Records and was still sometimes offered assignments there. Paley said the band members were 'easy to work with.' The photos on the front and back cover of the album were taken in front of a stone wall and though the exact location has been forgotten, Paley stated it 'must have been shot in Boston. I say that because I visited Peter's Cambridge apartment and my guess (regarding the timeframe of visiting the apartment) was when I went up there to photograph them.' As it turned out, in Wolf's already vast record collection were one or two 45s that Paley himself had produced.

For the cover photo, 'Peter (Wolf) was open to anything', said Paley. 'What he didn't want was a pretentious cover. He just wanted it to look raw, like the music, almost confrontational.' Paley added the band members were the first artists who gave him some input as to the graphic design of the album. 'I chose Lloyd Ziff (for album design), who was working at Columbia Records at the time. I did that because I never liked the way my Atlantic covers turned out and Peter gave me more input than I ever had in the past.' Wolf and Bladd, former art students, probably had a sense of what Paley wanted and instinctively trusted him.

The album's supporting tour included performances on 19 and 20 February 1971, opening for Black Sabbath at promoter Bill Graham's Fillmore East in New York. Although both bands' music was rooted in the blues, the music and showmanship of Geils were worlds apart from Black Sabbath's. As might be expected, the Sabbath fans were impatient for Sabbath, not wanting to sit through Geils, and made that clear. According to the September 2013 issue of *Classic Rock*, Graham came out early in the first show to admonish the crowd, urging them to give Geils some respect. With that, the crowd were more accepting and Geils ended up getting called back for several encores.

Graham was sufficiently impressed and a month later, Geils could be found at Graham's Fillmore West in San Francisco, this time opening for Eric Burdon and War. The tour also included what's likely the band's first gig in Detroit, in March of 1971 at Eastown Theater, building the foundation that made Detroit the band's second hometown. They returned to Detroit's Eastown Theater in April for two more shows, again in June for two shows, then performed at Detroit's Outdoor Rock Fest in July, and were at the Eastown Theater in September supporting Chuck Berry, which makes at least seven Detroit-area shows in 1971. On 27 June, Graham hired them to play the final show at Fillmore East in New York on a bill that included Albert King, Edgar Winter's White Trash, and The Allman Brothers. The show was broadcast live on NYC radio stations WPLJ and WNEW-FM. Geils performed about 50 minutes, and by this time, their setlist already included 'Whammer Jammer' and 'It Ain't What You Do (It's How You Do It!)', both of which would appear on the band's next album, *The Morning After*, issued at the end of 1971.

Despite the band's rapidly growing live reputation, the debut album barely made a ripple when it was released in late 1970, reaching only 195 on the US *Billboard* album chart, disappearing after two weeks, and failing to chart anywhere else. Like much of the band's Atlantic releases, *The J. Geils Band* was issued on CD in 1990 and then remastered by George Marino for cleaner sound and reissued on CD in the mid-1990s. Speakers Corner, a German audio company, remastered the original analogue recording and issued it on 180-gram virgin vinyl in 2018. The remastered and reissued recordings did not include any bonus material.

'Wait' (Justman, Wolf) (3:25)
The album opens with an original tune penned by Justman and Wolf, who quickly emerged as the band's primary songwriters. 'Wait', written on piano and said to have been inspired by the style of legendary jazz and blues pianist Mose Allison, is one of the first songs to come from the team. The r&b track slinks in on Justman's piano, accented by Bladd's cymbals and Klein's bass, soon joined by Jay's guitar before Wolf calls out, 'Come on.' Dick is there with harmonica, working it like a brass horn, and the band give the track an easy swagger.

Wolf sings about going down to the local bar where he eyes a woman looking 'so sharp, so petite', and who, according to the bartender, is 'disengaged.' There's a call-and-response chorus: 'I said now wait (*wait!*), stop a minute. I said now don't (*don't!*) go no farther.' It's perfect for engaging an audience to join in. Midway through, the instrumental break allows Dick to showcase his considerable harp skills. Later, when Wolf returns to the chorus and sings, 'I said now wait', there's a brief break where the band stomp and clap in rhythm for a measure, again perfect for a live audience to join in without interrupting the song's momentum.

'Wait' was the band's second single from the album but it failed to chart. Several artists have recorded covers of 'Wait', including Dutch band the Bintangs in 1974 and Dave Edmunds in 1983, with Paul Jones (Manfred Mann) handling the harmonica parts.

'Ice Breaker (For The Big 'M')' (Geils) (2:15)
A brief instrumental, 'Ice Breaker' is the sole track in the history of the band with songwriting credited solely to Jay, though the entire band had input. The tune was penned in honour of Mario Medious, known as The Big M, who heard the five-piece, unsigned band performing at The Boston Tea Party in 1968 and pushed tirelessly to get them signed to Atlantic Records. 'Ice Breaker' was a surprise to Medious, who said, 'I didn't know (about it) until I got the test pressing. Peter Wolf said, 'We put that on there for you, you broke the ice, you got us the record deal'.'

The song begins on guitar with a trace of echo from Jay before the rest of the band jump in. There's a funky easiness throughout the track, Klein's bass and Bladd's drums effortlessly carrying it without ever taking over. Jay lays down a solo, followed by Dick, and then Justman gets an opportunity to blast away on organ, and soon guitar and harp play atop and around each other. Though it's primarily showcasing Jay's guitar and Dick's harp, the barely two-minute track lets everyone show off. Paul Lanning, who'd videotaped Jay, Dick and Klein for his All-Stars student project in 1969, recalled being a guest of the band (pre-Justman) at the Boston Tea Party in early 1970, where they opened the set with a different 'shuffle-beat version' of 'Ice Breaker' before bringing Wolf out on stage.

'Cruisin' For A Love' (Juke Joint Jimmy) (2:32)
The album's blues-based third track introduces fans to the great Juke Joint Jimmy, who is listed as the song's author. Throughout the band's career, they've been coy about Juke Joint Jimmy, usually stating he's just a good friend of the band. In reality, Juke Joint Jimmy is the collective name for The J. Geils Band, and this track was written as a group effort (similar to The Rolling Stones' credit of 'Nanker Phelge' for group collaborations). A juke joint, incidentally, is a not-always-legal venue, often with no name or license, featuring music, sweaty dancing, food, drink, and possibly gambling, and being a place to hang out and have a good time. Exactly the type of place a six-piece band named J. Geils might be seen and heard.

'Cruisin' For A Love' begins with Dick's piercing harp before Wolf calls out, 'Alright.' Justman plays some honkytonk piano, and Jay coaxes subtle, warm tones from his guitar, providing background rhythm until he takes over for a solo. Wolf introduces the harp break by shouting, 'Alright, blow your horn, baby.' When it's time again for Jay on guitar, Wolf introduces him with 'Jay Geils!' The harmonica and guitar introductions are something Wolf would regularly do on various tracks on just about every album. 'Cruisin' For A Love' was the B-side to the 'Wait' single. The song was featured in the 2003 film *Anger Management*.

'Hard Drivin' Man' (Wolf, Geils) (2:18)
'Hard Drivin' Man' has the distinction of being the only co-write by Wolf and Jay in the band's canon (possibly written before Justman joined) and includes semi-autobiographical lyrics. On 14 and 15 March 1969, John Boyd, Barbara Boyd, and Steve Nelson (former manager of The Boston Tea Party) opened a new venue in western Massachusetts called The Woodrose Ballroom, on Route 5/10, about two miles down the highway from an eatery named The Four Winds Diner. The act they booked for that first weekend was the pre-Justman five-man J. Geils Blues Band. As Nelson tells it in his book *Gettin' Home*, money was tight, so the band 'camped out at the club in sleeping bags', hence the lyric 'ate at The Four Winds Diner, slept in The Woodrose Hall.' In a 9 May 2010 interview with Kevin O'Hare on *MassLive*, Wolf said playing venues like The Woodrose Ballroom and The Paramount

(another venue where Nelson and the Boyds promoted bands) in Springfield 'kept us alive for many years.'

The track is as much about physically moving forward as it is about the figurative hard drive to forge their reputation and build a following in town after town. The band tear through 'Hard Drivin' Man', bearing down like a speeding semi-truck, giving the track that sense of pistons pumping, wheels spinning, and making a living on the road, playing shows night after night after night. Thin Lizzy covered the song in their live shows around 1974, and Eddie and the Hot Rods also included the number in their sets by 1977.

'Serves You Right To Suffer' (John Lee Hooker) (5:01)
Jay pours his soul into this blistering blues number written by one of the band's idols, John Lee Hooker. Mississippi-born Hooker wrote and released the ragged 'Serves You Right To Suffer' (originally titled '*Serve* You Right To Suffer') in 1966. Hooker also had a version of the song retitled 'Serves Me Right To Suffer' with the same sentiment. Geils capture Hooker's biting misery of mistreatment by a woman and being prescribed 'milk, cream, and alcohol.' It's greasy and nasty and evokes every sentiment the song title implies.

Klein and Bladd hold the tempo, never forcing the song, letting it creep along and build as the rest of the band move in and out. Dick's harp and Justman's piano prove equal to Jay's raw guitar work. The band aren't just covering this song; they're living it. On the fadeout, Wolf plays the role of the burned lover, torn between emotions and who can't let go, and half sings, half talks in the blues tradition as he first says, 'You know you really hurt me', then pleads, 'Give me just a-one more, one more, one more night, one more night with you, baby.'

'Homework' (Otis Rush, Al Perkins, Dave Clark) (2:45)
Born in Mississippi, Otis Rush was a Chicago bluesman who wrote and released 'Homework' in 1962, though the original release doesn't list Rush as one of the writers. Fleetwood Mac (with Peter Green) performed an upbeat version on their 1969 *Blues Jam In Chicago*, but Geils stay closer to the same blues and r&b styling of Rush's take.

On his original recording, Rush makes great use of a horn section. As is often the case in the Geils catalogue, Dick covers those horn parts with harmonica, this time specifically a Hohner Marine band 'soloist.' The song chugs along on drums, bass and crisp piano, with the piano sometimes subtle enough that it might be overlooked. The lyrics tell of being so infatuated with a woman ('You got me so blind') that the singer can't concentrate on anything else ('I can't do my homework anymore'). Midway through, the instrumental break belongs to Dick on harp and Jay on guitar. 'Homework' was the album's first single in the US, under the title 'Homework (Ain't Gonna Do It Baby)', but it did not chart. The band clearly loved this song, as it pops up again on Wolf's 2002 album *Sleepless*, Klein's 2005 *Stonecrazy* and the 2012 *American Girl* CD by Jeff Pitchell with Jay.

'First I Look At The Purse' (Robert Rogers, William 'Smokey' Robinson) (3:54)
This r&b number was written by Smokey Robinson and Bobby Rogers in the early days of The Miracles and recorded by The Contours ('Do You Love Me') in 1965. Going against the grain of most pop songs at the time, it's not about love but about the realities of love, sizing up what kind of material assets a woman might have and chasing after those things. The Geils track is slightly grittier and fuller than The Contours' version and omits the hand claps, and again Dick covers the original horn parts on harmonica.

The track is about checking out women, with only one criterion: 'I don't care if she's underfed, why waste time looking at the waistline', sings Wolf, 'if the purse is fat, that's where it's at.' Justman handles the piano honkytonk style, Jay's guitar parts are straightforward, and Dick's harp is sharp as ever. Wolf adds a few lines not in the original recording: 'I want me a suit, I want me a car, I want me to look like a Hollywood star.' The song is another to feature a call-and-response, which Geils used to great effect over their career, whether involving the rest of the band or pulling in a live audience. When Wolf sings, 'I want money', he's answered with 'money', which sums up the track's sentiment. The song was the B-side to 'Homework.'

'What's Your Hurry' (Wolf, Justman) (2:44)
In a 1983 interview with radio personality Lisa Robinson, Justman said this was the first song he wrote with Wolf. Bladd handles harmony vocals as Wolf opens with the line, 'Baby, baby, baby, what's your hurry?' The woman in question is about to walk out the door, never to return after being treated so badly. The danceable, 1960s-style r&b track has a light feel as it bounds along, despite the lyrics telling of a breakup and a plea for another chance. 'All your bags are packed, you're leaving and now, baby, you ain't never coming back', sings Wolf, before begging, 'Give me just a little more time and we can make it work out fine.'

Justman has the right touch on the piano, embellishing the verses and choruses, with Dick, Klein, and Bladd pushing the rhythm forward. Jay intentionally keeps his guitar in the background until it's time for an instrumental break, when he casually lays down a few measures of just the right solo. The energy level is raised slightly when the chorus comes back around, with harp and cowbell growing louder and Wolf's vocals more urgent through the fadeout.

'On Borrowed Time' (Wolf, Justman) (3:03)
A rich, soulful ballad, 'On Borrowed Time' slows things down and provides contrast to the blues and r&b tracks comprising the rest of the album. The lyrics lament love lost with no hope of redemption: 'How fast it happened, how soon it was gone.' Bladd adds harmony vocals on the chorus of 'On borrowed time, on borrowed time, I borrowed some love, that never was

mine.' Jay turns in a heart-wrenching, uncomplicated solo, his guitar notes crying in sympathy with Wolf's anguished confessions. It's easy to picture Wolf on his knees in the spotlight, centre stage, Apollo Theater-style, as he dramatically cries out, 'Give me back my love! Whoa! Come on, baby!' There are no organ or harmonica solos. Instead, Justman and Dick fill out the sound from beneath, creating and adding emotion to the heartbreak. When Wolf did a short solo tour in 2019, 'On Borrowed Time' occasionally made it into his setlist.

'Pack Fair And Square' (Big Walter Price) (2:01)
Walter Price, also known as Thunderbird, was a Texas folk and blues singer and pianist. He released 'Pack Fair And Square' as the B-side of a single credited to Big Walter and His Thunderbirds in 1956, starting the track by drawing out the same 'Weeellllll' that Wolf adopted for the Geils version. Known for his barrelhouse piano skills, Price's version of 'Pack Fair and Square' surprisingly doesn't feature piano, though the song is still representative of his up-tempo blues swing music.

Geils infuse the track with the same 1950s feel as Price's recording, and Dick covers the original horn parts with harmonica. The band skip Price's middle verse of 'Look-a-here, woman, and tell me what you going to do' and instead move straight to the instrumental break, where Dick draws out the first harp notes, similar to the sax solo on Price's recording. In the following verse, Wolf changes the original lyric of 'From now on, darling, it seems I'm going to leave you alone' to 'If you gonna be my baby, now, hon, ya gotta stay at home.' The track was issued as a single in the UK in 1971, after Geils' second album *The Morning After* was issued, but it did not chart.

'Sno-Cone' (Albert Collins) (3:24)
The album closer is a hard-driving take on Texas-born Albert Collins' 1965 instrumental 'Sno-Cone (Part I)', which was nearly identical to Collins' own 'Stump Poker' (written by Jerry Foster and Bill Rice). Collins' distinctive Fender Telecaster playing earned him nicknames like 'The Ice Man', and songs like 'Freeze' and 'Frost Bite' were intentionally reflective of his 'cool' style. A sno-cone (or snow cone) is a shaved or crushed ice treat with fruit or sugar flavouring, so 'Sno-Cone' made a perfect Collins number. Of all the classic songs Geils have covered, this is probably the one they reworked and rearranged the most. Klein's bass and Bladd's drums carry the same thick, thumping beat, but much of the other instrumental parts differ considerably. In Collins' rendition, organ and guitar are more upfront when not soloing and the horns repeat a riff for the first half of the song and at the fadeout.

Bladd kicks off the Geils version of 'Sno-Cone', pounding away on the drumkit. Jay enters on guitar and the rhythm section steamrolls in, Klein playing a funky, repeating bassline to carry everyone. The tune was often the show-opener in the early days and it's easy to understand why. It's high energy, it sets the tone for the show, and every instrument gets to shine, though when all is said and done, the track belongs to Bladd. After giving an exhausting performance from the very start, about two-thirds through, Bladd delivers a 40-second unaccompanied solo that's just right in length. Of all the tracks on the debut album, this one captured the most energy.

The Morning After (1971)

Personnel:
Peter Wolf: vocals
Seth Justman: keyboards
Magic Dick: harp
J. Geils: guitar
Danny Klein: bass
Stephen Jo Bladd: drums, vocals
Producer: Bill Szymczyk
Engineers: Bill Szymczyk, Lee Kiefer
Record label: Atlantic Records
Released: 2 October 1971
Running time: 34:37
Highest chart place: US: 64, CA: 73, UK: –

Released just under a year after the first album, the appropriately titled *The Morning After* continued the exploration of grinding blues, r&b, and soul while pushing further into rock and roll. Seven of its ten tracks were originals, with two of those credited to the collective group moniker Juke Joint Jimmy and the rest to Wolf and Justman. Producer Bill Szymczyk – who had worked with the likes of B.B. King and The James Gang and would go on to produce everyone from The Eagles and REO Speedwagon to Bob Seger and The Who – was brought in to oversee this second Geils effort. Szymczyk had been working as a staff producer for ABC Dunhill in Los Angeles, but following an earthquake in February 1971, he moved to Denver, Colorado, and started Tumbleweed Records with Larry Ray (Szymczyk also briefly worked at radio station KFML). Jerry Greenberg from Atlantic, with A&R man Mark Myerson, soon approached Szymczyk to talk about recording Geils. Greenberg handed him the Geils debut album. 'That's the first I'd ever heard of them', stated Szymczyk. 'I took it home and listened to it and said, 'Yeah, I'd be all about that." Atlantic Records then sent Szymczyk to see Geils live and get to know them. 'I believe it was in Detroit. And I loved the show', he said. Afterwards, everyone went back to one of the band's hotel rooms. As Szymczyk explained, 'We were watching TV, and somebody had brought a watermelon in. We cut it open and everybody had a piece. And the watermelon was rotten. Something on the TV was not very good either, and I chucked my watermelon at the TV and Peter Wolf said, 'You're hired."

Szymczyk managed to put more muscle into the music and capture a bigger sound, though, as with the first album, the tracks fall short of the live sets and studio performances on future releases. In a 2002 *Sound On Sound* interview, Szymczyk stated that Geils 'always recorded ensemble' and 'there were really very few overdubs, occasionally a harp solo by Magic Dick. Even Peter Wolf's vocals were often cut live as the band was putting down the track. We made those records (the studio albums from *The Morning After* through 1975's

Hotline) in between three and four weeks (each).' According to a May 1972 *Hit Parader* article, the entire *The Morning After* record was cut in about eight working days using a 16-track recorder, though Szymczyk said it took a little longer than that. 'I brought them out to LA, to The Record Plant, Studio A. They were overjoyed to be in LA. It was like, 'Oh, boy, something new.' They dug being in LA. Everything went real smooth. It was a quick album; the tunes were all written. It went pretty quickly; I don't think we spent more than three weeks on it. Wolf stated in a May 1972 *Harmony* interview, 'The original title we had in mind for the album was 'Blow Your Face Out'.' That didn't happen, of course, but 'Blow Your Face Out' would also be considered (and discarded) for the album that became *Full House* and was finally used for 1976's live album.

The Morning After album cover, like the music itself, is stylistically similar to the first album, providing continuity. The band name and album title are scribbled in cursive on a black band above a black-and-white photo. The band's name dropped the article 'The' and is listed simply as 'J. Geils Band.' The shift of the band's name occurs a few times over the course of the band's output, with three albums showing 'J. Geils Band', one as 'Geils', and the rest as 'The J. Geils Band.' It made little difference, as throughout the years, most fans have called the band either 'J. Geils' or just 'Geils.'

The cover photograph finds the band in a trashed hotel room. Wolf stated in that same 1972 *Harmony* article that the photo happened after one of Geils' first headlining gigs in Virginia Beach, Virginia. The entire touring cast of *Jesus Christ Superstar* was staying at the same hotel as Geils and the party lasted until sunrise. The band cleaned up the hotel room a little, but Stephen Paley – who had taken the photos for the debut album and was briefly travelling with Geils – told the band members to stay where they were so he could capture a few photos. Wolf said a couple of weeks later, they were looking at the contact sheets (thumbnails of the photo negatives) at Columbia Records where the album packaging was done 'and this Columbia guy said, pointing to the cover photo on the contact sheet, 'Say, that looks like the morning after'.'

Photographer Paley didn't recall the exact location of the hotel but mostly echoed Wolf's recollections. 'I think (the trashed hotel room) was their idea', he said. The intent was to show the musicians in their hotel suite the morning following an all-night after-show party, with bedding strewn about and furniture overturned, the band in recovery mode. Paley preferred a more candid style over studio photography, which meant his back cover photo showing the band in an airport terminal wasn't staged. It captured the band on tour, waiting for their next flight. 'I took candid pictures as if I were doing them for a magazine', he explained. It was an appropriate setting, as Geils spent most of their career travelling from city to city, nearly always on tour.

The band's high-octane shows and relentless touring were bearing fruit. *The Morning After* climbed to 64 on the US album chart, where it spent 17 weeks, and made for the band's first chart appearance outside America, reaching 73 in Canada. The accompanying tour included the band's first billing at New York's Madison Square Garden, opening for Emerson, Lake and Palmer, and their first shows in Canada since those stints at Montreal's New Penelope Club in 1968. January 1972 found the band on the US television program *American Bandstand* and early April saw Geils on stage at the *Mar Y Sol Pop Festival* in Puerto Rico, a multi-day event featuring more than two dozen blues, soul, jazz, and rock acts. The tour made several stops in Detroit, including their April 1972 shows at the Cinderella Ballroom, which they recorded for their next album, a live one. 1972 also marked the band's first assault on Europe. The band had a short interview in the 5 February 1972 issue of the UK's *Melody Maker*, while the 17 June issue featured a concert photo of Jay, Wolf, and Klein on the cover. Later in June, Geils performed their first shows in Germany and the UK, with their first appearance on BBC's *Old Grey Whistle Test* airing on 27 June 1972, though no recording of it seems to have survived.

The Morning After was issued on CD in the US in 1990, then remastered and reissued on CD in 1995. In 2019, Mobile Fidelity remastered the analogue recording and issued a limited run of 3,000 vinyl copies, followed by a limited edition of 2,000 Super Audio Compact Discs (SACD) in 2020. The reissues did not contain any bonus tracks.

'I Don't Need You No More' (Wolf, Justman) (2:36)
The band jump right into this opening number. While Justman never gets a true solo, he shapes the track, pounding away on the piano keys, throwing in descending slides, and adding the right amount of organ near the end. Wolf can see the truth in a relationship as he sings, 'Lovin' you is a waste of my time.' The first instrumental break features Dick with some rapid riffs on the harp before Wolf is back. Jay commandeers the next break with biting guitar (finishing his solo with the slightest bit of feedback) before turning it back to Wolf. The track chugs along and it's over all too quickly. 'I Don't Need You No More' was the second single issued from the album but it did not chart. The track was used in the 2013 Australian surfing film *Drift*.

'Whammer Jammer' (Juke Joint Jimmy) (2:37)
One of the songs most identified with Geils, this rock/blues harmonica instrumental beast came about as a way to keep live shows moving when equipment or technical issues would otherwise delay the concert. Soon it became an essential part of the setlist toward the end of the shows, pushing Dick's stamina to the limit and testing his abilities after already having played harp for 90 minutes or more. Dick has often said the opening measures are greatly influenced by Sonny Boy Williamson II's 1963 'Bye Bye Bird', particularly the version heard on the live *Sonny Boy Williamson & The Yardbirds* LP (recorded in 1963 with the Eric Clapton lineup but not released until 1966).

The song's title comes from a phrase used by Mario 'The Big M' Medious, the man who discovered Geils at The Boston Tea Party and pushed to get them signed at Atlantic Records. When Medious was impressed with a woman (or anything), he'd say, 'That's a mammerjammer' – slang for 'motherf–ker' – meaning 'so fine.' But, as Medious explained, 'Peter Wolf told me, 'I can't say that" (at least not on an early 1970s record), so the title was changed to 'Whammer Jammer.'

The track begins on harp, with Dick twice executing an extended flutter and stab before launching into an extended solo without accompaniment. The band ease their way in, then tear it up, Bladd pounding away on drums, Justman hammering the keys, Jay and Klein providing the rhythm, everyone supporting Dick's tune through to the finish. The song was already in the band's live setlist at least as far back as June 1971, when they performed it at the Fillmore East final show. The tune even made its way into the 2010 Winter Olympics when Samuel Contesti of the Italian men's skating team used 'Whammer Jammer' in his routine short program.

'Whammer Jammer' was the B-side to 'Looking For A Love' in the US and was issued as an A-side in the Netherlands. This is a track that launched 10,000 harp players and likely frustrated all of them as they tried to learn Dick's incredible licks.

'So Sharp' (Arlester Christian) (3:10)

Dyke Christian fronted a funk group in Buffalo, New York, and recorded 'So Sharp' with The Blazers in 1967. Though they never recorded it, Geils had been performing 'Funky Broadway', another Dyke and The Blazers track, as far back as 1968. Dyke was killed in March 1971, in Phoenix, Arizona, aged 27, and when Geils recorded 'So Sharp' shortly afterwards for *The Morning After*, the track listing on the back cover of the album read, '(In memory of 'Dyke' Arlester Christian).'

Jay revs his guitar to announce 'So Sharp.' 'I used to have my fun, looong time ago', sings Wolf. The song tells the story of a man who's finally met his match in a woman who, even though she's 'all ragged and beat up', is still 'sharper than me' in attitude and style. Jay's guitar steers the track and he takes the first solo, followed by Justman on organ. As the song nears the end, Wolf sings his lines and the band calls back 'so sharp' each time through the fade.

'The Usual Place' (Don Covay, Leroy Randolph) (2:45)

Co-writer Don Covay began his career working with Little Richard and later penned hits for artists like Aretha Franklin ('Chain Of Fools') and Chubby Checker ('Pony Time'). 'The Usual Place' first appeared on Covay's *See-Saw* album in 1966 and served as the B-side to Don Covay and the Goodtimers' '40 Days – 40 Nights' single in 1967. Wolf had been a fan of Covay since his high school days watching Covay at the Apollo Theater and later Wolf and Covay would team up to write 'Lights Out' and 'It's Raining' for Wolf's solo albums. Dave Crawford and Brad Shapiro, producers of Geils' 1970 debut album, had worked with a lot of big soul acts. According to a February 2015 *Rolling Stone* article, when they asked Wolf if he'd like to meet any of those acts, Wolf instead said, 'I'd like to meet Don Covay.' Geils even had Covay join them on stage at Fillmore East in New York when they played 'The Usual Place.'

'The Usual Place' alludes to two lovers meeting in secret to conduct their affair, with Wolf singing, 'Please be there on time, the usual place' and 'been so long since I held you tight.' Justman fills out the track with a thick, swelling and swirling organ sound, while Jay's guitar break conveys the same sense of desperation and longing as the lyrics. Wolf even cries out in anguish during the guitar solo. It's an emotional number delivered with maximum effect.

'Gotta Have Your Love' (Wolf, Justman) (4:32)
It's probably intentional that three successive tracks feature 'Love' in the title. First is 'Gotta Have Your Love' to close side one of the LP. Then come 'Looking For A Love' and 'Gonna Find Me A New Love', with the three-song titles in themselves telling of moving through a relationship. 'Gotta Have Your Love' rolls in on a barrelhouse piano lick, signalling a change of mood from the yearning of the preceding 'The Usual Place.'

The song adds a light touch of humour in telling of a breakup and the aftermath, with the singer driving his girlfriend away, yet now missing her and on a quest to get her back: 'I tried every single Lost and Found, but they didn't see you around.' Dick's harp punctuates the choruses and after a couple of verses, Justman plays a swift piano solo. Wolf returns with another verse and then the song shifts into a funk-infused start-stop rhythm, perfect for getting a crowd on their feet and dancing. A harp solo is followed by guitar before the organ leads to the fadeout.

'Looking For A Love' (J.W. Alexander, Zelda Samuels) (3:47)
Highest chart place: US: 39, CA: 25, UK: –
Titled 'Lookin' for a Love' (without the *g*) when it was recorded by The Valentinos in 1962, that original version has a lighter doo-wop feel with the Womack brothers (including Bobby and Cecil) providing harmony and backing vocals.

On the Geils version, the drum/piano intro sets the pace and Wolf cries out, 'Somebody help me!' Harmony vocals fill out the chorus: 'I'm looking for a love, I'm looking for a love, I'm looking here and there, searching everywhere.' Backing vocals weave through the verses, answering Wolf's lines with 'I'm looking for a love to call my own.' The middle section hits hard and fast. First is Jay's guitar for a few measures, then Dick jumps in, followed by Justman on organ, before it's back to Jay, Dick, and Justman in sequence for a second round. Wolf returns, pleading, 'Somebody help me find my baby.' The song's ending becomes a rave-up, every instrument attacking with hurricane force. This was the first single from the album and the first Geils song to hit the top 40 in both the US and Canada. The band appeared on television's *American Bandstand* on 8 January 1972 to promote the track. Although it was a lip-synced (mimed) performance, as was standard for the program, Klein recalled that the band's playback was so loud that Monty Hall – host of the game show *Let's Make A Deal*, filming in the next studio – came over and requested the volume be turned down.

'Gonna Find Me A New Love' (Wolf, Justman) (3:24)
'Gonna Find Me A New Love' is a blues-styled rock tune about letting go of a failed love affair. There's no regret in the straightforward lyrics, just the satisfaction of moving on to something better after being unappreciated and mistreated: 'You just wanna make a fool outta me.' The song shuffles in on Jay's guitar and Wolf gets right to the chorus. Dick takes the first instrumental break, with Jay covering the second. Piano, drums, and bass push the rhythm along under it all. The song fades out, repeating 'Find me a new love' while Wolf screams and throws in a few adlibs like 'Give me a new love' and 'I want a new love.'

'Cry One More Time' (Wolf, Justman) (3:23)
With a feeling similar to 'On Borrowed Time' from the debut album, 'Cry One More Time' slows the pace and provides contrast to the faster, harder rock tunes. This is another song about a failed relationship and 'She just don't wanna stay.' While the singer knows he can't get her back, it seems he also doesn't want to get over her just yet. He'd rather be home alone, have another beer, wallow in his pain and suffering, and 'Cry one more time for you.' Justman, Jay and Dick maintain a light touch on piano, guitar (including some acoustic), and harp, supporting the tune through the verses and chorus. At the break, Jay lets loose with a solo fitting of the self-pity in the lyrics. The song finishes with Wolf repeating, 'I lost the best I had.'

Gram Parsons (The Byrds, The Flying Burrito Brothers) recorded a country rock version of the song for his 1973 solo album *GP*. Barry Tashian, a friend of Geils since their earliest days, assists with vocals and guitar on the Parsons recording.

'Floyd's Hotel' (Wolf, Justman) (3:11)
With a wink and a nod, 'Floyd's Hotel' paints a picture of a shady establishment with 'a lotta cheap rooms' and 'always somethin' nice to sell.' Justman starts with a few measures of impish piano before Jay's guitar enters, a drum roll fades in, and Wolf says, 'Let me tell you about it.'

Riding a punchy rhythm, the tune boasts several quirky characters. First is the woman with 'juicy red lips' who puts the singer in a taxi and drives him way 'cross town. There's big, fat Smilin' Jim at the front desk of Floyd's Hotel who 'don't ask where you're goin', he don't care where you been.' Dick comes in on harp for the first instrumental break. Wolf shouts, 'Come on, Tarzan, pound it' to introduce Justman's barrelhouse solo. Then, hanging out in the front hall is Tyrone: 'Just give him five dollars, he can really turn you on.' After the verse, Wolf calls, 'Jay Geils', and Jay steps forward with a short, lively guitar bit. One last chorus follows ('everybody sing it now') before the finish.

'It Ain't What You Do (It's How You Do It!)' (Juke Joint Jimmy) (5:12)
Possibly inspired by Little Richard's driving 'It Ain't Whatcha Do (It's The Way How You Do It)', the closing cut is another tune credited to Juke Joint Jimmy (aka the entire band) and is pure adrenaline. Over Bladd's driving beat, Wolf declares, 'We gonna get this one ca-razy, baby!' and bass, harp, and Hammond organ pounce like rabid animals. Wolf screams like a madman, and despite several verses and choruses, the song feels more like an instrumental than something centred around a set of lyrics. Klein holds the beat while everyone else gets an extended turn in the spotlight.

Of note, Wolf proclaims, 'Blow your face out, mama' before the harp break, the first time that expression appears on a Geils recording. Justman weaponises the organ when his turn comes around, and Jay's solo is equally inspired, with bass, drum, percussion, and harp relentlessly keeping time underneath. Over the extended outro jam, the Woofa Goofa starts improvising his 'dooba-dah dooba-dah dooba-dah' bit, later to surface on *Blow Your Face Out* during 'Give It To Me.' Like 'Whammer Jammer', this track was already part of the band's setlist at least four months before *The Morning After* was released, with Geils performing it at the final Fillmore East show in June. 'It Ain't What You Do' was used in a 15-second US television advertisement in late 2017 for Subway sandwiches, supporting the Feeding America charity. The song was also used in the 2022 Australian television series *Barons*, episode one. An edited version of 'It Ain't What You Do' is reportedly in the Atlantic Records vaults and was issued a catalogue number (23987) but has never been released. If so, that would indicate the track was considered for release as a single but later scrapped.

Related Tracks
'Dead Presidents' (Willie Dixon) (2:30) (1971)
Written by Mississippi-born Chicago bluesman Willie Dixon and recorded by Little Walter in 1964, 'Dead Presidents' is a reference to US paper currency, which features deceased presidents, from George Washington on the $1 up to William McKinley on the $500 and Grover Cleveland on the $1,000. Benjamin Franklin, the only non-president, graces the $100 bill and, for the sake of the song, is still one of the 'Dead Presidents.' The tune tells of the love of money and all it can or cannot do.

The track begins with a few measures of guitar from Jay before everyone else joins in. The lyrics make their way through the roster of dead presidents on paper currency: 'I looked at a Lincoln (on the $5), can't park my car, Washington, he can't go too far', up through McKinley and Cleveland, though the latter two haven't been in print since the 1940s. Justman shines on piano, as does Dick on harp, here covering the sax and harp parts from Little Walter's recording. Though it was relegated to the B-side of 'I Don't Need You No More', it sometimes made it into the band's live setlist. It did not appear on any album until 1993's *Anthology – Houseparty*.

'Get On My Airplane' By Canned Heat (Adolfo de la Parra) (4:40) (1972)
In February 1972, Canned Heat ('On The Road Again', 'Going Up The Country') recorded 'Get On My Airplane' with Wolf and Magic Dick for Boston radio station WBCN, where Wolf had been an overnight DJ in 1968. The Canned Heat lineup consisted of Bob Hite on vocals, Henry Vestine and Joel Scott Hill on guitars, Tony de la Barreda on bass, and Adolpho 'Fito' de la Parra on drums.

The recording is a loose mix of funk, blues, and boogie rock topped with a James Brown attitude. It begins with someone shouting, 'Key of D.' Dick is on harp from the start, settling in to jam with Heat's guitars and drums. Hite handles the initial verse ('Gonna get on my airplane') and Wolf takes the second, reaching for the high notes with, 'Oh baaaabe', before singing 'you some kind of wonderful…' From there, Hite and Wolf trade lines as the rest of the band work their magic. According to Alan Carter's 2013 book *Radio-Free Boston, The Rise And Fall Of WBCN*, the recording came about because the musicians were snowed in at the radio studio with time on their hands. Canned Heat singer Hite kept calling Wolf 'Jay', thinking he was J. Geils, and kept pronouncing Geils as 'Jeils.' Further, Wolf never corrected Hite. The 1972 recording surfaced on the 2004 release of Heat's *The Boogie House Tapes Vol 2 1969-1999* on their own Canned Heat Music label.

'Whammer Jammer' By Magic Dick & Jay Geils (Juke Joint Jimmy) (2:41) (2008)
This take of 'Whammer Jammer' was recorded specifically for Boulder, Colorado, radio station KBCO on 26 August 1994 as part of their *Studio C* program and released in 2008 on the *KBCO Studio C 20th Anniversary Edition* CD. The track is credited to 'Magic Dick and J. Geils', who were promoting their newly released *Bluestime* CD and likely includes the entire Bluestime band (Michael 'Mudcat' Ward on bass, Jerry Miller on guitar, Steve Ramsay on drums).

Dick announces the song by saying, 'Here's one called 'Whammer Jammer.' This one goes way, way back.' The playing is as intense as any version of the song but, at the same time, feels looser, partly due to Jay's jazz guitar beneath the harp riffs. KBCO regularly releases *Studio C* recordings, with proceeds donated to various charities.

'Cry One More Time' By Mary Chapin Carpenter And Peter Wolf
(Wolf, Justman) Lambent Light Records/Amazon Music (2:37) (2017)
In February 2017, Amazon Music Originals released two playlists, 'Love Me' and 'Love Me Not', to commemorate Valentine's Day. 'Love Me Not' included an exclusive recording of 'Cry One More Time' by country singer-songwriter Mary Chapin Carpenter and Wolf, recorded in late 2016 with Duke Levine producing. The Carpenter-Wolf recording sticks close to the original from Geils' *The Morning After* but with Chapin's acoustic guitar giving it a country touch.

'Funky', 'Mojo Train' and 'She Does It To Me Right' (Atlantic Records catalogue numbers 23236, 23293, 23294, respectively) are three tracks allegedly recorded at The Record Plant West on or about 29 July 1971 but never released. No information is available on 'Funky' or 'She Does Me Right.' Klein believes 'Mojo Train' is the song the band performed at places like King's Rook (later known as Stonehenge) when they worked the crowd into a conga line to dance through the venue, outside, and back in.

J. Geils Band ... *On Track*

'Live' Full House (1972)

Personnel:
Peter Wolf: vocals
Seth Justman: piano, organ
Magic Dick: harp
J. Geils: guitar
Daniel Klein: bass
Stephen Jo Bladd: drums, vocals
Producers: Geoffrey Haslam, J. Geils Band
Engineer: Geoffrey Haslam
Record label: Atlantic Records
Recorded: Cinderella Ballroom, Detroit, Michigan on 21 and 22 April 1972
Released: 26 September 1972
Running time: 32:54; 35:45 with crowd noise/spoken intros
Highest chart place: US: 54, CA: 65, UK: –
Tracklisting: 'First I Look At The Purse' (22 April), 'Homework' (22 April), 'Pack Fair And Square' (21 April), 'Whammer Jammer' (22 April), 'Hard Drivin' Man' (22 April), 'Serves You Right To Suffer' (22 April), 'Cruisin' For A Love' (22 April), 'Looking For A Love' (22 April)

'Alright, are you ready to get down? I said, are you ready for some rock and roll? Let's hear it for J. Geils Band!' With that introduction, fans are blasted with 35 minutes of live Geils on *Full House*. The J. Geils Band had a well-earned reputation for explosive live performances even before their first studio album was released, but it wasn't until their third album, this live set, that fans who hadn't yet seen the band could finally get a taste of a Geils show. While the first two studio LPs showcased the musicians' skills and love for blues, r&b, and rock, it was *Full House* that best captured the performances, which were simultaneously manic and focused. Manager Dee Anthony was the one who recommended putting out a live album, which anyone else might've thought premature after just two studio records. But another of Anthony's acts had just broken into the mainstream with a live release (Humble Pie's *Performance – Rockin' The Fillmore*) and Anthony knew he could do it again with Geils. He believed the studio records hadn't truly captured the essence and power of the band and, of course, was proved right. The volcanic energy on this recording nearly blew the needle out of the vinyl groove.

Inciting and schooling the crowd on r&b and blues is what the record was all about. It's said the audience was so raucous that the crowd noise had to be pushed lower in the final mix so the music could be properly heard. The album's eight tracks were culled from two nights in April 1972 at the Cinderella Ballroom on East Jefferson Avenue in the band's second home of Detroit, Michigan. Billing for both nights was J. Geils with Doctor Hook & the Medicine Show ('Sylvia's Mother', 'The Cover Of The Rolling Stone'). Capacity at the Cinderella Ballroom was just under 1,900 and admission for Geils and Doctor Hook was $4.50. Of the two nights recorded, only one of *Full House*'s eight songs was taken from Friday 21 April, with the remaining tracks pulled from the 22nd. The bulk of the songs were from the debut album, with two ('Whammer Jammer' and 'Looking For A Love') from *The Morning After*. The band's stage performances were modelled after the r&b shows at New York's Apollo Theater, and in a 12 April 2010 interview on National Public Radio, Wolf said *Full House* was patterned after James Brown's *Live At The Apollo, Volume 1*. Wolf stated *Full House* truly represents the band and is probably his favourite Geils record.

'First I Look At The Purse' opens the album with a take-no-prisoners attitude. The moment the emcee finishes his introduction, Bladd attacks the snare drum to launch the track and the entire band take off like a runaway freight train. Organ, bass, and drums push the rhythm as Wolf begins, 'Some fellas look at the eyes.' Dick blows a short harp solo, Wolf is back with a few more verses, and Bladd pummels the drumkit, never letting up until the last note. Before the listener can recover, Wolf introduces 'Homework' by shouting, 'The college of musical knowledge', a line likely borrowed from the US radio (and later TV) music and quiz show *Kay Kyser's Kollege Of Musical Knowledge* that aired from the late 1930s through 1950. With 'Homework', the band settle into a slower groove without losing any momentum and Jay and Dick get to shine during their brief solos. Wolf announces 'Pack Fair And Square' with that now famous line, 'This is called 'Take Out Your False Teeth, Mama, I Wanna Ssssuck On Your Gums'.' Justman's piano is more prominent than in the studio version and he tickles the piano keys as Wolf drags out 'Weelllllll.' At the right moment, the band jump in and cram everything they have into a mean performance lasting not even two minutes.

'Whammer Jammer' captures the brilliance of Dick's harp skills (blowing and drawing, grunting and wheezing, hitting those impossible notes) while guitar, bass, drums, and keyboards complement the tune. In an odd bit of sampling, Missy Elliot uses this version of 'Whammer Jammer' on her 2005 track 'Partytime.' The intro to Elliot's track features *Full House*'s entire 15-second verbal exchange between Magic Dick and Wolf from 'We gotta get it crazy tonight, you gonna get it crazy tonight?' through 'Whammer Jammer, let me hear ya, Dickie!' to start her track. But that's all she uses and 'Partytime' then strangely transitions into something else entirely, with 'Whammer Jammer' never heard from again. 'Whammer Jammer' also made its way into the 2008 Will Smith movie *Hancock*.

'Hard Drivin' Man' finds Justman flying across the keys, the band rapidly chugging along. First, Dick gets in a solo, then Justman ('we're gonna get a little piano in there'), followed by Jay ('a little chicken pickin', let me hear ya'). Wolf works the crowd by calling out the names of several dances (Boogaloo, Boston Monkey, Philly Freeze) before lifting the crowd higher by mentioning 'Detroit Demolition' and the band go full throttle to the end.

If the studio version of 'Serves You Right To Suffer' was smouldering, here it practically sets the stereo speakers aflame with Jay's ferocious guitar on this nearly ten-minute version. Wolf introduces the most vicious song on the album by proclaiming, 'Serve you right to suffer, baby, serve you right. You gonna live a *lonnng* time.' Jay hits with a gut punch from his guitar, Bladd rolls in, and harp, Hammond organ, and bass slam down to kick the blues into gear. The track brings some sweaty, greasy solos, first with 'on the lickin' stick, Mr. Magic Dick', then Justman shines on organ, and Jay on guitar. After 'Serves You Right To Suffer', the band shift gears as Wolf yells, 'Everybody gotta get it crazy with us. Blow your face out, baby' before Dick kicks off 'Cruisin' For A Love' on harmonica. At the time, 'Blow Your Face Out' was considered for the album's title. That didn't happen, but it did surface as the title of Geils' next live album in 1976. Closing *Full House*, the band tear through their top 40 hit 'Looking For A Love', with Wolf pleading, 'Somebody help me, somebody help me now!' Unlike the studio version, where the solos are a round of guitar, harp, and organ, followed by a second round of guitar, harp, and organ, here it's a single round with extended guitar, extended harp, and extended organ. There's a false ending around the 3:30 mark, giving Wolf a moment to work the crowd before the whole band return for the finish.

The *Full House* album cover was conceived by Wolf and Bladd, who had both been art students. The title was not only a reference to the crowded venue where the album was recorded but also a hand of playing cards. Those cards displayed on the front cover, however, are not a true full house, which the band make clear. Instead of three of a kind and a pair, it shows three jacks, a king, and a winking queen. Geoffrey Haslam, who had produced or engineered acts like Velvet Underground and MC5 and who served as the remix engineer on Geils' debut album, shared production duties with The J. Geils Band on *Full House*. It was the first time the band had been credited with production. After his success with *The Morning After*, Bill Szymczyk would've been the obvious choice for producer here. He would've been happy to take on the role but wasn't even asked, an arbitrary decision likely coming from the executives at Atlantic.

In early 2010, Rhino Handmade Records, under Atlantic Records, announced a limited, 2-CD deluxe set of both nights of Cinderella Ballroom shows in their entirety, along with six commemorative playing cards representing the members of the band. The expected August 2010 issue date came and went, and the release was cancelled. Allegedly, Rhino had never coordinated with the band, who felt that the best of that two-night stand was already available as the official *Full House* single disc. Although it never saw the light of day, Rhino's deluxe edition track listing was briefly advertised. Both nights had a nearly identical setlist: 'Sno-Cone', 'Wait', 'Gonna Find Me A New Love', '(Ain't Nothin' But A) House Party' (the studio version would appear on the following year's *Bloodshot* album), 'Homework', 'Pack Fair And Square', 'Looking For A Love', 'Cry One More Time', 'Whammer Jammer', 'Cruisin' For A Love', 'Serves You Right

To Suffer', 'First I Look At The Purse', 'Floyd's Hotel', 'Hard Drivin' Man' and 'I Don't Need You No More.' The one difference is the second night featured an additional performance of '(Ain't Nothin' But A) House Party' as an encore.

After *Full House* was recorded but before it was released, Anthony, who also managed Emerson, Lake & Palmer, put Geils on tour with ELP in Europe in June 1972, a pairing that gave Geils valuable exposure in Europe but was not ideal. Audiences buying tickets for an ELP show probably were not expecting such a rowdy opening act. After *Full House* was released, Geils continued touring across the US and included some dates in Canada. In 1973, they made a second appearance on BBC's *Old Grey Whistle Test* on 9 January, performing 'Floyd's Hotel' and 'Looking For A Love', then remained in England for a short tour of about a dozen shows.

Around the time *Full House* hit the record stores, Wolf met actress Faye Dunaway (*Bonnie and Clyde*). Several accounts have them meeting in San Francisco in September when the band were performing at the Fillmore West, but all known Geils concert dates that month were in the Midwest and eastern US. It was likely a promotion party, not a concert, but Wolf and Dunaway were soon spending time together. She even visited the studio while Geils were recording their next album, *Bloodshot*.

'Hard Drivin' Man' was the only single released from the album, with 'Whammer Jammer' as the B-side. Despite the success of the album, the single did not chart, though 'Whammer Jammer' received significant airplay. The album was the band's second US gold album (500,000 copies in the 1970s), receiving a certification in February 1974, in the wake of their next record, *Bloodshot*, receiving gold certification in late 1973. *Full House* was originally released on the standard formats of vinyl LP, cassette, and 8-track tape in 1972, then on CD in 1989, and remastered CD in October 1995. In 2009, Audio Fidelity issued a limited-edition analogue remastered 180-gram virgin vinyl pressing of *Full House*.

Related Tracks
'This Old Fool' (Buddy Guy) (4:43) Atco (1972)
Some Geils members had known Buddy Guy and Junior Wells since mid-1967 when Guy and Wells came over after their own performance at Boston's Club 47 to see The J. Geils Blues Band play at The Unicorn and jam together. From the album *Buddy Guy & Junior Wells Play The Blues*, 'This Old Fool' features Buddy Guy along with Justman, Jay, Klein, Bladd, and Magic Dick. Guy and Wells had recorded most of their album together in 1970, but Atlantic Records chose not to release it. Producer Michael Cuscuna invited The J. Geils Band to finish two tracks on the album in April 1972, and once Geils were involved, Atlantic had enough confidence to issue the album. Junior Wells didn't perform on 'This Old Fool' or 'Honeydripper', and as Dick mentioned in a November 2020 interview with *Blues Blast Magazine*, Buddy Guy wasn't present when he and Jay showed up to record their parts. Dick added, 'It has

never been one of my favourite records.' That may be true for Dick, but it's a great-sounding cut. The blues number rocks along as Guy sings, 'This old fool, lord, is falling in love again.' Guy plays a tight guitar solo, but aside from Dick's harp, it's not obvious the Geils members are performing on the song.

Klein recalled that the Geils band 'met at a bar (Kentucky Tavern) before we went into the studio and Jay said, 'I got married today.' And we went and recorded.' Klein added that even though he and the others already knew Buddy Guy and Junior Wells, 'I went in completely terrified, but it worked out all right. It was a lot of fun.'

'Honeydripper' (Joe Liggins) (3:29) Atco (1972)
From the same album as 'This Old Fool', 'Honeydripper' was featured as the B-side on Guy's 'A Man Of Many Words' single. The A-side was shown as Buddy Guy with Dr. John and Eric Clapton and the B-side as Buddy Guy with The J. Geils Band. As with 'This Old Fool', in addition to Buddy Guy on vocals and guitars, the band is credited as J. Geils, rhythm guitar; Magic Dick, harmonica; Seth Justman, piano; Danny Klein, bass; Stephen Bladd, drums; Juke Joint Jimmy, foot tapping; and 'Special thanks to Peter Wolf.'

It's difficult to hear what Guy says at the start, but it's something like, 'Roll it, we'll make it with The Honeydripper.' After a count-in of 'one, two, one, two, three, four', Guy strums his guitar and the foot tapping begins, driving the beat through the entire song. It's upbeat and laidback, with nice piano work from Justman as he plays off Guy's guitar licks. There's no harmonica, so it's possible Dick is playing only on 'This Old Fool' and not on 'Honeydripper.'

'Looking For A Love' (J.W. Alexander, Zelda Samuels) (5:16) Atco (1972)
Less than three weeks before the band recorded *Full House*, they appeared at the four-day *Mar Y Sol: The First International Puerto Rico Pop Festival* on 3 April. A two-LP set of performances from 12 bands was released later in the year, featuring 'Looking For A Love' as the opening track, showcasing what Geils had to offer. Not surprisingly, the song has the same high energy as the *Full House* recording (perhaps even more energetic) and features the same false ending around the 3:30 mark. Although 'Looking For A Love' was their sole track selected for the *Mar Y Sol* album, Geils' 25-minute set also included 'Sno-Cone', 'Cruisin' For A Love', 'Homework', 'Wait' and 'Whammer Jammer.' Those five cuts have never been released.

'(Ain't Nothin' But A) House Party' and 'Southside Shuffle' are tracks allegedly in the Atlantic vaults (catalogue numbers 27248 and 27249, respectively), recorded a month after the Cinderella Ballroom *Full House* concerts on or about 22 May 1972 at Electric Lady Studios in New York. These would be different recordings from those that later appeared on *Bloodshot*, which was recorded at New York's Hit Factory.

Bloodshot (1973)

Personnel:
Peter Wolf: vocals
Seth Justman: keyboards, vocals
Magic Dick: harp
J. Geils: guitar
Danny Klein: bass
Stephen Jo Bladd: percussion, vocals
Mike Hunt: saxophone
Special assistance: Juke Joint Jimmy
Producers: Bill Szymczyk, Allan Blazek
Engineer: Bill Szymczyk
Record label: Atlantic Records
Released: 12 April 1973
Running time: 36:27
Highest chart place: US: 10, CA: 17, UK: –

With *Bloodshot*, Geils' third studio album and fourth overall, the band cracked the top ten in the US and top 20 in Canada; record sales were starting to catch up to the band's concert reputation. Not only did the album mark a shift to a more rock and r&b sound without losing its blues roots, but it also showed J. Geils as one of the first rock acts to incorporate reggae. Seven of the nine tracks were originals, with Justman and Wolf as writers. Unlike previous albums, Juke Joint Jimmy gets no writing credits but does warrant a back cover note for 'Special assistance.' The *Bloodshot* title might've been alluding to the endless travel, late nights, hard-partying and lack of sleep the band were enduring.

Bill Szymczyk, who handled production and engineering duties on *The Morning After*, returned, this time with Allan Blazek assisting with production. The Szymczyk-Blazek team would work on the next four Geils albums, up to and including *Blow Your Face Out*, and would continue to work together over the next decade as producers and engineers for other acts like The Eagles, REO Speedwagon, and The Outlaws. The team were able to capture a livelier, truer sound on *Bloodshot* than on the first two studio releases. As Szymczyk stated in a January 2006 *MusicRadar* interview, Geils 'were a very hot live band, but they needed to establish themselves on record. (*Bloodshot*) introduced them to a whole new audience, one that was radio- and record-driven as opposed to performance-driven. The musicianship was killer on this record, and the songs were truly fantastic. The whole band was really getting their act together.' He added, 'They brought in a lot of songs that were very close to finished – they weren't just parts – so we worked on the arrangements quite a bit.'

Intentional or not, *Bloodshot* set a template that seven of the next eight studio albums followed (the exception being *Ladies Invited*), serving up nine tracks total, with five on side one of the LP and four on side two. *Bloodshot*'s album cover is black and red with white lettering. In keeping with the previous two studio albums, the band's photo graces the front cover but features individual headshots on the back. David Gahr took the cover photo in New York on 4 October 1972 in front of a dilapidated concrete building, which was erased from the background of the final image. Gahr, whose career spanned more than 50 years, photographing everyone from Buddy Guy to Bruce Springsteen, also provided the band photo for the back cover of Geils' 1979 *Best Of* collection. The inner paper sleeve was black.

Initial pressings of *Bloodshot* were on translucent red vinyl, in keeping with the 'bloodshot' theme, and etched into the dead wax/runout groove on side two was, 'NICE TO SEE YOUR FACE IN THE PLACE.' The 'vinyl graffiti' was courtesy of producer Szymczyk. 'When I was just in the music business and I was learning how to be an engineer, I was cutting acetates in Regent Sound in New York', he said. It was around 1965 and Szymczyk was a huge Phil Spector fan. When The Righteous Brothers' 'You've Lost That Lovin' Feelin'' came out on Spector's Philles Records label, the time was listed as 3:05 to facilitate airplay, but the song was actually much longer, so Szymczyk put the record on a cutting lathe to study it. 'These grooves are smashed right up against each other. I'm looking at the grooves through the microscope on the lathe and I get to the runout and it says 'Phil + Annette' on there. And I went, 'What? You can write stuff in there?' And as soon as I started making records as a producer, I was writing stuff in there on my albums.' To that end, Szymczyk would take the final mixed tapes from his productions to mastering engineer Lee Hulko at Sterling Sound, telling him what the vinyl graffiti would be. Hulko, whose work was often accompanied by 'LH', would then scribe a message on the mother plate that was sent to the pressing plant. Szymczyk always made it relevant to the record itself, often a catchphrase that came up during the recording. For *Bloodshot*, it was the idea that 'If you're looking at this record, then it's nice to see your face in the place.'

Promotion for *Bloodshot* included a spot on American television's *In Concert*, which aired on Friday 13 April. Two months later, on 24 June 1973, Geils appeared on the new US *King Biscuit Flower Hour* syndicated FM radio show. Six selections taken from the band's 4-5 May shows at The Academy of Music in New York City were aired, with three of those being from the new record: '(Ain't Nothin' But A) House Party', 'Give It To Me' and 'Back To Get Ya.' The show was broadcast in quadraphonic sound, though it's unknown how many listeners could've taken advantage of that new technology, the assumption being that most listened on their regular two-channel stereo equipment or mono automobile speakers rather than the high-end specialised audio gear required for quad playback. Atlantic Records may have intended to issue *Bloodshot* itself in quadrophonic sound, as some 1973 test pressings have surfaced, but nothing has been released.

Bloodshot is one of producer Szymczyk's two favourite Geils albums (1974's *Nightmares* being the other). It quickly became the best-selling J. Geils

Band album to date and earned a US Gold Record award (500,000 copies) in September 1973, five months after its release. Its success propelled the previous year's *Full House* to gold status in February 1974. A limited-edition red vinyl LP was reissued in 2015 on the Real Gone Music label.

'(Ain't Nothin' But A) House Party' (Del Sharh, Joseph Thomas) (4:43)
Already in the setlist at least a year earlier when the band were touring behind *The Morning After*, '(Ain't Nothin' But A) House Party' opens the album. Philadelphia r&b group The Showstoppers (sometimes The Show Stoppers) recorded the song – under the title 'Ain't Nothing But A House Party' – in 1967, taking it to number 87 in the US and all the way to number 11 in the UK.

Jay starts the tune with a ringing guitar riff and Bladd attacks the cowbell, providing a harder edge than the Showstoppers' version and serving to announce a harder rocking Geils album as a whole. As with so many of the cover songs Geils did, Dick covers the original horn section on harp. Background vocals punctuate the verses with 'doot-doot, doot-doooo' and join in on the chorus. Wolf alters the lyrics slightly and omits an entire verse ('You shake it from your nose to your toes, 'cause that's the way the dance goes, shake it fast and shake it slow, shake it till you can't no more'). Organ and harp work together on the break, followed by guitar with Bladd brightly tapping the ride cymbal; then they're all weaving through, in, and out of each other before Wolf sings, 'I know it's cold outside.' When the final verse hits, Justman adds a punch on piano with thick, lumbering bass notes to supplement Klein's bass and Bladd's drums before the chorus repeats on the fadeout while everyone plays at full bore. 'House Party' was never released as a single but received airplay in markets like Boston and Detroit. The song was featured in a 15-second Toyota automobile television advertisement in the US in 2018. A performance of the track with Wolf on vocals is captured on Little Steven Van Zandt's 2021 release *Summer Of Sorcery Live!*

'Make Up Your Mind' (Wolf, Justman) (3:31)
Highest chart place: US: 98, CA: –, UK: –
Justman's boogie piano and syncopated rhythm announce 'Make Up Your Mind.' Bladd's drumming provides a Latin-tinged undercurrent as Wolf contemplates waiting on a woman who's indifferent toward him despite his affection for her. 'I don't mind waiting for you, it's what I really, really want to do', sings Wolf before telling her, 'Girl, make up your mind before it's too late.' Jay's guitar, like Wolf's vocal, is restrained yet sincere throughout and his relaxed, extended solo gives the impression of someone hanging around, waiting for a decision. The whole tune has a casual feel to it.

This was the second single released from the album but wasn't as successful as 'Give It To Me', barely touching the US *Billboard* singles chart. 'Make Up

Your Mind' was issued in a picture sleeve featuring a shot from the same photo session as the album cover, but in this image, the background of the dilapidated building remains visible.

'Back To Get Ya' (Wolf, Justman) (5:22)

The band are in a groove from the start, with bass and drums driving the down-and-dirty 'Back To Get Ya.' Jay hits the right notes with jangling guitar, Justman works the piano, Wolf channels a bit of James Brown, and Dick chugs along on harp. 'Think I found something's gonna wreck my mind', sings Wolf and it's soon clear it's not a song about love. Rather, it's unapologetically about sex and infatuation: 'You looked so good when I first met ya, told you then I'd be back to get ya.'

At the start of the instrumental break, Wolf shouts, 'Scramble my eggs, honey, come on.' The band take their time, riding the groove for several measures, waiting for the right moment. Justman holds down the track on organ and Dick takes flight with a brilliant harp solo through to the next verse, where Wolf reminds the woman he's with what they're there for: 'Don't get shy or play polite, ha ha ha, just shut your mouth, turn off the light.' Jay takes the second break with piercing guitar, followed by Justman's solo at the fadeout, swiping across the organ keys while Klein and Bladd keep it moving.

'Struttin' With My Baby' (Wolf, Justman) (3:16)

'Struttin' With My Baby' is exactly what the song title implies – going out with a fine-looking lady at the end of the work week and 'strutting down the boulevard.' The light-hearted tune builds from a bit of tentative piano, winding up to a bigger start, with guitar, harp, bass, and drums piling on. Harp and guitar work in tandem during the mid-point break, playing off each other while piano bounds along beneath. After the break, Wolf returns for two more verses and a chorus and the song ends with a big finish.

Swedish band Low Budget Blues Band recorded 'Struttin' With My Baby' in 1983, reworking the tune with a slower tempo and a bluesier feeling.

'Don't Try To Hide It' (Wolf, Justman) (2:35)

Conjuring up images of an inebriated one-man band with a bass drum strapped to his chest, cymbals tied to his knees, and saxophone hanging around his neck, Geils let the good times roll in this bawdy number that closes side one. The lyrics are intentionally infantile ('I see your heinie, it's nice and shiny, don't try to fight it, you know I'll bite it') and give the impression of a drunken group singalong. The saxophone has a thick tuba oompah sound, with some intentional flat notes. The sax is credited to 'Mike Hunt', the popular fictitious name (say it quickly) used by hordes of snickering juveniles in the 1970s making crank phone calls – but both Magic Dick and producer Szymcyzk confirm it was Jay.

'Southside Shuffle' (Wolf, Justman) (3:43)
Side two opens with a funky dance number that quickly became a Geils favourite. 'Southside Shuffle' begins with an old-style r&b call-and-response of 'Do you wanna dance? (*yeahhh*).' Guitar climbs around the first chorus, harp is there the second time the chorus comes around, and then Jay delivers some raunchy guitar for the break. After a couple more verses and choruses, there's another call-and-response, this time with 'All night long (*all night long*).' The long outro invites the listener to join in with the repeating, 'Got to do it, got to do it, yeah, you got to do it.'

'Southside Shuffle' was the B-side to 'Make Up Your Mind.' It was sampled in Saigon's 'Come On Baby' from the 2009 *Fighting* soundtrack, but it seems the only part of the song that was actually used is a repeated '*yeahhh*' from the intro on the Geils track.

'Hold Your Loving' (Titus Turner, Bernice Snelson) (2:30)
Singer/songwriter Titus Turner released 'Hold Your Loving' in 1957 as the B-side to his 'Stop The Pain' single and it probably would've languished in obscurity were it not for Geils' (Wolf in particular) gift for unearthing such gems. Although his 'Hold Your Loving' was initially overlooked, Turner had great success in the 1950s as a songwriter with other songs like 'Leave My Kitten Alone' (later recorded by Elvis Costello) and 'Tell Me Why' (covered by Elvis Presley).

With a count of, 'One, two, one, two, three, four', the Geils track kicks off. The band stick close to the original jump blues tune but give 'Hold Your Loving' the rave-up treatment, performing it at a faster tempo, and Dick handles the horn parts on harmonica. The band are in a rowdy mood and when the instrumental break hits, Dick takes the lead, Klein runs up and down the neck of his bass, and Justman pounds away on piano while the band clap and whoop and sing background lines. The track served as the B-side to 'Give It To Me' and has the distinction of being the only Geils song where Wolf gets to sing about how his baby makes 'my meatballs bounce.'

'Start All Over Again' (Wolf, Justman) (4:15)
After the high energy of 'Hold Your Loving' comes this ballad. 'Start All Over Again' starts on piano, with Justman setting the mood before the rest of the band enter. Wolf demonstrates his emotional range by delivering the anguish and heartbreak of someone who has to accept a broken relationship and build a new life with someone else. There have been good times, but after the latest time she let him down, 'I'm gonna start all over, over again, all over again.'

Justman turns in a tight organ solo and after the next verses, the music continues to swell, growing bigger and more emotional, as Wolf screams and the band repeat 'start all over, start all over' in the background.

'Give It To Me' (Wolf, Justman) (6:32)
Highest chart place: US: 30, CA: 39, UK: –

Reggae music, with its off-beat rhythms, came out of Jamaica in the mid-to late-1960s and was gaining a foothold in the pop music scene in places like the UK in the early 1970s. Wolf's girlfriend at the time had recently returned to the US from England and brought with her several reggae records, which caught Wolf and Justman's attention. Along with Led Zeppelin's 'D'yer Mak'er', Geils were one of the first rock acts to incorporate reggae, though 'Give It To Me' had only hints of it when they brought the song to Szymczyk. Szymczyk was already a huge reggae fan, and he was the one who pushed to make it 'as reggae as possible.'

    The track begins with a hoarse count-in of 'One, two.' Drums tumble in, followed by the rest of the band and the groove is set with its reggae beat. Wolf tells whoever's working the recording console something like, 'Now don't touch the knobs 'cause I feel we're gonna have some fun with this one here. Oh yeah.' After the bridge comes an organ solo and by the song's mid-point (around the time Wolf blasts a traffic whistle), the song transitions toward rock with a lengthy breakdown. Szymczyk described the jam at the end as 'an all-time winner.' Klein's bass propels the groove while Dick blasts away on harp. Jay replies with a greasy solo of his own, wringing everything he can from each note. Another whistle burst from Wolf, and then Bladd is in the spotlight with drums and percussion while Klein continues pushing the rhythm along. Wolf returns in the background, calling 'All night (*all night*)' through the extended funky fadeout.

    Edited to 3:07, 'Give It To Me' was the first single released from the album. It made the top 40 in Canada and the US *Billboard* chart (and all the way to 15 on the now defunct *Cash Box* chart) but lost momentum when radio stations deemed it too sexually suggestive based on the title and lyrics like, 'Why keep me cold when it's so warm inside.' But as many fans (and band members) have pointed out, just a few months earlier, Chuck Berry's rendition of 'My Ding-A-Ling' made it all the way to number one in the US with its double-entendres and much more overt lyrics. Geils' live performances around this time often featured a manic instrumental break, bringing Bladd and Justman center stage to bang it out on drums and percussion. Their work, along with Wolf's call and response ('ohhh, yeah (*ohhh, yeah*), all night (*all night*)'), stretched out the song to nearly ten minutes.

    The studio track was used in a Heineken beer TV commercial in 2002 as a man at a house party has to decide between offering the last beer to a woman or keeping it for himself. Also in 2002, ska punk band Reel Big Fish covered 'Give It To Me' on their *Cheer Up* album, initially as a 'hidden track.' Their take has a faster tempo, as expected, and uses horns to great effect and ends with a bit of humour. In 2013, the Geils track appeared in the *Grown Ups 2* film.

Related Tracks
'Give It To Me' By Peter Wolf (Wolf, Justman) (FM 101.9/Virgin) (1996)
Prior to a July 1996 show at West Hollywood's House of Blues, Wolf and The Street Ensemble (formerly Houseparty 5) visited Los Angeles radio station KSCA as part of the station's *Music Hall* series. Wolf turns in a relatively short (3:40), semi-acoustic but still rowdy rendition of 'Give It To Me.' Though Wolf also performed 'Long Line' from his 1996 solo album of the same name, that track is not included on the *Live From The Music Hall Volume Three* CD. Half of the proceeds from the CD were donated to charity.

'Hate To See You Go' is another unreleased track waiting in the Atlantic vaults (catalogue number 26318), recorded at New York's Hit Factory studios on or about 4 October 1972. It's likely a cover of the 1955 blues number (sometimes titled 'I Hate To See You Go') by Little Walter and His Jukes.

Ladies Invited (1973)

Personnel:
Peter Wolf: vocals
Seth Justman: keyboards
Magic Dick: harp
J. Geils: guitar
Danny Klein: bass
Stephen Jo Bladd: drums, vocals
Producer: Bill Szymczyk
Engineers: Bill Szymczyk, Allan Blazek
Record label: Atlantic Records
Released: 9 November 1973
Running time: 41:16
Highest chart place: US: 51; CA: 85; UK: –

Arriving the same calendar year and barely seven months behind *Bloodshot*, the band's fourth studio album was the first of entirely original material, ten tracks from the Wolf-Justman team. *Ladies Invited* (the title allegedly inspired by a sign hanging in a bar) builds on the rock foundation of *Bloodshot*, still moored to r&b, soul, and blues, but doesn't include the reggae touch which had proved successful with 'Give It To Me.' The album was the first with Dick on chromatic harp, which allows a player to switch between two sets of reeds. The chromatic is more difficult to play than a Marine band or diatonic, but offers greater range, providing complete scales in any key.

Production was again handled by Bill Szymczyk. He stated in a *Colorado Music Experience* interview with G. Brown that he wanted to get Geils out to Colorado to use the isolated Caribou Ranch Studios, where he'd produced Joe Walsh and others, but Geils preferred to stay in New York with its nightlife. Szymczyk said to the band, 'At least let me mix it there (at Caribou)', to which they agreed. 'I don't think all of them came out', he said. 'I think four of them did. And within two days, three of them left, and only Seth stayed' to finish mixing *Ladies Invited*.

As beautiful as the album cover was, it may not have presented the rock and roll image fans expected and perhaps hindered, rather than helped, sales. The album jacket was a colourful piece by Puerto Rican-born New York fashion illustrator Antonio Lopez. Actress Faye Dunaway served as the model, her eyes and red lips painted on a white background within a silver foil frame, and 'Ladies Invited' scrawled as if in lipstick. As Dunaway explained in *Looking For Gatsby: My Life*, Wolf visited her in Spain while she was working on the film *The Four Musketeers* and 'Peter had an idea for an album cover he wanted to have done while we were in Europe.' Dunaway said once filming was complete, they 'were to go together to Paris where the artist, Antonio, was going to paint my eyes and lips for the new J. Geils album.'

The back cover was a reflective silver monochrome photo of the band, along with the track listing and album credits. The inner sleeve was silver paper with female mannequin heads and roses along the bottom on one side and a plain silver colour on the other. Album credits note, 'inner sleeve design by Douglas T. Slade', Wolf and Bladd's bandmate from their Hallucinations days. Initial vinyl pressings had 'MEZZ IS BACK' etched into the side one runout groove and 'PASS THE WORD' etched into side two. During the recording sessions, Dick was known to wander through the studio proclaiming, 'Mezz is back, Mezz is back.' 'MEZZ' refers to Milton Mesirow, aka Mezz Mezzro, a jazz clarinettist who became known as much for the high-quality marijuana he sold as for his musicianship, with 'Mezz' or 'Mezzrolls' often slang for pot in music circles. Mesirow passed away aged 72 in 1972, just over a year before *Ladies Invited* was released.

Ladies Invited is often unfairly overshadowed by the record before (*Bloodshot*) and the one that followed (*Nightmares*). Although several tracks would've made excellent radio material, only one was released as a single and it failed to chart. As great as the record was, it didn't sell as well as *Bloodshot*, which could be attributed to a lack of airplay and record label promotion rather than the songs themselves. A *Record World* article from 1 December 1973 stated that based on the success of *Bloodshot*, *Ladies Invited* 'shipped gold' (500,000 copies in the US), but by mid-1974, the album was found in the cut-out bin in many record shops in the US and was soon out of print. In the days of physical forms of music (vinyl records, cassettes, 8-track and reel-to-reel tapes), record store inventory was a guessing game. Stock too few copies and sales were lost when consumers couldn't find the product. Stock too many copies and stores were stuck with unsold inventory. Cut-outs, similar to book remainders, were overstock merchandise that retailers returned to record distributors. Record labels would then mark the records – typically with a notch cut into the side of the album cover or spine of the cassette cover or with a corner of the cover snipped off – and sell them back to retailers in large lots at a discount. The physical cut in the cover didn't damage the music but ensured the product could not be sold or returned at full price. Because of those initial returns in 1974, a gold record certification was never officially awarded.

Promotion for the album included a 45-minute documentary of the band on tour, directed by Seth Justman's brother Paul, who would film several Geils music videos in the early 1980s and direct the 2002 documentary *Standing In The Shadows Of Motown*. As part of the US Public Broadcasting Service Independent Focus series, Paul's 1974 film *Post Cards* captured live performances, backstage and offstage bits, and interviews. It also showed the band rehearsing the call-and-response for live performances of 'Give It To Me', working out the 'ohhh, yeah (*ohhh, yeah*)' and 'all night (*all night*)' parts. *Post Cards* provides possibly the only video of Geils performing 'Did You No Wrong' and 'I Can't Go On' from *Ladies Invited*. Notably, Jay is seen playing his flying V guitar and Klein is on a flying V bass. Klein's bass was custom-made from a flying V guitar since there was no such thing as a flying V bass. When it's time for the break in 'I Can't Go On', Wolf shouts, 'Magic Dick, let me hear you blow your face out!' Other concert footage includes part of 'Hard Drivin' Man' and 'Whammer Jammer.' Viewers also get treated to Dick singing Sonny Boy Williamson's 'Peach Tree.' The documentary wraps up with a nearly 12-minute 'Give It To Me', spotlighting Bladd and Justman, Bladd on timbale and Justman on bongos. At the end of the show, the band creates its now-famous pyramid: Dick, Wolf, and Jay at the base, Bladd and Klein above, and Justman climbing to the top. Music critic Lester Bangs, who was briefly caught by the camera in *Post Cards*, once joined Geils on stage, as recounted in *Creem*'s August 1974 issue. The article never stated the exact date, just that Bangs, performing on typewriter, joined Geils for the encore of 'Give It To Me' at Cobo Hall.

The tour included a headlining gig at New York's Madison Square Garden on 30 November. *Billboard* reported on some of the new tunes featured in Geils' set that night, including 'That's Why I'm Thinking Of You', 'Take A Chance On Romance' and 'Chimes.' Also already in the setlist was 'Truck Drivin' Man', later to appear on 1976's *Blow Your Face Out*. After the show, Atlantic's Jerry Wexler presented Mario Medious (who pushed to get the band signed to the label) and band members with awards for *Bloodshot*, which had been certified gold in the US in September. Later on the same *Ladies Invited* tour, a 10 August 1974 *Cash Box* article mentioned Geils' recent headlining gig at the Los Angeles Forum, where Geils 'took the occasion to debut material from their upcoming *Nightmares...* album', with the songs in question likely being 'Detroit Breakdown' and 'Must Of Got Lost.'

The same month *Ladies Invited* was released, Michael Stanley's *Friends And Legends* (also engineered and produced by Szymczyk) arrived in record stores. Although Jay didn't perform on the recording, the credits state, 'saxophones produced by Michael Stanley and J. Geils.'

In the early 1980s, in the wake of the success of *Love Stinks* and *Freeze-Frame*, Atlantic briefly restored and reissued *Ladies Invited* in its original packaging at full price. It was later released on CD in the mid-1990s with the rest of the Geils Atlantic catalogue, and in 2004, Wounded Bird Records, under license from Atlantic, reissued *Ladies Invited* on CD.

'Did You No Wrong' (Wolf, Justman) (4:08)
Highest chart place: US: 104; CA: –; UK: –
The opening track begins with several measures of heavy foot stomping before Klein plunges in with dexterous bass lines, giving the rock track r&b undertones. A few measures of vibraphone are heard before Justman's piano enters. The tune – about a lover's betrayal ('I did you no wrong, why'd you hurt me baby?') – moves swiftly, Dick's harp bolstering the choruses. Close to the mid-point, the tune dives into a slower tempo for the bridge, Jay's

scorching guitar and Justman's swirling organ conveying misery as Wolf, in the role of a spurned lover, laments his hopeless situation: 'I find myself walking and I got no place to go.'

The tempo picks up for the next verse, which brings a change of attitude. Backing vocals accent each line with 'doot... doot.' The lead vocals are more confident, as if the song's protagonist has now accepted his loss and come to realise he's not the one at fault: 'Love can do tricks, make you too blind to see.' The track grows more raucous as Bladd hammers away, Dick's harp becomes more prominent, Justman attacks the piano, and Wolf continues to wail, 'Why'd you hurt me, baby?' 'Did You No Wrong' was the album's only single, edited to 3:39. It appeared on *Billboard*'s Bubbling Under chart for six weeks.

'I Can't Go On' (Wolf, Justman) (5:05)
With its jerky start/stop beat, 'I Can't Go On' is a high-energy party tune in the best J. Geils tradition. Thick bass and punchy organ create a tight funkiness while the tune tells of being pulled – rather than gracefully falling – into love. It's almost a warning, with lines like 'Watch out for your heart, it can lead you on and make you do harm', yet at the same time, Wolf sings that he 'can't go on without your love.'

Bladd introduces the lengthy instrumental break with some quick work on the drumkit. Dick takes over on harp while organ, percussion and bass support. Then it's Justman on organ, climbing, descending, and swiping across the keys. As Wolf sings the last choruses, smooth 'Oooh, oooh, baby, baby' backing vocals carry the track to the end. The track has a distinct Rolling Stones feel yet remains all Geils.

'Lay Your Good Thing Down' (Wolf, Justman) (4:36)
'Lay Your Good Thing Down' is a rock track with a bit of soul thrown in. A few measures of Jay's guitar begin the tune before the rhythm section enters. As he does on many tracks, Justman handles both piano and organ. Harp is introduced with the first verse, accenting the lyrics. A woman has been toying with her boyfriend and now he's begging for more: 'Look here, you always teasin' when you should be a-pleasin', now I'm a man insane.'

Guitar, harp, and keyboards lead into the instrumental break together before Wolf shouts out some of his 'yabba jabba gooba looba labba be bah' jive talk and Justman is turned loose with a soulful organ piece. After the break, the lyrics make clear nothing's changed. 'Every time I move in, you always movin' out', sings Wolf as the woman in question continues to send mixed signals. Wolf continues to plead for a little sex as the track fades out.

'That's Why I'm Thinking Of You' (Wolf, Justman) (3:14)
A laid-back ballad with a Stonesy sensibility that also brings to mind Otis Redding, 'That's Why I'm Thinking Of You' mourns a painful breakup and all the memories of that ill-fated relationship. Wolf sings from the viewpoint

of a man in sorrow who's looking back at what his former girlfriend meant to him and 'all the things we used to do.' Justman's deft organ work defines the track, giving the song its soul. Jay's guitar is sparse but effective. There's no big instrumental break, no blistering solos, just solid playing throughout in support of Wolf's plaintive vocals. Despite the grief-stricken lines ('I lost a lover and a friend', 'Early morning finds me wanting you', 'That's why I'm still missing you'), there is no push for reconciliation, no plea for things to go back to the way they used to be. Wolf's lyrics instead wallow in pain and loss but without a way to move forward. 'That's Why I'm Thinking Of You' was the B-side of 'Did You No Wrong.'

'No Doubt About It' (Wolf, Justman) (3:50)
This blues rock tune begins as if it's going to be a warning about the pain of failed romance: 'The flame of love is so hot to touch, it's bound to hurt because it burns so much.' Maybe it is a warning, but it builds up and soon becomes a down-and-dirty pounding party track. The verses move in a start-stop rhythm, Bladd and Klein pouncing with each beat. Dick shines on harp, riding over and under the lyrics before taking the lead with a boogie break while Justman plays rollicking piano beneath. The latter part of the song is unleashed in a rave-up jam. Every instrument seems to solo at the same time, yet it remains cohesive. That this track was never released as a single or promoted for radio play reflects poorly on the record company.

'The Lady Makes Demands' (Wolf, Justman) (4:22)
Side two of the LP opens with a change of pace after 'No Doubt About It.' The song's intro provides a sweet r&b sentimentality as it builds toward the first chorus. Wolf sings about a woman who drives him out of his mind, yet 'she's the best thing I can find.' He's flustered and frustrated, wanting to be with her despite her faults: 'She says she wants me near her, then she don't want me to stay.' Under the chorus, Dick's harp and Justman's piano are played in a light-hearted fashion, providing a playful attitude. Then, Justman switches to organ during the verses for a more earnest feeling. The break brings a tempo change, with harp and percussion in double time before settling back down for a couple more verses. Another musical shift finds Wolf gently asking, 'Don't you love me, baby?' He's soon joined by soft backing vocals repeating the same line before the song returns to the chorus. The track fades as Wolf continues to proclaim his love and his frustration, even tossing in a few falsetto vocals.

'My Baby Don't Love Me' (Wolf, Justman) (3:43)
A heart-wrenching tune reminiscent of something from the 1950s and early 1960s, 'My Baby Don't Love Me' begins with Justman's grand-sounding keyboards. Wolf lays down emotional vocals, proving the band could create sincere ballads in addition to the expected rock and roll boogie numbers.

Wolf portrays a man lost and alone after a breakup, crying in his beer as he reflects on what went wrong. The gentle call-and-response verses add a level of weepiness to the woe-is-me lyrics: 'I thought if I loved her (*she would love me*)', and 'When I come home (*she won't be there*).'

The playing is low-key but emotional, with Bladd getting in some understated drum fills in the mid-section as Justman works piano and organ. The song surges toward the end, Wolf cataloguing every moment of his days when he'll be missing her: 'When I feel sad', 'when I get lonely', 'early in the morning', each line bringing the soft refrain of '*she won't be there*' to drive home the emptiness.

'Diddyboppin" (Wolf, Justman) (3:32)
'Oh, darlin', falling in love is *wonderful*', proclaims Wolf at the start of this slightly giddy number. He reminds the listener that 'every good story has a beginning, a middle, and an *end*.' It's an easygoing, light-hearted number that, despite the humorous spoken intro and sometimes nonsensical lyrics, avoids becoming a novelty piece. Keyboards, bass, and drums provide the funky 'diddybop' foundation of the song's title as Wolf sings, 'I went to Spain, had some quiche Lorraine' and 'I went to France, I learned to dance.'

Wolf introduces the instrumental break with, 'Hot stuff, can't get enough, come on', and Justman steps in with a punchy organ solo over Bladd's drumming, flirting with a Latin beat. Wolf returns with another verse before things get goofier: 'You know what I'm gonna do? I'm gonna *dormez-vous* all over you' and 'Uh, that's no gentleman, that's my wife' as the track moves into the fadeout. Intentional or coincidental, the next album's 'Detroit Breakdown' has Wolf still thinking about diddy-bopping with the line, 'Everybody diddy-boppin' right in the street.'

'Take A Chance (On Romance)' (Wolf, Justman) (3:41)
Driving piano and organ launch the fast-moving, high-energy 'Take A Chance (On Romance).' Bladd's powerful drumming and Klein's bass steer the groove while Dick's harp accents the verses. In the verse before the break, Jay turns up his guitar and Bladd effortlessly adds some muscular drum fills to inject another level of energy. When that first break does hit, Jay lets loose with a raunchy solo, wrapping it up over more of Bladd's fills and Justman's pounding piano. The extended outro gives Dick a chance to shine with some rapid-fire harp over Wolf's madman howling. Had the promotion people at the record label been paying attention, 'Take A Chance (On Romance)' is another track that would've been a solid choice for a single.

'Chimes' (Wolf, Justman) (5:05)
From the start, Justman sets the mood on organ for this closing track, Bladd keeping time on cymbal. A piano chord strikes and the music opens up slowly, guitar and bass skulking in. Wolf sets the scene: 'It's long past

midnight, long past gettin' any sleep.' This brooding track is different from the others on *Ladies Invited*, and different from most songs on any Geils album. A dark piece evoking paranoia and desperation, 'Chimes' creeps into the listener's consciousness, creating a sense of claustrophobia. The chimes in the title seem to be wind chimes moving in the dead of night but also might be the chimes of a clock, slowly counting the minutes through a night of terror.

Wolf alternately confides and howls, conveying his torment without ever naming what's preying on him. Dick delivers a solo on a chromatic harp, taking his time, calling up sleepless nights, fear of the unknown and unseen, and the endless hours waiting for dawn. Jay comes in behind with an equally brilliant stinging guitar solo. Following another chorus, organ and cymbal come to the forefront again, driving the track through the fadeout with the same ominous feeling as the intro.

Related Tracks
Soul Pole No. 1 (25 December 1973)
Soul Pole Records was a project Bill Szymczyk assembled as souvenirs of his recording sessions. Over time, it has achieved mythical status, as only a handful of titles were ever created, with each limited to 50 pressings given as gifts to artists and others associated with the sessions. *SP1* features J. Geils with some assistance from Barnstorm (Joe Walsh, Joe Vitale, Kenny Passarelli and Rocke Grace).

The tracks comprising side one include 'bits and pieces from things that happened in the studio with the Geils band.' It makes clear why Szymczyk often referred to Geils as 'six comedians disguised as a band.' Working snatches of 'Did You No Wrong', 'The Lady Makes Demands' and 'My Baby Don't Love Me' are dropped in with comedic chatter, funky jamming, talk of 'Mezz is back' and a bit of echo, under the title 'Hot Left-Overs.' Another track brings Dean Martin and Jerry Lewis getting raunchy as they record promos for their 1953 film *The Caddy*. Barnstorm's Vitale and Passarelli jam on the short 'Funky Drummer.' 'Get Those Tapes' provides more song bits and clowning around. Wolf jokes that Szymczyk has recorded too much incriminating and compromising chatter.

Three jams are featured. 'My other band I was working with was Barnstorm', said Szymcyzk. 'They were playing in New York. I was recording the Geils band at the Hit Factory. I took both bands out to dinner... just to introduce everybody.' Dinner was served at the House of Chan Chinese restaurant. Alcohol flowed. They were eventually tossed out of the establishment and 'We all went back to the studio and jammed together.' The laid-back 'Geilsstorm No. 1' moves between jazz and funk, with a sax that would be at home on Traffic's 'The Low Spark Of High Heeled Boys.' 'Geilsstorm No. 2' is a funkier, punchy track with prominent organ, guitar and sax. Side two (the centre label states 'side three') consists of a single number titled 'Allan, I Need You (Or – Chinese Aftermath).' Szymczyk explained it was 'the last jam of the evening/morning, no edits, no overdubs, just two great bands getting to know each other and having a blast.' It's a 20-minute loose, funky workout. There's cowbell, guitar, organ, bass, drums and piano, along with plenty of sax, courtesy of Jay and Dick. Around the 17-minute mark, it slows and soon Szymczyk cuts in to get his engineer's attention to change the tape reels: 'Allan, I need you.'

Typical for a Szymczyk production, Lee Hulko cut the plate for mastering. The vinyl graffiti on side one states, 'SOUL POLE NO. 1 SIDE A' and 'HAVE YOU SEEN BEN?' Side two reads, 'SOUL POLE NO 1 SIDE B' and 'With Love From Al + Bill.'

Above: The famous Geils show-closer pyramid, Boston Garden, 1982. Bottom L-R: Dick, Jay, Bladd. Middle: Wolf, Klein. Top: Justman. (*Derek Szabo*)

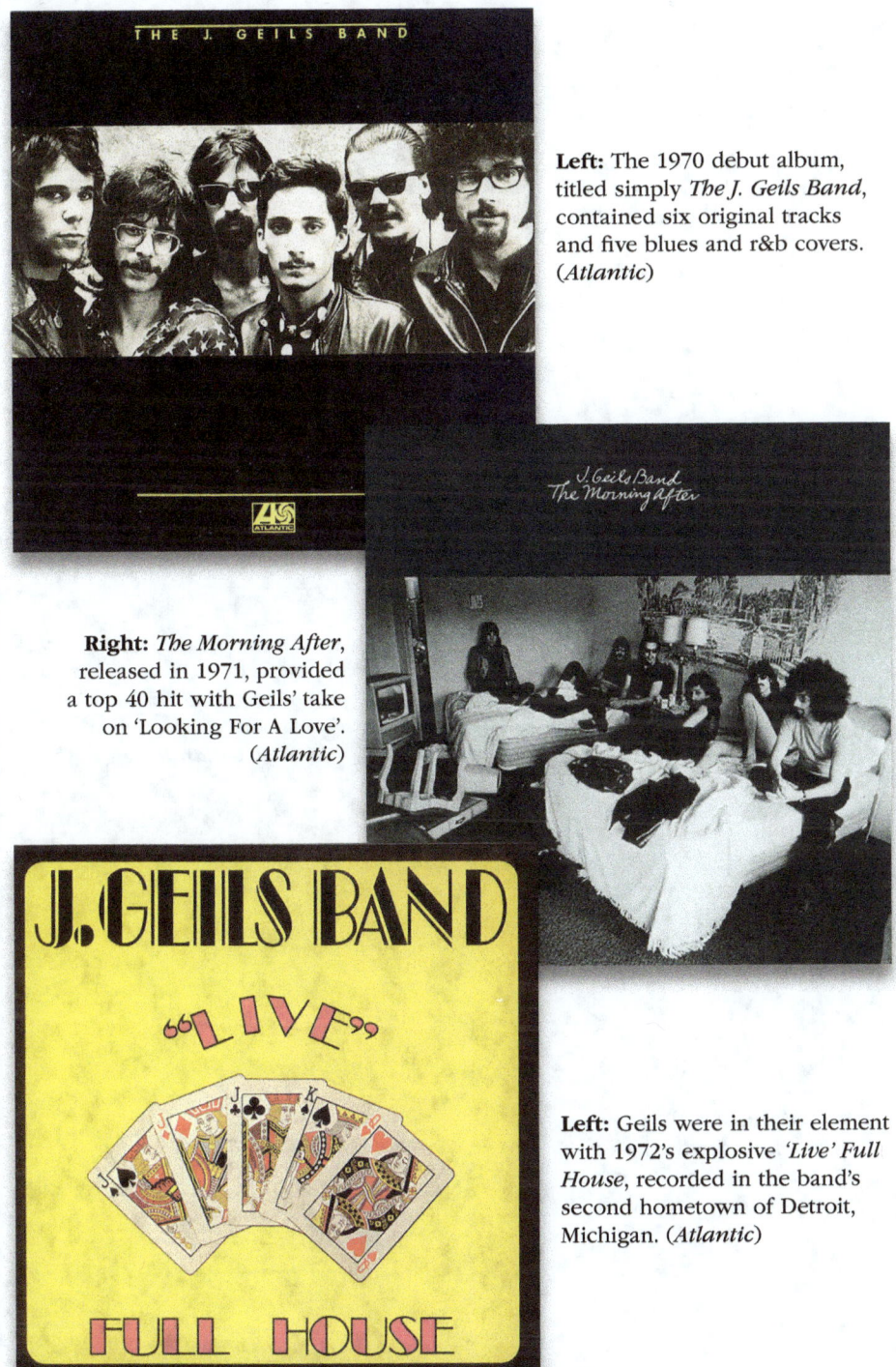

Left: The 1970 debut album, titled simply *The J. Geils Band*, contained six original tracks and five blues and r&b covers. (*Atlantic*)

Right: *The Morning After*, released in 1971, provided a top 40 hit with Geils' take on 'Looking For A Love'. (*Atlantic*)

Left: Geils were in their element with 1972's explosive *'Live' Full House*, recorded in the band's second hometown of Detroit, Michigan. (*Atlantic*)

Right: 1973's *Bloodshot*, a US gold record, brought a harder rock sound and contained the reggae-influenced hit 'Give It To Me'. (*Atlantic*)

Left: Actress Faye Dunaway was the model for the cover artwork of 1973's *Ladies Invited*, Geils' first album of all original material. (*Atlantic*)

Right: The 1974 release *Nightmares* featured 'Detroit Breakdown' and the band's biggest hit to date with 'Must Of Got Lost'. (*Atlantic*)

Above: The J. Geils Blues Band at Cambridge Common, April 1968. (*Tom Benedek Collection (PH 073), Robert S. Cox Special Collections and University Archives Research Center, UMass Amherst Libraries*)

Below: Mario Medious (The Big M) and Geils with *Bloodshot* gold records. L-R: Medious, Klein, Dick, Wolf, Jay, Bladd, Atlantic's Jerry Wexler. (*Mario Medious*)

Above: L-R: Mario Medious and Wolf in 1974. Medious (The Big M) was instrumental in getting Geils signed to Atlantic Records. (*Mario Medious*)

Left: Dick and Jay trading licks sometime around 1974 or 1975, probably at New York's Academy of Music. (*Lance Kovar*)

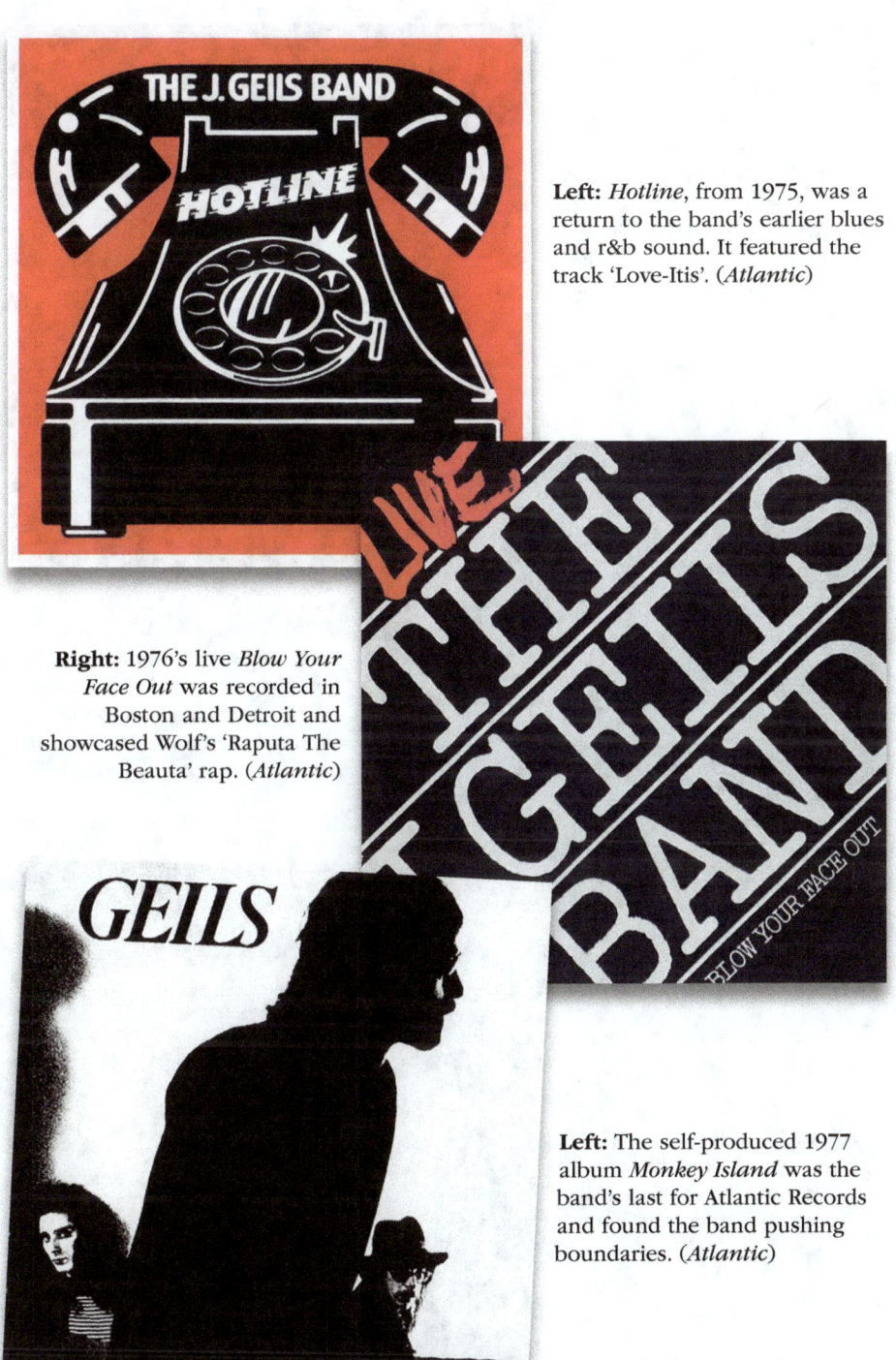

Left: *Hotline*, from 1975, was a return to the band's earlier blues and r&b sound. It featured the track 'Love-Itis'. (*Atlantic*)

Right: 1976's live *Blow Your Face Out* was recorded in Boston and Detroit and showcased Wolf's 'Raputa The Beauta' rap. (*Atlantic*)

Left: The self-produced 1977 album *Monkey Island* was the band's last for Atlantic Records and found the band pushing boundaries. (*Atlantic*)

Right: Geils' first album for a new record label, 1978's *Sanctuary*, gave the band its first UK hit with 'One Last Kiss'. (*EMI America*)

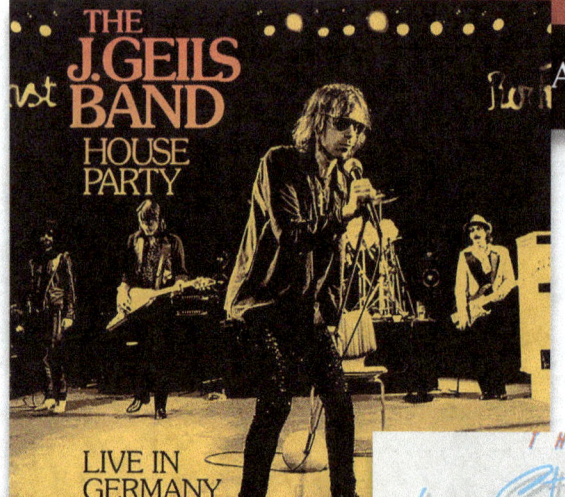

Left: Recorded in 1979 but not released until 2014/2015, *House Party Live In Germany* captured the band's *Rockpalast* performance. (*Eagle Vision*)

Right: *Love Stinks*, from 1980, retained the band's r&b and rock roots but marked a shift towards a new wave sound. (*EMI America*)

Left: Seth Justman on stage at the Calderone Theater, West Hempstead, New York, August 1975, shortly before the release of *Hotline*. (*Steve Tomlinson*)

Right: L-R: Jay, Wolf, Bladd and Klein performing at the Calderone Theater, West Hempstead, New York, in August 1975. (*Steve Tomlinson*)

Left: The harbour cruise celebrating Geils on EMI America. Shown here are Capitol-EMI Boston branch manager Jim Johnson, label president Jim Mazza and executive Giles 'Frenchy' Gauthier. (*Paul Lanning, photographer unknown*)

Above: Those Bad Boys onstage at The Warehouse, New Orleans, Louisiana, 1979. L-R: Bladd, Dick (in shadows), Klein, Justman, Jay (in shadows). (*J. Douglas*)

Left: Jay in the spotlight for a Flying V solo at The Warehouse in New Orleans in 1979 on the *Sanctuary* tour. (*J. Douglas*)

Right: L-R: EMI America president Jim Mazza, Wolf and Madame Wong at Madam Wong's restaurant and live music venue in 1980. (*Jim Mazza*)

Above: Preparing for a photo shoot on Long View Farm property, 1978. Seated, L-R: Wolf, Dick, Justman, Klein. Standing: Jay, Bladd. (*Patricia Glennon*)

Below: Working at Long View Farm studios in North Brookfield. Seated, L-R: Jay, Justman, engineer Dave Thoener. Standing: Dick, Wolf. (*Photo by Bruce Arnold, restored by Patricia Glennon*)

Above: Wolf inciting the crowd as only the Woofa Goofa can. Captured here at The Warehouse, New Orleans, Louisiana, in 1979. (*J. Douglas*)

Right: Magic Dick on stage performing on soprano saxophone. Jay is in the shadows just out of the spotlight. (*David Thoener*)

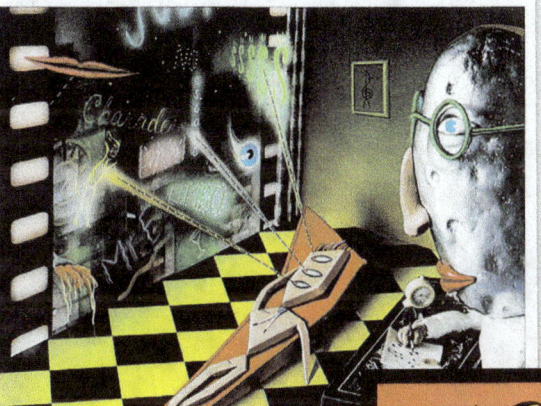

Left: Released in late 1981, *Freeze-Frame* put Geils on the top of the charts around the world with 'Centerfold' and the title track. (*EMI America*)

Right: Recorded at Pine Knob Theater near Detroit, 1982's live *Showtime!* was the last album to feature the six-man lineup. (*EMI America*)

Left: *You're Gettin' Even While I'm Gettin' Odd*, recorded as a five-piece band, proved to be the final Geils studio record. (*EMI America*)

Above: Promotional photo taken from the band's appearance on *The Joe Franklin Show* in New York, February 1982. L-R: Franklin, Wolf. (*EMI America*)

Left: Jay tearin' it up at Madison Square Garden on 20 February 1982 on the *Freeze-Frame* tour. It was Jay's 36th birthday. (*David Plastik*)

Above: Hanging around for a photo shoot at Model Café in Union Square, Boston, circa 1981. L-R: Dick, Wolf, Justman, Klein. (*Derek Szabo*)

Left: Magic Dick on harmonica, gettin' down to it at Boston Garden in February 1982 on the lengthy *Freeze-Frame* tour. (*Derek Szabo*)

Right: The college of musical knowledge is in session. Peter Wolf in the spotlight at Boston Garden, February 1982. (*Derek Szabo*)

Below: Hard-drivin' man Peter Wolf brings the house party to the crowd at Boston Garden, February 1982, in support of *Freeze-Frame*. (*Derek Szabo*)

Left: Released in 1979, *Best Of The J. Geils Band* pulled together nine tracks from five of the band's Atlantic albums. (*Atlantic*)

Right: *Flashback – The Best Of The J. Geils Band*, from 1985, showcased the band's big hits like 'Love Stinks' and 'Centerfold'. (*EMI America*)

Left: Packed with 18 tracks, 2006's *Best Of The J. Geils Band* compiled numbers from both the Atlantic and the EMI years. (*Capitol Records*)

Nightmares ...And Other Tales From The Vinyl Jungle (1974)

Personnel:
Peter Wolf: vocals
Seth Justman: keyboards, vocals
Magic Dick: marine band, chromatic, bass and chord harmonicas
J. Geils: guitars, mandolin
Danny Klein: bass
Stephen Jo Bladd: percussion, vocals
George Jessel: spoken words on Funky Judge
Producer: Bill Szymczyk
Engineers: Bill Szymczyk, Allan Blazek, Kevin Herron
Special assistance: Juke Joint Jimmy
Record label: Atlantic Records
Released: 25 September 1974
Running time: 40:19
Highest chart place: US: 26; CA: 32; UK –

Nightmares ...And Other Tales From The Vinyl Jungle is the third album (following *The Morning After* and *Full House*) to show the band's name as 'J. Geils Band', rather than 'The J. Geils Band', but there was no intention behind it. *Nightmares* – the recording of which may or may not have been assisted by a bit of nitrous oxide – consisted of eight Wolf-Justman tracks and one cover tune. Wolf based the title on one of producer Szymczyk's expressions while making records: 'just another tale from the vinyl jungle.' The album provided a rebound for the disappointing sales of *Ladies Invited*, becoming the band's second highest-charting album to date in both the US and Canada. It also spawned Geils' highest-charting single until 1981's 'Centerfold.'

The band had most of May 1974 off from touring and prior to the recording sessions in New York, Wolf was in Los Angeles, where he ended up in a studio with John Lennon during Lennon's legendary 'Lost Weekend.' Wolf and Lennon's time together lasted a few days and as Wolf told Terry Gross in a 2010 National Public Radio interview, 'there was a lot of Remy Martin and milk, and Harry Nilsson.' A month before *Nightmare*'s release, on 7 August, Wolf married actress Faye Dunaway. The couple intentionally kept their marriage out of the public eye, focusing on their respective careers while doing their best to maintain a relationship despite considerable time apart due to tours and filmmaking.

Wolf wasn't happy with the art director at Atlantic Records, so when it came time to design the album cover, either Ahmet or his brother Nesuhi Ertegun brought in Peter Corriston and Pam Vassil from Album Graphics, Inc. 'Basically, they just needed someone to assemble it', said Corriston. 'So they picked up this illustration and got the rights to it and asked me and Pam

Vassil (to work on it). That's how I met (Wolf).' Wolf was obviously happy with Corriston's efforts, as Corriston worked on Geils' next three albums through 1977's *Monkey Island*. Among other pieces, Corriston designed Led Zeppelin's *Physical Graffiti* and The Rolling Stones' *Tattoo You* (winning a Grammy Award for that album package).

The surreal *Nightmares* cover image showed a man sinking into a tightly made bed, his face, hands, knees, and some toes poking through the blanket, similar to being sucked into quicksand. The painting, titled *I Wish For Peace*, was something Wolf had come across by abstract expressionist Jean Lagarrigue that fit the album's *Nightmare* title. The LP's inner sleeve was specific to the album. One side of the black sleeve displayed headshots of the band members, while the reverse contained lyrics for all nine tracks – a first for Geils. The headshots were taken by Shanghai-born fashion photographer Yasuhiro Wakabayashi, known as Hiro. Hiro had already done some album photography for the likes of Johnny Winter and Rick Derringer before *Nightmares*.

The supporting tour included two nights at Cobo Arena in Detroit, on 3 and 4 November 1974, where the band was given the Key to the City of Detroit. The 'Key to the City' tradition dates back to medieval days and, in modern times is a symbolic gesture to show appreciation and honour the recipient for reflecting well on the city. The 3 November show was recorded for US radio program *King Biscuit Flower Hour* and broadcast in quadraphonic sound in December. It was the band's second time on *King Biscuit* and their segment consisted of '(Ain't Nothin' But A) House Party', 'Detroit Breakdown', 'Must Of Got Lost', 'Give It To Me', and 'Looking For A Love.'

Similar to *Bloodshot* and *Ladies Invited*, initial pressings of *Nightmares* had a humorous note etched into the runout groove. Side two asked, 'SO DIS IS A REKID, HUH?' (*So this is a record, huh?*). Although two of the band's live shows had by now been recorded and later broadcast in quadrophonic sound as part of the *King Biscuit* radio show, *Nightmares* was the only Geils album available in quadraphonic sound, which entailed a slightly different mix. Quad records required specialised stereo equipment for playback and provided a surround-sound atmosphere, with separate audio channels typically placed in the four corners of a listening room, creating a soundscape that enveloped the listener. In June 2023, Rhino Records, under Atlantic, rereleased *Nightmares* with its quadraphonic mix on a limited-edition CD as part of Rhino's Quadio series.

'Detroit Breakdown' (Wolf, Justman) (6:00)

The album opens with a blast of funky rock and roll in tribute to the band's second hometown of Detroit, Michigan. In barely three years, from March 1971 to the release of *Nightmares* in September 1974, Geils had played two dozen shows in and around Detroit, tearin' it up from the Eastown Theatre to the Cinderella Ballroom to Cobo Arena. 'Detroit Breakdown' begins on a crescendo, jangling guitar, drums, bass, and piano swelling louder, Dick adding a punch on harp. At the moment the band reaches a climax, Justman takes a swipe down the keyboard and starts pounding away with a piano riff while Bladd keeps time on cymbals. The entire band joins in by the first line: 'Music is blastin', we're havin' a ball.' Wolf screams and howls about getting out of control, passing limits, and hot, sweaty dancing.

In and around the bass and drums, Justman lays down some piano work that might be overlooked initially, given Klein and Bladd's hard-driving rhythm section. The bridge is ushered in with some funky bass and a call of 'breakdown!' Wolf references being 'out on Woodward', a nod to Woodward Avenue, one of Detroit's north-south main streets. When he announces, 'I'm gettin' ready, man, to blow my top', that's Dick's cue to blast away on chromatic harmonica. Another verse and chorus follow before Wolf calls out 'Let me hear ya, Jerome' for a guitar break. Most fans know Jay's first name is John, but over the course of many records, Wolf sometimes refers to him as Jerome. It's a Woofa-Goofa nickname with no underlying meaning, though it may initially have been an off-the-cuff reference to Jerome Green, who played maracas in Bo Diddley's band (Diddley had a song called 'Bring It To Jerome' and later another titled, 'Hey, Jerome'). 'Detroit Breakdown' was never released as a single but has always been one of Geils' biggest numbers.

'Givin' It All Up' (Wolf, Justman) (3:43)
Highest chart place: US: 106; CA: –; UK: –
After the heavier opening track comes a more pop/r&b number, reminiscent of Geils from a few years earlier. Dick works the harp with ease, delivering the equivalent of a horn section, laying down more than a dozen overdubs. Justman's piano is often part of the rhythm section, creating a rich sound as Wolf sings about leaving behind the playboy single life: 'I'm giving it all up for you.' He's happy despite knowing 'the promises you made can easily fade.'

The song builds even as the extended fadeout begins, background vocals repeating, 'give it up, givin' it all up' while Wolf continues screaming and proclaiming his love. An edited version (3:11) of 'Givin' It All Up' was released as a single. It didn't make the US Top Pop Singles Chart but did appear on *Billboard*'s Bubbling Under chart for one week.

'Must Of Got Lost' (Wolf, Justman) (5:04)
Highest chart place: US: 12; CA: 27; UK –
From a grammar perspective, it should be '*Must've*' rather than '*Must of*', but that's incidental to the greatness of the tune. Wolf reiterated the song's origins on Redbeard's *In The Studio* radio program, telling how he wrote most of the lyrics on an envelope during an airplane trip, and had some of the melody in mind when he sat down with Justman, who worked out the arrangement. The tune eases in on drums, bass, and guitar, and Wolf's lyrics set the tone: 'Never thought about tomorrow, seemed like a long time to come.' The song's

narrator blames himself for letting love slip away while pondering things that could've been if he'd not been 'so blind, baby.' It's not until almost two-thirds through that Jay comes to the front with a few measures of guitar before Justman takes flight on organ as Wolf repeats the chorus. Jay then returns with more blazing guitar to carry the track through to the end.

Although it's always been a concert favourite and drives crowds wild, it's a song of regret that has a sombre inspiration. It's based on Wolf's high school girlfriend and longtime companion Edie, whom he loved but never married. Out on the road with the band, somewhere along the way, he 'got lost' and let her slip away without realizing what a good thing he had. Tragically, she later died in a car accident. Wolf also dedicated 'Never Let It Go' from his 1990 album *Up To No Good* to her. Whittled down to 2:53, 'Must Of Got Lost' became the band's highest charting single in the US and cracked Canada's top 30. It was the first Geils record to make the charts in Australia, at 72. The song appeared in the 2004 film *Miracle*, about the 1980 US men's Olympic hockey team, and was featured in season four of the US sports comedy television show *East Bound And Down* in 2013.

'Look Me In The Eye' (Wolf, Justman) (3:57)
In contrast to the previous track, here Wolf is singing about intentionally walking away from a relationship and this time, he's the one who's been neglected and hurt. His urgent vocals carry conviction as he asks, 'Do you think I'd let you hurt me again?' But first, he demands she admit she's in the wrong: 'Look me in the eye and tell me.' Harp and piano join drums and bass, pulsing under the verses. After holding steady in the background, Jay steps forward at the right moment for the break and churns out a solo. Another chorus follows, and with the next verse, Jay dives in and out over Justman's piano and organ riffs. As Wolf continues to demand, 'Look me in the eye', the band carry the song through the fadeout.

'Nightmares' (Wolf, Justman) (1:14)
Revisiting some of the paranoia from the previous album's 'Chimes', this album's title track speaks of someone who's gone over the edge of sanity and 'you ain't neeevvvver comin' back.' Though the wild track may seem improvised, 'That was thoroughly planned', said Szymczyk. 'It was like, 'We wanna do something really off the wall.'' He continued, 'Pete had that rap, Stephen beating the hell out of congas and all kinds of percussion. It was, 'Let's do something completely bizarre.''

At just over a minute long, the frantic cut packs a wallop. Rabid drumming and percussion from Bladd, combined with screaming vocals from Wolf – all of it over background vocals repeating, 'whoa, ooh-oh oh ohhh oh' – frame the piece to create the horror of a nightmare. This is the first Geils album with a 'title track.' The song 'Nightmares' was featured in the 2021 film *Cruella* but was not included on the accompanying soundtrack.

'Stoop Down #39' (Wolf, Justman) (6:50)
Wild harp work introduces 'Stoop Down #39.' Dick said that while Geils worked on their albums, he would often record a practice session, then take the tape home or into another small studio room to practice and work out his parts. The harmonica served as 'frosting' on many of the band's songs, taking something that was already great to a higher level. For *Nightmares*, the band convened in New York and as luck would have it, one of Dick's trumpet heroes was performing near the band's hotel. Jazz royalty Roy 'Little Jazz' Eldridge was the house band leader at Jimmy Ryan's jazz club and Dick would watch Eldridge perform nearly every night, with Dick even bringing in his own trumpet at one point, which Eldrige used on stage. The harp intro to 'Stoop Down' was heavily inspired by Eldridge's style of playing. Dick didn't imitate any Eldridge licks but said that he was working to capture Eldridge's intensity and approach, 'going for a badness about it' and 'soaring over the backup, flying over everything.'

After the intro, the tempo downshifts as the track celebrates 'my lady lover, and I don't want another' and Wolf's lyrics list her best qualities, from being a 'real sweet kisser' to 'an all-night mover.' Midpoint, Wolf calls out, 'Awww, crank it!' and Dick returns for another solo before Jay takes the spotlight. All the while, handclaps keep it upbeat and moving briskly before boogie piano brings it back to the next verse. The 'na nana na na, stoop, stoop, stoop down baby' party attitude carries to the end, with everyone blazing away. Dick said he prefers this studio version of 'Stoop Down' to the take on 1982's live *Showtime!*

'I'll Be Coming Home' (Wolf, Justman) (4:30)
'I'll Be Coming Home' fades in on organ, piano, bass, and percussion over ambient restaurant noise. The track has a laidback feeling despite the yearning in the lyrics. Wolf sings, 'It's so hard to love this way when the one you love is so far away' while promising he's on his way back home. The album credits mention 'Mr. Du Midi and his restaurant' for the song's ambient noise. Klein recalled producer Szymczyk recording some local musicians in a restaurant but wasn't sure where. 'That was at the Du Midi on West 48th Street in New York', confirmed Szymczyk. 'A bunch of us had been there more than once. It was a great little French restaurant. I took a tape deck over, a couple of mics, and recorded a whole dinner.' That recording was then mixed into the Geils track, painting a picture of a small bistro with local musicians performing for diners.

The instrumental break brings a mandolin solo from Jay. It's so effective; it's a wonder he didn't use mandolin on any other songs. Close to the 3:00 mark, in the middle of Jay's mandolin piece, comes the pop of a cork. 'I think it's a wine cork and I think I added that later', said Szymczyk. The song's fadeout brings more ambient restaurant noise, including accordion and singing.

'Funky Judge' (Andre Williams, Leo Hutton) (3:15)
Originally done by East St Louis, Illinois, band Bull & the Matadors in 1968, 'Funky Judge (Part 1)' is a good time tune about standing before a judge/magistrate and pleading a case that's never made clear: 'I didn't do it, your honour, what she told you was a lie.' Was it a criminal act, or was it a lovers' misunderstanding? The Geils track opens with 'Aawwwww, order in the court!' and Bladd hammers the drumkit like a gavel in a courtroom.

Justman and Bladd were huge fans of American singer, actor, and comedian George Jessel, who turned out to be easier to get for the recording of 'Funky Judge' than expected, though he didn't join the band in the studio. Instead, said Szymczyk, Wolf (possibly facilitated through Faye Dunaway's connections) recorded Jessel on a cassette tape and brought it in for use on the song. Jessel plays the role of the judge, declaring, 'I want no shenanigans in my court room. Please bring on the first case.' Over a loose, funky groove with prominent bass and harmonica, Wolf shouts, 'I didn't do it. Get my lawyer!' The Geils version is mostly true to the Matadors' original, but when Jessel asks, 'Where do you come from, young man?' Wolf replies, 'I'm from the Bronx, your honour', as opposed to Bull's response of Alabama. And while Bull gets a sentence of 17 years, Wolf gets 14. 'Funky Judge' was the B-side to 'Must Of Got Lost.'

'Gettin' Out' (Wolf, Justman) (5:46)
The band throw everything they have into this fast tempo number. Justman kicks it off with a rapid descending glide on the piano, moving from right to left on the stereo speakers. Staccato, jazzy piano and pounding bass and drums drive the intro. The track is a perfect package of paranoia and desperation, with Wolf in the role of a madman. Lines like, 'I'm high on the ledge, it's getting me uptight' and 'everyone around me wants to do me harm' stir that feeling of panic.

The Klein and Bladd rhythm section throws fuel on the fire, burning up the tune under a break that lasts over two glorious minutes. Dick enters with blistering harp, then Justman delivers on piano, and finally, Jay is there with gritty guitar. Another verse and chorus follow before staccato piano, bass, and drums carry the track through the outro, never relenting. As with the song 'Nightmares', 'Gettin' Out' was featured in the 2021 film *Cruella* but was not on the soundtrack. Edited to 2:46, 'Gettin' Out' was the B-side of 'Givin' It All Up' in the US and Canada.

Related Tracks
The Brandy Bunch – Drunken Sessions In 1974 [Bootleg]
So named because of the amount of Remy Martin brandy consumed during the process, *The Brandy Bunch* – the title a play on the US 1969-1974 television show *The Brady Bunch* – was compiled from time in the studio in Los Angeles in May 1974 during John Lennon's 18-month 'Lost Weekend.'

At the time, Lennon would've been working on Harry Nilsson's *Pussy Cats* and his own *Walls And Bridges*. Wolf, Lennon, Nilsson, and Dennis Dunaway (Alice Cooper Group) ended up in a studio, soon joined by Paul Simon and Art Garfunkel and actress Diane Keaton. Jimmy Iovine, one of the engineers on *Pussy Cats* and *Walls And Bridges*, and who would later produce acts like Stevie Nicks and U2, recorded the sessions. While certainly novel, the shambolic results that have been leaked don't amount to much other than a rambling, sometimes raunchy, drunken good time.

Not all tracks on the one-hour and 40-minute bootleg include Wolf, as when Lennon is working out 'It's All Down To Goodnight Vienna' (for Ringo Starr), but Wolf is mostly present. During some jamming, Wolf calls out for brandy. Later, he's heard shouting, 'Let the good times roll' and the musicians very loosely take up that 1956 Shirley & Lee tune (which Nilsson had covered on his 1971 *Nilsson Schmilsson* album). When Lennon tosses up Little Richard's 'Send Me Some Lovin' or Ben E. King's 'Stand By Me', Wolf adds enthusiastic backing vocals. Bobby Freeman's 'Do You Want To Dance' gets the same treatment. Wolf takes lead vocals as he starts to improvise with 'I Could Have Danced All Night' (definitely not the Lerner and Loewe tune) and Sam Cooke's 'Having A Party.'

Hotline (1975)

Personnel:
Peter Wolf: vocals
Seth Justman: keyboards, vocals
Magic Dick: harmonicas
J. Geils: guitars
Danny Klein: bass
Stephen Jo Bladd: percussion, vocals
Producers: Bill Szymczyk, Allan Blazek
Engineers: Bill Szymczyk, Allan Blazek, Dave Thoener
Special assistance: Juke Joint Jimmy
Record label: Atlantic Records
Released: 9 September 1975
Running time: 41:28
Highest chart place: US: 36, CA: –, UK: –

The band's seventh release was a return to their earlier style and included four covers of blues and r&b songs alongside five Wolf-Justman originals. *Hotline* also had more of a live feel in regard to the studio performances. As Wolf stated in a September 1977 *Circus* interview, *Hotline* was 'pretty much the type of stuff we'd play in the dressing rooms before shows.' In terms of sales and chart activity, it made less of an impact than *Nightmares*, due possibly to lack of airplay or a hit single.

Production was again handled by Bill Szymcyzk and Allan Blazek. David Thoener was an assistant engineer at The Record Plant, where *Hotline* was recorded and is listed in the album credits as one of the engineers. That wasn't the case, but Thoener was still part of the recording team. 'I was chosen to work with Bill because I was on the cusp of becoming an engineer,' said Thoener, 'and the studio wanted to provide Bill with an assistant that could double as an engineer if needed.' Blazek was already filling that role, so Thoener 'was never needed in an engineering capacity. Bill and Allan were wonderful to work with. It was this album that solidified the friendship between the band and myself and led to years of future albums.' Indeed, the band were clearly happy with Thoener, who went on to engineer *Monkey Island* through *Freeze-Frame*.

Hotline's bold cover, created by Peter Corriston, consisted of a stylised black and white rotary-dial telephone against a red background, with HOTLINE emblazoned near the top of the phone. Geils had already worked with Corriston (as half of 'Pam & Peter') on *Nightmares*, and for *Hotline*, Corriston presented an idea he'd had while working in California for an act Lou Adler was producing. 'I just had this idea sitting there', said Corriston, 'and I showed it to Peter and he liked it, liked the idea of 'Hotline', and that's how it evolved.' The album's back cover displayed a cartoon illustration by artist Lou Brooks that was later used for the front cover of 1980's *Best Of The*

J. Geils Band Two. Above Brooks' drawing of the band members for *Hotline* were the album's track listing and credits. Brooks' graphic style was based on art Corriston had noticed on an old matchbook for The Pep Boys (aka Manny, Moe & Jack), an American auto parts store. As Corriston explained, 'I showed something to Peter and Seth, relating to Manny, Moe, and Jack and thought they could be portrayed like that.' With Wolf and Justman agreeing to the idea, Corriston moved forward. He said, 'I showed him (Brooks) a matchbook cover' and had the band members illustrated in the same fashion.

Brooks passed away in 2021, but in a 2018 blog post on his website, he wrote about how he came to work on *Hotline*, saying, 'I had been dragging my portfolio up to New York each Wednesday and leaving it at magazines and record companies. Somewhere along the line, Atlantic Records and Peter Wolf, lead singer for The J. Geils Band, saw what I was doing and hired me to illustrate the band's next album.' It didn't hurt that Brooks was already a Geils fan. In his blog, he mentioned seeing the band in concert many times, stating, 'no one could touch the Geils Band for live performance.' Among other artwork, Brooks redesigned Mr. Monopoly in 1985 for the classic board game.

Corriston's design style aims for album 'packages' over basic, bland covers that might be only a band photo, something more than 'just eyes and teeth on the cover.' *Hotline*'s die-cut design meant the inner sleeve was extracted from the top, like answering an old telephone, rather than the viewer's right side, as was usual. Additionally, Wolf wanted an extra red colour for the cover. In pre-digital days, printing was done through an offset process that required a separate printing plate for each colour, with four colours being typical (and cheapest) to create most images. Wolf's 'extra red' request meant six printing plates rather than four. The unique cover design and colour request meant additional printing costs, which likely required a meeting with Atlantic's Ahmet Ertegun so Wolf could plead his case.

Lyrics were printed on the front side of the inner sleeve, visible only after lifting the receiver. This was just the second time, after *Nightmares*, that lyrics were included with a Geils album. The reverse of the inner sleeve had strips of black and white photobooth shots – the kind that would've cost 25 cents for a strip of four pictures in 1975 – of each band member clowning around. The photo booth was likely located in the back of the Cha Cha Pool and Game Parlor in New York, as listed on the album's credits. Each band member's autograph was printed below his own strip of photos. Similar to the previous three studio albums, *Hotline* featured a note in the vinyl runout groove. On side two was the question, 'WHEN DO WE GO TO MIAMI?' It was a reference to Szymczyk pushing the band to record at Criteria Studios in Miami, where he'd had success with acts like The Eagles and Elvin Bishop. The way the album was engineered and mastered, the expected silent gap of one or two seconds between tracks does not exist, with each track intentionally segueing immediately from one to the next, fusing the songs together with no dead air between.

In support of the album, Geils appeared on US television's *Midnight Special* on 31 October 1975. Songs performed were 'Love-Itis' and 'Orange Driver' from *Hotline*, plus *Bloodshot*'s 'Give It To Me.' By this point – though it likely had been in place for a while – the band's contract rider called for, among other things, '(1) quart Thunderbird wine 18 proof.' A rider is a supplement to the basic contract detailing additional requirements, and it wouldn't be long before the rider also included a bottle of Dom Perignon champagne. Thunderbird (a cheap wine) served as a reminder of Geils' roots and where they started, and Dom Perignon was a testament to how far they'd come.

As great as the record was, it suffered from a lack of promotion. *Hotline* was the first Geils album since the 1970 debut that did not chart in Canada. One single was released from the record, though it failed to chart anywhere. Similar to the fate of *Ladies Invited*, by mid-1976, unsold overstock of *Hotline* was relegated to the cut-out bin in many record shops in the US and soon out of print. By the early 1980s, following the commercial breakout of *Love Stinks* and *Freeze-Frame*, Atlantic reissued *Hotline* on vinyl at full price and later released it on CD in the mid-1990s, along with the rest of the Geils Atlantic catalogue. In 2004, Wounded Bird Records, under license from Atlantic, reissued *Hotline* on CD.

'Love-Itis' (Harvey Scales, Albert Vance) (4:40)
Written by Milwaukee, Wisconsin-based Harvey Scales and Albert Vance for their band Harvey Scales & The 7 Sounds, 'Love-Itis' was the B-side of their 1967 hit 'Get Down.' Though it was their only hit single, Scales and Vance found continued success as songwriters, penning hits like Johnnie Taylor's 'Disco Lady.' The 7 Sounds' original 'Love-Itis' recording has a soulful, slower groove and features a three-piece horn section. The tune was later recorded by American garage band The Sonics in 1967 and Canadian r&b/soul group Mandala in 1968, but it was Geils' version that brought the song its greatest exposure.

Geils give 'Love-Itis' the boogie rock treatment. Guitar and cowbell open the track – about being caught in the fever of love – and Wolf proclaims, 'My family doctor could find me no cure.' When the instrumental section comes around (as Wolf shouts, 'Shake what mama gave ya!'), the instruments lock together and play off each other. It's a quick measure of harp, a bit of guitar, harp and guitar again, then a longer solo on harp answered by a longer solo on guitar. Wolf returns, singing, 'It's got me, man, it's got me, it's really, really got me', and the backing vocals repeat 'Love-itis' as the band continue jamming. The track ends with Wolf declaring, 'It's got me!' This was the only single issued from *Hotline*, edited to 3:08. It did not chart.

'Easy Way Out' (Wolf, Justman) (4:06)
As 'Love-Itis' ends, 'Easy Way Out' begins without a pause between the two. Bladd's drumming launches the fast-moving track before guitar, bass, and

organ join the mix. Wolf calls out, 'Yeah! Come on!' before proclaiming, 'My coins are all bent, they can't fit in the slot.' After a couple of verses and choruses, the instrumental section begins with a quick blast of organ and Jay rips it up on guitar, tossing in some surf-style playing at the end before another blast of organ. 'Confusion and delusion, oh, man they got the best of me', sings Wolf as he remembers how it used to be. The second break starts with a few measures of Justman on organ and soon ('Let me hear ya') Dick is there on harp. Wolf continues to scream out lines like 'Rough, tough, had enough' with Bladd and Justman admonishing, 'Better take it easy.'

'Think It Over' (Wolf, Justman) (4:41)

The contemplative, r&b-infused 'Think It Over' opens with gentle but insistent guitar over Klein's thumping bass work to give it a Motown sensibility. Justman arranges and stacks piano and organ throughout and Wolf's vocals are restrained as he takes the role of someone whose girlfriend is walking out on him. Though she's clearly been unfaithful, he doesn't want her to leave and begs her, 'Take one more look, I think you should.'

Like a 1950s-era rock and roll love song, the tempo slows each time the chorus comes around, emphasizing the heartbreak as Wolf sings, 'Girl, you better think it over.' Justman takes the first instrumental break, layering the Hammond organ and lifting the tempo before Wolf returns with the next verses. A second short break brings guitar and bass, repeating the motif from the intro before Wolf starts pleading with his girlfriend again. Backing vocals repeat the 'you better think it over' line and Justman works the piano through the fadeout. 'Think It Over' was the B-side to 'Love-Itis.'

'Be Careful (What You Do)' (John Brim) (4:06)

John Brim was a Chicago-based blues artist who released the unsuccessful single 'I Would Hate To See You Go' on the Chess record label in 1956 under the name John Brim and His Gary Kings (from the city of Gary, Indiana, near Chicago). The track later found a home on the 1969 John Brim-Elmore James album *Whose Muddy Shoes*, retitled 'Be Careful' (sometimes also 'Be Careful What You Do'). Although it's an upbeat blues track, the sentiment is dark. Brim sings from the perspective of a man whose woman put him down 'for someone new' and he warns, 'You know if you tempted to quit me, that's when you gonna die.' Among other songs Brim wrote, he's noted for 'Ice Cream Man', which Van Halen recorded for their debut album.

The Geils track starts with a bit of studio chatter (including an imitation of a rooster crowing) and Bladd hitting an eight count on his drumsticks before guitar, harp, and the rest of the band come in. Wolf alters some of Brim's lyrics, completely omitting one verse ('You know I love you, which you know is true, you talk about leavin' me for someone new, it ain't no telling what I might do') and shuffling Brim's final verse to the middle of the song. The break is announced with 'Magic Dick, slide on it, baby.' After Dick's solo,

Justman has a short keyboard part until Wolf screams, 'guee-tar!' It's Jay's turn, but soon harp, piano, and guitar are all working together over bass and drums. Wolf returns for another verse and draws out the following chorus, singing, 'I'd hate mighty bad to have to do awaaaaayyy with' before he stops the song with, 'wait a second, wait a second...' The band start whistling and chattering and someone's honking a squeeze horn before Wolf picks it back up with, 'I'm gonna have to do away with you.' The instrumental outro, just over a minute long, brings plenty of jamming. Juke Joint Jimmy is credited with 'second guitar' on the track.

'Jealous Love' (Wolf, Justman) (4:10)
'Jealous Love' is set in motion with a drumbeat and a glide down the piano keys like a 1960s dance tune. Wolf's lyrics come from the perspective of a jealous, infatuated lover who's now realizing 'you had me acting like your fool.' He understands he's being jealous and irrational, yet he can't give her up, claiming, 'I don't know what to do.' Dick's harp accents the verses and chorus, weaving around and accenting Wolf's vocals. Jay draws out a solo just before the track's midpoint, incorporating slide guitar, and then Wolf returns with another verse.

Musically, it's an upbeat, fun number, but underneath lies a disturbing message: 'But if I find out you've been foolin' about, I'm gonna make a mess outta you.' After a final chorus of 'jealous love, jealous heart, jealous mind over you, and I don't know what to do', Wolf's singing grows more insistent and agitated ('you're walkin' down the street, shakin' what you got, makin' everybody hot, messin' up my mind'), punctuated by Dick's harp through to the end.

'Mean Love' (Wolf, Justman) (5:06)
Side two creeps in with organ and brushed cymbal before turning gritty and rough. While the previous track, 'Jealous Love', was slightly playful despite its darker lyrics, the appropriately titled 'Mean Love' brings a contrast. Wolf's vocals are harsher, Dick lays down Jimi Hendrix-inspired harp that snarls and peals, Jay's guitar pierces deeper, and the whole thing has a malicious, vicious attitude. The song carries a primal bite, but it's not about a fractured relationship or a nasty breakup. Quite the opposite. Relentless desire and lust shape the lyrics while the rhythm section pulses and assaults.

The break begins with a jerky groove to generate tension, with bass, drums, harp, and guitar punching out the rhythm. When Dick is turned loose, he unleashes a sharp, squealing solo, taking flight before turning it over to Jay on guitar. Jay climbs and dives, throwing in everything he can before Wolf comes screaming back for another verse. At the tail end, as the song begins to fade, a very short organ solo is squeezed in. Justman's playing style is considerably different from his organ work on the song's intro but bookends the track nicely.

'Orange Driver' (Eddie Burns) (4:29)
Blues musician Eddie 'Guitar' Burns released 'Orange Driver' as a single in 1961 on the Detroit-based Harvey Records label. The song, about a man whose woman is telling everyone around town that she doesn't love him and is making him 'look like a clown', is closely based on Sonny Boy Williamson's 1942 'My Black Name Blues.' The original 'Orange Driver' features Burns on vocals and guitar, with a young Marvin Gaye on drums, and although Burns was known for playing harmonica, his recording doesn't feature any harp work.

Geils tackle 'Orange Driver' with an unvarnished attitude. 'Give me the key on it', says Wolf at the start before howling, 'I can hear my name a-ringing, baby.' The band stick close to Burns' arrangement (with some lyric changes) and treat the number as a straight blues tune. Wolf serves up his vocals with urgency and the musicians wring out emotion with every note. An extended harp solo is followed by an extended guitar solo, Justman slamming piano keys under all of it.

Wolf's altered lyrics are a curiosity. He leaves out Burns' verse about 'blues before sunrise' and adds his own lines about 'on my bedroom floor, rollin' and tumblin' all night long.' On top of that, the Orange Driver of the song's title is an *extremely* cheap white wine with orange flavouring and colouring, and Burns sings, 'you were drinking that Orange Driver, baby, and were talking all out your head.' Yet, Wolf completely omits that line, probably confusing some who were left wondering what the song title was all about, and instead sings, 'you said you loved me baby, how I won't forget.' 'Orange Driver' had been in the Geils repertoire as far back as the pre-Justman days, when the band performed it at The New Penelope Club in Montreal in 1968. In the radio broadcast recording captured there, the lyrics stick closely to Burns' original rather than the version on *Hotline*.

'Believe In Me' (Curtis Mayfield) (4:44)
Curtis Mayfield's 'You Must Believe Me' was released as a single in 1964 when he was a member of The Impressions and included on their album *People Get Ready*. The Impressions serve up 'You Must Believe Me' as a soulful number with smooth harmony vocals, horns, and understated guitar. The track is about a man trying to persuade his girlfriend that rumours about him with another woman at a party are not true and 'darlin', it just didn't happen that way.'

The Geils rendition is retitled 'Believe In Me' and the band give it a different flavour, with Klein injecting funky bass lines and Wolf adding grit to the vocals. Instead of opening with the chorus, the way The Impressions' version does, Wolf starts with a verse. Later, Wolf changes the last line of one verse with, 'There's nothing else to say about this kind of mess', rather than Mayfield's line, 'There's nothing else to say about whom I love best.' Dick gives another stellar harp solo, Jay responds in kind, and Wolf repeats some verses before the next instrumental section. Klein and Justman ease in with bass and piano and things start to build as the line 'Oh, it's alright' is repeated. Wolf interjects further pleas about his innocence while harp and organ take the song higher through to the end. The instrumental introduction to 'Believe In Me' has been used as the theme music for Germany's *Rockpalast* music television program since the show debuted in 1976. Geils appeared on *Rockpalast* in 1979 on their *Sanctuary* tour but did not perform 'Believe In Me.'

'Fancy Footwork' (Wolf, Justman) (5:26)
Wolf playfully announces, 'Hey, everybody, it's dance time!' at the start of 'Fancy Footwork.' Getting up and moving is what this funky track is all about: 'dance, dance, all night long.' Guitar, bass, piano and drums set the groove, initially sounding like a Jackson 5 number. It manages to be light and breezy without becoming lightweight. When Wolf sings, 'Ain't gonna hang up my rock and roll shoes', it's likely a nod to Chuck Willis' 1958 hit '(I Don't Want To) Hang Up My Rock And Roll Shoes.'

The instrumental break arrives with an exchange between guitar and organ, building anticipation while Wolf urges everybody to get out on the dance floor ('don't be afraid to make a fool of yourself, darlin''). Soon he calls out, 'Magic Dick, let me hear you blow. Come on, daddy', and Dick wails away on harmonica over the funky rhythm section. Jay returns with a smooth riff, settling into the groove before Wolf says, 'Come on, Jerome, play your guee-tar', and Jay steps up with a ringing solo for the fadeout while Klein's bass pulses underneath, guaranteed to get everybody dancing.

Related Tracks
Soul Pole No. 2 (25 December 1975)
As with 1973's *Soul Pole No. 1*, Szymczyk pressed just 50 copies of *SP2* and gave them as Christmas presents to band members and other relevant parties. *SP2* is a double LP with 19 tracks of studio chatter and joking, good vibes, music snippets and jamming. As Szymczyk stated, 'Most of the record was a night of jamming at the Record Plant LA, Studio B. I was working on *One Of These Nights* (The Eagles) and had a night off. Somehow, both the Geils band and Barnstorm were in town that night, so, of course, we went to the studio and beat up The Eagles' gear! The players were Jay, Seth, Steven and Dick … and Joe Vitale, Kenny (Passarelli) and Bob Webb from Barnstorm and Al Kooper. Dick only played trumpet!! And played very well!! No Peter Wolf (during the jam sessions), so no banter, but there is some *serious* jammin' goin' on!!'

SP2 track titles include 'Hot Left Overs', 'Nightmares '75', 'Gettin' Out' and 'The Snowballs', with the 27 minutes on side four consisting solely of 'Nitrous Oxide (It Doesn't Have To Go On Tape).' The only song that's ever been heard publicly is 'The Snowballs', which was aired once as 'Come On To The Christmas Party.'

'Come On To The Christmas Party' By The Snowballs (Wolf, Justman) (1975) (3:07) [Unreleased]
On Christmas Day 1980, Boston radio station WBCN (where Wolf held court with his overnight show just over a decade earlier) broadcast 'Come On To The Christmas Party', performed by The Snowballs. The Snowballs were, in reality, The J. Geils Band, but the vocals were done Chipmunk-style. In the pre-digital days of recording, it wasn't possible to speed up the vocals without changing the tone of the instruments. As Klein explained, the entire track was recorded in half-time, then sped up for the final mastering. The instruments then sounded 'normal', but the voices were high-pitched for the intended effect.

Recording a Christmas single was Wolf's idea, and though it wasn't heard until late 1980, the song was done several years earlier. 'That was one or two of the last records I did with them', said producer Szymczyk. 'We did it at some studio up in Boston; I was only there for a couple of days. It didn't take long.'

The brief intro includes sleighbells and laughter, with Wolf asking, 'Hey, Jerome, where ya going?' 'Well, I'm going to the Christmas party, daddy-o.' Bass and drums provide a bouncy groove and the midsection brings Jay on saxophone. The call-and-response towards the end asks, 'Who's gonna be there? *Everybody I know.* Who's gonna be there? *Everybody you know.*' It's a great track with chatter and bright playing. The band cared enough to spend the time to get the performance and production right and the track deserves to be officially released.

'Top Secret' and 'Hold Me Just A Little Bit Longer' are unreleased tracks in the Atlantic archives (catalogue numbers 30686 and 30687, respectively) recorded at New York's Record Plant studios on or about April 1975.

Live – Blow Your Face Out (1976)

Personnel:
Peter Wolf: vocals
Seth Justman: keyboards, vocals
J. Geils: guitar
Magic Dick: harp
Danny Klein: bass
Stephen Jo Bladd: percussion, vocals
Producers: Allan Blazek, Bill Szymczyk, with The J. Geils Band
Engineers: Allan Blazek, Bill Szymczyk
Assistant Engineer: Mike Getlin
Special assistance: Juke Joint Jimmy
Record label: Atlantic Records
Recorded: 15 November 1975 Boston Garden, 19 November 1975 Cobo Hall Detroit
Released: 22 April 1976
Running time: 74:46
Highest chart place: US: 40, CA: 78, UK: –
Tracklisting: 'Southside Shuffle', 'Back To Get Ya', 'Shoot Your Shot', 'Musta Got Lost', 'Where Did Our Love Go', 'Truck Drivin' Man', 'Love-Itis', 'Intro:', 'Houseparty', 'So Sharp', 'Detroit Breakdown', 'Chimes', 'Sno-Cone', 'Wait', 'Raise Your Hand', 'Start All Over', 'Give It To Me'

There was never any doubt fans were ready for a second live album, but the bar had been set so high with the first that it was a question of whether *Blow Your Face Out* could be as good as, or better than, 1972's *Full House*. The vocals and playing on *Blow Your Face Out* shake the ground, everyone gets a turn in the spotlight, and the result is pure, unadulterated live Geils, the way it was meant to be experienced. There will likely be debates until the end of time as to which is better, but both *Full House* and *Blow Your Face Out* capture the band as they were at those points in their career. Geils were experts at creating shows that took the crowd to the edge, brought them back, pushed harder and took the crowd higher, then slowed everything down and hit hard again. The contrast between the tempos and emotions made each shift feel that much more extreme and heightened the experience to the very last note for every ticket holder.

The album, again designed by Peter Corriston, featured a monochromatic cover with the band's name typewritten in large capital letters and the title in smaller letters on a black background, except for 'LIVE' scribbled in red in the upper left corner. The back cover lists song titles and credits, with shadowy black and white headshots of the band members. Like the front, all lettering is at a 45-degree angle, as are the photos. The bottom right corner states, 'MADE LOUD TO PLAY LOUD', the type of statement Szymczyk included on many of the albums he produced, going back at least to The James Gang's

1969 *Yer' Album*. The inside of the gatefold album displays over a hundred black and white images across more than a dozen diagonal strips of 35mm film of the band (mostly on stage). Funky Judge George Jessel, who appeared on *Nightmares*, can be seen toward the upper left. Each side of the two paper inner sleeves features a large photo of random objects and various smaller photos scattered atop a vinyl copy of *Nightmares*. Dirty ashtrays, matchbooks, airline tickets, playing cards, coins, backstage passes, car keys, guitar strings, a microphone, and more can be seen, some of it representing the band's previous albums. The photographers credited for the cover and inner sleeves are Magic Dick, Seth Justman's brother Paul, album designer Corriston, and David Heffernan.

For the music, every studio album to date is represented without overlapping the track listing on *Full House*, save for a snippet of a slower, reworked 'Looking For A Love.' Fans get five tracks from *Bloodshot*, two from each of the first two albums, two pulled from *Nightmares*, and one each from *Ladies Invited* and *Hotline*, along with a few new tracks to fill four sides of vinyl. Jay said on a 2006 edition of the Groton, Massachusetts, show *Around Town With Jane Bouvier* that by 1976 the band were trying to get out of their contract with Atlantic Records, which called for ten albums. By putting out a double album with *Blow Your Face Out*, it would legally count as two towards that ten.

The album begins with the announcer shouting over the noise of the rowdy crowd, 'Ladies and gentlemen, welcome to the stage those Bad Boys from Boston, the funkiest band in the land, the incomparable J. Geils Band!' The audience and the band are primed even before Wolf shouts, 'It's good to be back home! Let me hear the key, baby' and asks the crowd, 'Do you wanna dance?' There's no turning back as the band rip into 'Southside Shuffle.' Jay and Justman shine on guitar and keyboards while harp, bass and drums drive relentlessly beneath it all. Immediately following 'Southside Shuffle', the band slide into another track from *Bloodshot*, showcasing the funk of 'Back To Get Ya.' Keyboards, bass, guitar, and harmonica punctuate the verses. Dick's harp break tears up the tune, riding atop the groove. Jay proves just as hungry with his guitar on the next break and through to the ending. Then the band change course and work a new track into the setlist. Wolf announces, 'We gonna do the slow grind to ya', and the band slip into Junior Walker's 'Shoot Your Shot.' Organ and harp spiral over and under each other. Wolf sings, 'They know what a J. Geils party is all about' and mentions Juke Joint Jimmy, all in the same verse.

While Wolf has always been known for his extemporised Woofa Goofa with the Green Teeth wild stage patter, his now-classic extended rap for 'Musta Got Lost' (titled 'Must Of Got Lost' on *Nightmares*) was, as he reiterated in a May 2016 *Stereophile* interview, 'Totally unplanned, totally spontaneous.' Bladd strikes the drum kit for attention and Wolf begins, 'Now hold on, this song has a little introduction to it.' Anyone who's listened to the album has probably memorised the entire bit and knows the point where Wolf can't recall fairy tale princess Rapunzel's name ('What's the name of that chick with the long hair?') and ends up with 'Hey, Raputa. Raputa the Beauta.' The slightly over two-minute rap finishes with Wolf declaring, 'And I believe I musta, you know I think I musta, you know, baby, I think I musta, you know I think I musta, I musta got *loooost*.' Justman delivers a brief organ solo during the number and Wolf sings a snatch of Jackie Wilson's 1967 'Higher And Higher' ('I said your love's got me higher than I ever been lifted before'). After the album was released, crowds were calling for the rap at every show and Wolf had to listen to *Blow Your Face Out* to learn his own introduction to the song.

Side two begins with 'Where Did Our Love Go', the 1964 Motown hit for The Supremes. 'Doin' it to it in Detroit City, let me hear ya, like this', says Wolf. At the time of this recording from a November 1975 performance, it hadn't yet been issued as a studio single (that would come in March 1976). Even so, the first notes would've been instantly recognisable to the Detroit audience. Geils follow 'Where Did Our Love Go' with another new track, 'Truck Drivin' Man' (not to be confused with the band's 'Hard Drivin' Man'). Wolf tells the crowd, 'We'd like to do this one by special request', but the song had previously popped up in the setlist on occasion.

'Love-Itis' is even more energised than the studio cut from *Hotline*. Cowbell and harp are more prominent, and the solos are slightly altered. Similar to the studio version, the instrumental break features interplay between Dick and Jay, bouncing between harp, guitar, harp, guitar, and then a longer harp piece, but instead of an extended guitar break next, fans get a brilliant organ solo. After 'Love-Itis' the band take things down for an abridged 'Looking For A Love.' Listed simply as 'Intro:' on the album cover (but 'Intro: (Lookin' For A Love)' on the LP centre label and the cassette, and shown on previous albums as 'Looking For A Love' with a *g*), the crowd sense something big coming. The band maintain a slow-burning groove as they work through two minutes of the song and let the tension grow before Wolf shouts, 'We are gonna blow... your... face... OOUUT!' Bladd starts pounding and the band explode with 'Houseparty' (listed as '(Ain't Nothin' But A) House Party' on the LP centre label and on *Bloodshot*).

'So Sharp', from the second Geils album, leads side three. Instead of a big hard finish, guitar and organ draw out the last notes and Wolf says, 'Now hold on a minute. The moment of truth has finally come.' He stirs up the crowd and his bandmates and asks, 'Are you ready to do some stomping, baby? Are you ready on the bandstand?' before shouting, 'Detroit Breakdown!' Wolf revises the lyrics slightly here. The first verse now includes the line 'blow out your face' and later, instead of 'I passed my limit, honey, I don't care' is 'I lost my nerve and my underwear.' After a stinging instrumental break, Wolf works the audience, first calling out 'Detroit Breakdown', getting the climbing response of 'Yeah, yeah, yeah, yeah', then calling, 'Motor City Shakedown' with the descending response of 'Yeah, yeah, yeah, yeah.' After another instrumental break, the song hits a false ending and the band freeze on stage. Anticipation builds. After 15 seconds or so, Wolf yells, 'Ugh!' and the song continues to its raucous finish. 'Chimes' closes side three. The performance is darker and moodier than on *Ladies Invited* and stretches out about three minutes longer. The band work the groove, taking their time as harmonica, organ, and guitar all get to burn.

A pair of selections from the debut album open side four. With the fast-moving instrumental 'Sno-Cone', everyone gets a workout. Klein keeps it moving as guitar, harp, organ, and drum solos push the track. Next up, 'Wait' features some funky harp and piano. Another new track, Eddie Floyd's 'Raise Your Hand', follows. Wolf again works the audience, connecting with fans in the front, up in the balcony, and 'way, way in the back.' Then a heart-wrenching, stripped down, slower rendition of 'Start All Over' (titled 'Start All Over Again' on *Bloodshot*) simmers and builds suspense until Wolf calls out, 'Give It to Me!' and the band erupt. It's a frenzied performance, the band giving their all and the crowd returning the energy, shouting along, providing background vocals. Wolf perfects the call-and-response, singing, 'Doobadah doobadah doobadah yeah (*doobadah doobadah doobadah yeah*)', drawing the crowd in even further. It's a perfect ending to a concert and a Geils live album, leaving everyone wanting more. The track's running time is listed as 5:02 on the album, but it's closer to 7:00 (including the crowd noise fadeout). The live '(Ain't Nothing But A) Houseparty' was released as a single, with 'Give It To Me' as the B-side. The single did not chart.

At a show at Boston's Music Hall on 28 April 1976, Boston Mayor Kevin White declared 'J. Geils Band Day' in honor of the band. As soon as the presentation was complete, the band launched into 'Give It To Me.' A month later, on 25 June, the band pressed their handprints and signatures into wet cement on the Walk of Fame in front of Peaches Records and Tapes in Atlanta, Georgia (Peaches was a chain of about 50 record superstores across the US).

The same year *Blow Your Face Out* was released, Justman contributed organ to Michael Stanley Band's 'Heavy Weight' from *Ladies' Choice*, which was also produced by Bill Szymczyk. The credit stated, 'Seth Justman appears through the courtesy of Juke Joint Jimmie' (note the misspelling of 'Jimmy').

The New Songs
'Shoot Your Shot' (Junior Walker (Autry DeWalt), James Graves, Lawrence Horn) (4:42)
Junior Walker and the All-Stars recorded the funky 'Shoot Your Shot' in 1965. The song, released on the Motown label, features a horn section with Walker on saxophone. When Geils perform the track on *Blow Your Face Out*, the lyrics are changed considerably, but both renditions mention 'The Twine', a 1964 mostly instrumental dance hit by Alvin Cash & The Crawlers, and the groove from 'The Twine' is probably the inspiration for 'Shoot Your Shot.'

'Truck Drivin' Man' (Terry Fell) (1:44)
Written and recorded by country musician Terry Fell in 1954, it was the B-side to his 'Don't Drop It' but became a hit on its own and everyone from Buck Owens to Leon Russell has covered it. Wolf's love for r&b music is well-known, but he's always had equal admiration for the country greats. On *Blow Your Face Out*, Wolf introduces the song by claiming it's by special request, though it wasn't the first time they'd performed the song on stage, and they would also sometimes play it backstage. Wolf begins the track with a drawn-out, 'Weeelllll' over Justman's piano, and the band kick into hillbilly country mode. Wolf doesn't sing all the song's verses before it wraps up with a shave-and-a-haircut ending. A recording from a month earlier, in October 1975, at the Augusta Civic Center in Maine (available at wolfgangs.com) captures a different arrangement of the song with different lyrics.

'Raise Your Hand' (Steve Cropper, Eddie Floyd, Alvertis Isbell) (3:56)
'Raise Your Hand' was first recorded by Eddie Floyd ('Knock On Wood') on the Stax record label in 1967. Though it's often associated with Janis Joplin, Geils had it in their setlist as far back as 1968 or 1969, before Justman joined, while they were still a five-piece. The Geils version on *Blow Your Face Out* prominently features organ and harp and is another song that allows Wolf to engage the audience. It's performed with slightly altered lyrics and a faster tempo than Floyd's original track.

Related Tracks
'Where Did Our Love Go' (Brian Holland, Lamont Dozier, Eddie Holland) (3:00) (March 1976)
Highest chart place: US: 68, CA: –, UK: –
Despite the live version of 'Where Did Our Love Go' being better known and likely receiving more airplay, this studio track was released shortly before *Blow Your Face Out* and is the version that made the singles charts. It was released as a single only but eventually surfaced on 1993's *Anthology – Houseparty* (1979's *Best Of* used the live track). The single was produced by Atlantic Records co-founder and Geils advocate Ahmet Ertegun. The B-side was 'What's Your Hurry', from the band's debut album.

Though they weren't credited as The J. Geils Band due to legal reasons at the time, Justman, Magic Dick, Wolf, Klein, Duke Levine, and Tom Arey can be glimpsed performing 'Where Did Our Love Go' in a party scene in Adam Sandler's 2013 film *Grown Ups 2*. The credits list the musicians' individual names but not the band name.

Monkey Island (1977)

Personnel:
Peter Wolf: vocals
Seth Justman: keyboards, vocals
Magic Dick: harmonicas
J. Geils: guitars
Danny Klein: bass
Stephen Jo Bladd: percussion, vocals
Frank Vicari, Lew Del Gatto, Micheal Brecker, Ron Cuber: saxophone
Alan Rubin, Lew Soloff, Randy Brecker: trumpet
Barbara Ingram, Evette Benton, Harriet Tharpe, Luther Vandross, G Diane Sumler, Michelle Cobbs, Theresa V. Reed, Cissy Houston: vocals
Producer: The J. Geils Band
Engineer: Dave Thoener
Assistant Engineer: Corky Stasiak
Special assistance: Juke Joint Jimmy
Record label: Atlantic Records
Released: 9 June 1977
Running time: 41:44
Highest chart place: US: 51, CA: –, UK: –

For their seventh studio record, the band made some changes. The most visible was the shift in name from The J. Geils Band to just Geils, prominently displayed in all capitals on *Monkey Island*'s cover. In a February 1980 interview with *Sweet Potato* magazine, Justman said the change to 'Geils' was nothing more than 'the graphic artist's idea. The only place it was changed was on the cover of the album.' This may or may not be true, as the centre label on the vinyl record also states just 'Geils' and any advertisements reflect the same. The music itself signalled a shift as the band branched further into pop and rock with an air of experimentation.

Making *Monkey Island* left the band in serious debt but fulfilled their Atlantic contract, and as it was their last album for the company, the band seemed to take some chances. The record encompassed an array of pop, r&b, rock, doo-wop, and Latin-infused music. With each new studio record, Geils would never forget their roots, never forget their audience, yet would push a little further and try new things. The result is another great album.

Outside musicians were brought in on horns and backing vocals, with production credited solely to The J. Geils Band (after sharing production on *Full House* and *Blow Your Face Out*). The Bill Szymczyk-Allen Blazek team wasn't available when Geils went into the studio to start *Monkey Island*, with Szymczyk and Blazek still busy with their 'day jobs' finishing The Eagles' *Hotel California*, which had become a full-time endeavour for them (Szymczyk would win a Record of the Year Grammy award for 'Hotel California.') It was Szymczyk who felt Geils – Justman and Wolf in particular – were ready to produce themselves and suggested it. 'I kept telling them, 'You guys, you're ready to produce yourself. I've taught you everything I know and you don't need me anymore." The result was a group production, with Justman leading the effort. 'We weren't trying to be commercial, we were just trying to do something different', Wolf stated in an 11 November 1977 *Los Angeles Times* article. 'When he was producing us, Szymczyk always tried to get us to do more elaborate things in the studio, but we always resisted. He was happy to hear about what we had done with the album. He told us, 'Welcome to the '70s'.' Reflecting on his work with Geils, Szymczyk stated the sessions 'were all *up*. There were very few hassles and very few disagreements. It was a fun band to work with. I always describe them as six comedians disguised as a rock band.'

David Thoener, who had served on *Hotline*, returned for *Monkey Island*. Thoener explained, 'The band enjoyed working at (Record Plant New York) and called the owner/engineer Roy Cicala to engineer the album. He accepted and booked me as his assistant because he knew the band and I had a good relationship. I set everything up on the first day, including getting sounds and recording levels on the band. He walked in and stayed for halfway through the first take, then walked out, telling me, 'If you need me, call me; if not, then you're on your own.' The band walked in after about three takes and asked where Roy was. I told them and they said 'Great, let's keep going'.' Typical pay for engineers at the time was 15% of the studio billing. Thoener's cut was 7% despite working solo, but Thoener was happy even so: 'I have gone on record to say that The J. Geils Band took a chance on a 21-year-old kid (his age while working on *Hotline*) from Yonkers, New York, and therefore kept my loyalty. They gave me a chance when there were few that would. I am also grateful to Roy Cicala, the owner of Record Plant New York, for throwing me in the deep end. He believed in the swim-or-sink method of success and I'm forever grateful for his belief that I could swim.'

Monkey Island included the most guest artists of any album to that point. Thoener stated it 'was the first time Seth Justman had a chance to experiment and record what he felt the direction of the band should go.' While putting the album together, Geils played sporadic shows but were on stage fewer than two dozen times from late 1976 to early 1977. Time off from touring meant a lack of income, so time in the studio put the band in debt.

Peter Corriston was back as album designer, his fourth time with the band. His concept for *Monkey Island* was for it 'to be somewhat minimalist. You're just trying to create more impact to get the package noticed.' Alen MacWeeney, who has worked with Corriston on many albums over the years, served as photographer. Both Corriston and MacWeeney stated that putting all six band members on the front cover wouldn't be effective when trying to create an impact. The final image was a sober, grainy, shadowy black and white photo that wrapped from front to back of the gatefold album. Justman, Wolf, and Klein were on the right half (front), with Bladd, Jay, and Dick on the left half (back). The inside of the gatefold cover was white with black lettering showing the track listing and musician credits overlaid on another black and white band photograph.

The *Monkey Island* photo session took place in Faye Dunaway's New York apartment. As MacWeeney recalled, the shoot was scheduled for one o'clock in the afternoon but didn't get started until about five hours later. Once underway, the session lasted four or five hours and MacWeeney said that despite the sombre cover image, 'There was a lot of hilarity in doing the photograph.' He gave each of the band members nicknames as he corralled them for the photos, calling one of them The Baron of Bayonne. 'We all enjoyed it and I was very pleased with how it looked.' He added, 'Maybe it's just the way I take pictures. I don't like people to be artificially humorous or fake. I did want to get a kind of serious picture and it had to wrap around the album. It was a consideration where the fold would be. There couldn't be a face right there (in the fold).' Using black and white film was probably MacWeeney's idea, though he and Corriston worked closely together, and MacWeeney 'probably told the band members to wear black.' He printed the photo using a point-source enlarger – something more difficult than using a diffused light source – which creates micro-resolution and makes the grain very distinct.

The paper inner sleeve was black with lyrics printed in white lettering, but only for the seven Wolf-Justman tracks and not the two cover tunes (possibly due to copyright or publishing restrictions), and not in the same order as on the album itself.

Beginning in May 1977, the *Monkey Island* tour included headlining shows and multiple supporting dates with Peter Frampton, who shared management with Geils and who was still riding high with the previous year's *Frampton Comes Alive!* After completing *Monkey Island*, Thoener stated, 'The (Record Plant) studio was going to put me back as an assistant.' Instead, 'the band offered me the job of front of house engineer on their upcoming live shows. We were playing huge stadiums, opening up for Peter Frampton.' Thoener spent his 23rd birthday in Las Vegas, where the band opened for Roy Orbison. In total, he 'lasted the first leg of the tour (a few months) and went back to (the Record Plant) as an assistant for one record with the Blue Oyster Cult band' and then engineered David Johansen's (New York Dolls) first solo album.

In October, Tom Petty and the Heartbreakers, who had just released their debut album, opened several shows. Though the date is difficult to pin down, it was probably late 1977 or early 1978 that Petty had a song he'd written back in 1974 which he offered to Geils, feeling it would be a good fit. Due mostly to timing, Geils opted not to use it. Petty ended up keeping and using it on his own *Damn The Torpedoes* in 1979, and the track – 'Don't Do Me Like That' – became a US and Canadian top ten hit for Petty.

The *Monkey Island* tour setlist at various times included 'Monkey Island', 'I'm Falling', 'Somebody', 'Surrender' and 'Wreckage.' Also appearing sometimes were Sonny Boy Williamson's 'Peach Tree' (with Dick on vocals) and 'It Ain't Right', originally recorded by Little Walter and His Jukes in 1956.

Like 1975's *Hotline*, *Monkey Island* failed to chart in Canada, though it was the band's first album to chart in Australia, coming in at 97.

'Surrender' (Wolf, Justman) (3:49)
Anybody dropping the needle on *Monkey Island* the first time might've done a double take when the vocals that emerged from the speakers belonged not to Wolf but to a woman. Gospel and soul singer Cissy Houston (mother of Whitney Houston) was a member of The Sweet Inspirations in the late 1960s before finding fame as a solo artist in the 1970s. She was also an in-demand session singer who had already performed on records by everyone from Wilson Picket and Aretha Franklin to Paul Simon and David Bowie when she duetted with Wolf.

Bladd slams the drum kit once, crashes the cymbals, and immediately guitar, bass, and organ launch 'Surrender', creating a funky r&b foundation before Houston sings, 'Could it be mind over matter, or maybe you just can't see.' It might've been a risk having Houston come in first on vocals, but it pays off. Houston takes the role of the woman unsure how much to trust this man pursuing her and Wolf is the man under her spell pleading for a chance. After the second chorus, Dick is there with a fat-sounding harp, climbing and dropping, conveying the conflicting sentiment of the two lovers. Justman's clavinet adds funk. Backing vocals were handled by r&b singer Luther Vandross, G. Diane Sumler (who had already worked with Vandross in the band Luther), and Michelle Cobbs, who was later in Chic ('Good Times'). 'Surrender' was the second single from the album, edited to 3:17, though it did not chart.

'You're The Only One' (Wolf, Justman) (3:05)
Highest chart place: US: 83, CA: –, UK: –
The album's second track, a bluesy love song, presents an immediate change of pace. Dick brings tender, sweet-sounding harp to the slower-tempo tune, reminiscent of Stevie Wonder's style. Here, Dick employs a chromatic harp and plays it acoustically – rather than through an amplifier – in front of a vocal microphone, the way a singer would normally be recorded. Bladd is solid but restrained on drums, Wolf's vocal delivery brings sincerity, and Jay's understated guitar adds to the tune's gentleness and honesty.

The song begins with a brief spotlight on Dick's harp before the first verse. Harmony vocals add softness to Wolf's singing. There are no grand solos, just a brief, heartfelt organ break after the second chorus. 'You're The Only One' was the first *Monkey Island* single, charting only in the US.

'I Do' (Johnny Paden, Frank Paden, Jesse Smith, Willie Stephenson, Melvin Mason) (3:09)
A horn-saturated doo-wop number, 'I Do' was a top 40 hit for Chicago vocal group The Marvelows (sometimes The Mighty Marvelows) in 1965. Geils remain faithful to that recording while putting their own stamp on it.

'I Do' is an exuberant dance number. Saxophones and trumpets, handclaps, and backing 'doot doo-doo, doot doo-doo' vocals bring an energy that can't be denied. Justman's piano, Klein's bass, and Jay's guitar rip it up in the background and add a punch while Bladd jumps in with some brilliant drum fills. Midway, the instrumental break begins with horns, and then it's Dick's turn on harp before Wolf returns with another verse. 'I Do' was issued as the third single from *Monkey Island* but did not chart. Its B-side was the non-album track 'Trying To Live My Life Without You.' It's surprising the single didn't make the charts, but the song found renewed life when a live version was released from *Showtime!* in 1982. 'I Do' was one of three Geils tracks used in Adam Sandler's 2010 film *Grown Ups*.

'Somebody' (Wolf, Justman) (5:13)
Jay's grinding riff starts 'Somebody.' There's an underlying sense of paranoia, thematically similar to 1973's 'Chimes' and 1974's 'Nightmares', though musically the songs are completely different and, in this case, the paranoia is valid. Wolf's lyrics lay out a shadowy scene where he's mired in criminal activity and double-crossed some treacherous partners: 'I realised I could take all mine and skip off with theirs too.' He's hiding out, going stir-crazy, so he calls a friend and foolishly tells her what he's done. Now the bad guys are outside his door, 'I'm bound to wake up dead', and the friend is long gone.

After the second chorus, Dick lays down a driving harp solo. The second instrumental break brings Jay's piercing guitar, accented by Bladd's percussion. After another chorus, harp and guitar take the track to the end as the backing vocals call out, 'somebody, somebody.' It is a gritty, satisfying number.

'I'm Falling' (Wolf, Justman) (5:41)
'Into the spotlight, alone, just waiting for my cue', sings Wolf in this introspective number, making the listener wonder if the lyrics are autobiographical. Perhaps the band were weary of life on the road? Or getting tired of always being so close to that next level of success but finding it still slightly out of reach? The song begins sparsely, painting a picture of despair. Wolf imparts a sense of exhaustion in his vocals. At the song's midpoint, strings are added and the song begins to escalate, providing a sliver of hope before dropping back down, with Justman's piano projecting loneliness and isolation. When Wolf sings, 'and I'm, and I'm, and I'm, and I'm, and I'm tired and so all alone', the heartbreak bleeds through.

Against expectations, the mood transitions from despair to optimism. Horns build up, strings return, and Michael Brecker plays tenor sax for all he's worth. After pulling the listener down into an abyss of hopelessness, the horns and strings shift the song from mournful to uplifting, soaring at the end. This is a song of survival and triumph. On the *Monkey Island* tour, Jay handled most of the horn parts on guitar.

'Monkey Island' (Wolf, Justman) (9:02)

Side two opens with the ambitious, experimental 'Monkey Island', the band's longest cut from any of their studio albums. It starts with a Roland Rhythm Machine, percussion, and acoustic guitar, followed by organ, bass, and crisp piano, and Dick gets a chance to shine on trumpet. The song has a jazzy, Latin-styled flavour, creating an exotic atmosphere. The instrumental three-minute introduction winds down with keyboards and horns before Klein's bass creates an eerie backdrop with his *bomp-bomp, bomp-bomp-bomp, bomp-bomp*. Klein said the bass part took a little while to learn and work out, but 'it came out good.' Wolf's first lines are delivered in a tone somewhere between narration and song: 'No one could explain it, what went on that night.' The imagery is gothic and the tale consists of mystery and horror. The song is based on a story Justman had read or heard about a place called Monkey Island, where the inhabitants mysteriously disappeared. Alternately, it's believed the track is a commentary of their time at Atlantic Records.

At the break, Dick blasts out a dark, cutting solo on harp, climbing back up for the next chorus. Another softer break follows with Justman on piano and Jay on guitar, followed by Justman on organ with Klein's bass and Bladd's dampened drums adding more depth. The track escalates as the chorus repeats and Jay delivers a blistering guitar solo through the fadeout. When the song was performed on tour, Dick also played coronet. The track served as the B-side to 'Surrender', but as a truncated 2:59 version titled 'Monkey Island – Pt. I', consisting of the introduction, which ends as the song is about to settle into Klein's bass riff. An instrumental snippet of the song's opening was used in American television's *Burn Notice* Season 2 'Good Soldier' episode in 2008.

'I'm Not Rough' (Louis Armstrong) (3:03)

Jazz legend Louis 'Satchmo' Armstrong and His Hot Five recorded 'I'm Not Rough' in 1927, featuring Armstrong's wife Lil on piano. It was Magic Dick, a huge fan of Armstrong, who brought the track to Geils and pushed for it to be part of *Monkey Island*. He told the band, 'There's a song I think we could do that I think would fit us pretty cool.' He explained his vision, saying, 'It's sort of like this country thing, it's very old', and by the ending, the band could 'take it into this Chicago amplified, more modern blues.'

The band remain true to Armstrong's recording, with a small change of lyric. Justman begins the track on piano, followed first by harp and then the entire band. Dick used an amplified harp sound throughout the track and meticulously transcribed Armstrong's solo, playing it note for note on diatonic harmonica. Jay covers the original 1927 guitar and banjo parts and replicates Kid Ory's trombone solo with slide guitar. It's more than halfway through the cut before Wolf sings the first verse: 'Well, I'm not rough, and I don't bite. The woman that gets me got to treat me right.' This is the oldest track that Geils ever covered for one of their albums.

'So Good' (Wolf, Justman) (3:19)
'So Good' is an upbeat r&b-styled pop song telling of falling in love, perhaps when least expected, with the song's narrator letting the world know how happy he is to change his ways and settle down. Piano starts the dance track, along with percussion and handclaps, before bright horns ease in. 'I was wild', sings Wolf, 'I was always on the run.' The jangly guitar and funky bass are subtle, never in the forefront but always there lifting the song and moving it forward. After the second chorus, Justman comes forward on piano, accompanied by horns. The backing vocals build, beginning with a sultry, 'Love so good, love so good, love so good, it's so darn good!' A harp break follows, adding to the exuberance.

The song provides another example of how the band knew how to pick the perfect guest musicians. Barbara Ingram, Evette Benton, and Harriet Tharpe provide soulful backing vocals. Ingram and Benton performed on Billy Paul's 1972 hit 'Me And Mrs. Jones', and Ingram, Benton, and Tharpe later were in Teddy Pendergrass' backing vocal group, The Teddy Bears.

'Wreckage' (Wolf, Justman) (5:23)
After the joyous 'So Good' comes the anguish of 'Wreckage', about getting back up and finding a way forward after suffering crushing defeat and disappointment. It might even be a look back at their time on Atlantic Records. Moody keyboards (including Wurlitzer organ) from Justman open the track, accompanied by Jay's acoustic guitar. The music is stripped down to a barren frame, conveying weariness, pain, and near surrender. Wolf bites into the lyrics, the chorus saying, 'Only few return, only few will learn, about the wreckage along the way.' After a final chorus, Dick enters with a short, mournful harp solo and the song begins to fade, only to resurrect itself with a nearly two-minute coda. Drums and bass pound away, accenting the brutality of the track. At the right moment, Jay attacks with some of his best, most vicious guitar work, pushing the track to the end with a feeling of conquest.

The final track on the final studio album for Atlantic, 'Wreckage' has Geils leaving on a high note, exposing their souls, giving their all, and proving they weren't even close to being finished.

Related Tracks
'Peanut Butter' (Hidle Barnum, Martin Cooper, Fred Smith, Clifford Goldsmith) (2:23) (December 1976)
Wolf stated in a 1980 *Sweet Potato* interview, 'We were doing *Monkey Island* and we figured, man, some of these songs were takin' weeks and weeks to get down. So we went in one night and we recorded 'Peanut Butter' and 'Magic's Mood' and called up the record company and said, 'We got our first single for you!' (laughter) So they released it.'

Recorded by The Marathons (legally, The Vibrations) in 1961, it was based on The Olympics' 1959 '(Baby) Hully Gully' dance number written by Clifford

Goldsmith and Fred Smith, who later co-wrote 'Peanut Butter.' The music and melody are the same, but most of the lyrics are different. One line from 'Hully Gully' is, 'I went to a party, and what did they do? Hully, hully gully', with the 'Peanut Butter' lyric being, 'I went to a dinner, and what did they eat? Peanut, peanut butter.'

Bladd's drums introduce 'Peanut Butter', the rest of the band enter, Justman slides down the piano keys, and Wolf begins, 'There's a food going around that's a sticky, sticky goo.' Klein said that during the recording session, 'I remember Wolf on the phone to a DJ in Boston, getting the words to 'Peanut Butter'.' The US had just elected a new president the month prior – Jimmy Carter, a peanut farmer from Georgia – so the original lyric of 'I went to a dinner...' was changed to, 'I went to the White House, and what did they eat?'

The band keep the mood playful without turning the tune into a pure novelty number. Midway through, Dick drops a harp solo over hand claps and a chugging rhythm before the chorus returns: 'I like peanut butter, creamy peanut butter, chunky peanut butter too.' Wolf ends it by proclaiming, 'Awww, nuts!' 'Peanut Butter' was released as a single in late 1976, about six months before the *Monkey Island* LP, but it did not chart. It was later included in 1993's *Anthology – Houseparty*.

'Magic's Mood' (Juke Joint Jimmy) (2:29) (December 1976)
The mesmerizing instrumental 'Magic's Mood' is the last song in the Geils catalogue to credit Juke Joint Jimmy as the songwriter. With some of the tracks on *Monkey Island* taking weeks to record, the band went into the studio one night for a quick session and recorded both 'Peanut Butter' and 'Magic's Mood.' This track was issued as the B-side to 'Peanut Butter' and has never appeared on any album.

The opening notes are a nod to Charlie Parker's 'Parker's Mood' (featuring Miles Davis and Max Roach) from around 1948. The track belongs to Dick, whose harp carries the tune over a blues bass and drums rhythm section. Justman's piano is at the back of the mix, barely noticeable. Jay's subtle but jazzy guitar is more upfront but never takes the spotlight from the harp.

'Trying To Live My Life Without You' (Eugene Williams) (3:08) (1977)
Recorded by Mississippi-born r&b and soul singer (and Blues Hall of Famer) Otis Clay in 1972, the lyrics of 'Trying To Live My Life Without You' tell of a man who was able to overcome bad habits and addictions like womanizing, smoking, and drinking but getting over his latest lover is nearly impossible.

Geils stick close to Clay's soulful recording, from the horns to the background vocals, but add a guitar and keyboard break. Klein's bass is funky but understated and he said he was doing 'slides and fretless things' for the track. Recorded during the *Monkey Island* sessions, 'Trying To Live My Life Without You' uses the same backing singers and horn section as on 'Surrender.' The track was the B-side to 'I Do' but never released on an album until *Best Of Two* in 1980. Bob Seger popularised the song in the US when he released his live version in 1981.

'Harp Tune', 'Ain't No Joke' and 'Gettin' Out' are reportedly three unissued tracks sitting in the Atlantic Records vaults, assigned catalogue numbers 34523, 34524, and 34525, respectively. The tracks were recorded at the Hit Factory in New York in November 1977, after Geils had released *Monkey Island* and fulfilled their contract with Atlantic, so perhaps they were thinking of signing with Atlantic again. 'Gettin' Out' is likely a rerecording of the same-named track from 1974's *Nightmares*.

'Untitled Track' is another recording in the Atlantic archives, this one under catalogue number 34664, so it can be assumed to be a complete track that was never given a proper title. It was recorded at New York's Cutting Room in December 1977.

'Jam' and another 'Untitled Track' are the final two recordings believed held in the Atlantic vaults, with catalogue numbers 34702 and 34703, respectively. These tracks were recorded in December 1977 at The Record Plant in New York.

Sanctuary. (1978)

Personnel:
Peter Wolf: vocals
Seth Justman: keyboards, vocals
Magic Dick: harmonicas
J. Geils: guitars
Danny Klein: bass
Stephen Jo Bladd: drums, vocals
Producer: Joe Wissert
Engineers: Dave Thoener with Jon Mathias, Steve Satter, Jess Henderson
Record label: EMI America
Released: 13 November 1978
Running time: 36:41
Highest chart place: US: 49, CA: 53, UK: –

What a difference a change of record label made. With *Sanctuary*, the band had the full backing of a new record company, giving Geils their first gold record since 1973's *Bloodshot* and their first top 40 hit since 1974's 'Must Of Got Lost.' For the second time in their career, after *Ladies Invited*, the album contained all original songs. The songwriting and performance on the nine tracks, all by the Wolf-Justman team, carried a sense of confidence and vigour. Even the title of the record was a statement, the word 'Sanctuary' ending with a period as if proclaiming the band were now exactly where they needed to be. The songs still carried the influence of blues and r&b, but *Sanctuary* is more of a rock album than anything else. Geils were still making dance music but avoided the disco trends that many other bands of the day were cashing in on.

It's fair to say the band's string of gold and platinum records in the late 1970s and early 1980s came about in large part because of Jim Mazza, founding president of record label EMI America in 1977 (and later president of Capitol Records). Mazza had been part of Capitol Records for over a decade by then, having worked his way up to Vice President of International and Domestic Marketing. During his time at Capitol, he worked with everyone from The Beatles to Grand Funk Railroad, and with the launch of a new label, Mazza understood exactly what he was doing. He had the clout of a major label but could act like an independent. Mazza knew how to break new acts and revitalise established acts, which was precisely what he did with J. Geils.

Mazza said it was sometime in 1977 and, 'I ran into Peter Wolf at some industry function. I said, 'Do you want to be on a new label?' (Wolf asked) 'What's the name?' (I said) 'We don't have a name yet.' (Wolf replied) 'We record for Atlantic.' (I replied) 'You want to be on a brand-new label?' We sat there and laughed, telling stories. We just hit it off. That was the impetus of J. Geils to EMI America. Their relationship with Atlantic was faltering at the time.'

A *Cash Box* article from 29 July 1978 reported EMI America celebrated the signing of Geils by hiring a cruise ship for 'some 450 New England radio personnel' for a three-hour event in Boston Harbor. At that signing, Mazza surprised the band by hiring an airplane to tow a banner across the harbour announcing, 'The J. Geils Band on EMI America.' Paul Lanning, a friend of the band who had filmed Jay, Dick and Klein in 1969 for his TV production class, was, by this time, a sales account manager at EMI and was one of those aboard the ship. Mazza also took out ads in the music trade publications featuring a photo of New York's Apollo Theater with a message on the marquee stating, 'Welcome The J. Geils Band.' It was clear that Mazza was a huge fan and believed in the band as much as – and possibly more than – the band believed in themselves at that point. Following success with Geils, Mazza signed and boosted acts like David Bowie and George Thorogood, giving them some of the biggest records of their careers.

Around the time of their signing with EMI America, Geils parted ways with manager Dee Anthony, who was focusing his energies on another of his clients, Peter Frampton. Wolf considered managing the band himself, but Mazza put Geils in touch with Ken Kragen. Kragen was already a successful manager when he took on Geils, but he gained further fame as a driving force behind USA for Africa's 1985 charity single 'We Are The World.' Kragen partnered with Bob Hinkle and Jeb Hart, who managed acts like Harry Chapin, Manfred Mann, and Kenny Rogers. Hinkle, incidentally, saw his first Geils concert back 'around 1969, playing with Creedence Clearwater Revival at The Fillmore East.'

Sanctuary, like all the EMI America studio releases to follow, was recorded at Long View Farm Studios in North Brookfield, Massachusetts. Long View, located around 60 miles west of Boston, wasn't just a studio but a working farm on about 150 acres of land, offering considerable privacy. A converted farmhouse and barn provided not only a studio but also kitchens and lodging, allowing the band to live and work with as few distractions as possible (and still go home on weekends). Joe Wissert, who had just come off Boz Scaggs' *Silk Degrees*, was brought in as producer. Wissert oversaw a more polished sound without turning it slick or lifeless.

David Thoener, who was like a seventh member of the band by this time, returned as engineer. It was his first time working at Long View. Though it's something many listeners may not notice, he explained, 'I approached recording using the studio attached to the control room, like a normal situation. That's why the drums are dryer with less ambiance than future records because the studio was dead.' Thoener gave further insight into the recording process and the many hours spent with each musician: 'For example, when it came time for Magic Dick to record, it was an overdub and I'd sit with him late at night, usually starting at 10 pm or 11 pm and going until midnight or 1 am. This would be after the band and Joe Wissert and I would have worked from 10 am until they were exhausted, usually around

10 pm. The next morning, the band and Wissert would listen to what we'd recorded and sometimes accept it or sometimes would listen to alternative takes and make an edit. Again, sometimes, the final take was a combination of several performances. Overdubs with Seth playing keys were usually Seth and I in the control room and sometimes Jay would sit in. Vocals were Seth and I and Peter, naturally. (For) basic tracks, it was usually the whole band, although once basics were finished, Stephen Bladd and Danny would usually go home unless needed for overdubs. We always went back to (The Record Plant New York) to mix because I knew the room and monitors. The studio would let me use whatever equipment I needed for free.'

The album cover had a striking red background with a yellow circle in the middle and a purple/blue palmprint within the circle. Black banners across the top and bottom carried the band name and album title in white lettering. A November 1978 *Cash Box* stated, 'The group has switched its name back to The J. Geils Band after radio resisted its recent change to Geils' on *Monkey Island*. The palmprint was based on an image Wolf and Mazza spotted coming off the boat in Boston harbour after the signing and promotion party. 'There was a building there, and on the wall of the building was the handprint', said Mazza. 'He's (Wolf) a spiritual kind of guy, he took that moment and said, 'This represents something. That handprint sort of solidifies the relationship (between EMI and Geils) and that's the cover of the album'.' Mazza continued, 'It became sort of an inside thing, it represents the moment in time when we all came together on the same page, with the same thoughts and the same dreams and the same ideals.'

The palmprint image used for the album cover belonged to Bobby Andrea DiMarzo, a friend of Wolf who later took photos for Wolf's second solo album *Up To No Good*. The *Sanctuary* back cover listed the songs and credits, with photos of the band beneath. Photography was split between Alen MacWeeney, who had worked on *Monkey Island*, and Rob Van Petten. The record's inner sleeve was yellow, with one side featuring a black band across the middle with the word 'SANCTUARY.' (with a period) on it and the EMI logo on the bottom. The reverse had monochrome headshots of the band members (again by MacWeeney and Van Petten) with a small palmprint logo below, but no lyrics were included. The centre labels on the vinyl record also carried the palmprint. A limited-edition picture disc was released in Europe, pressed on yellow vinyl displaying a large purple/blue palmprint.

Not only did Geils make a strong showing on the US charts, they jumped back on the Canada album and single charts and *Sanctuary* proved to be the second album to chart in Australia, reaching 82. After years of hard work, Geils finally had their first single on the UK charts. The Geils-EMI America partnership was bearing immediate results.

The band were on tour as soon as the album was released, making their way across the US. EMI America had planned to film the 16 December 1978 show at Detroit's Cobo Arena, with the intent of distributing it for overseas promotion, but that apparently did not happen. However, a 10 February 1979 Boston Garden concert was filmed and broadcast in the US on 21 April. By late April, the tour took Geils to Europe, with shows in Germany, Holland, and France. The 24 April show in Amsterdam was recorded for radio broadcast and included the new tracks 'I Could Hurt You', 'Sanctuary', 'One Last Kiss' and 'Teresa.' A day later, the band performed two songs (lip-syncing 'Wild Man' and 'Take It Back') on the Dutch *TopPop* television program for broadcast the first week of May. After a 3 May concert at London's Hammersmith Odeon, Geils returned stateside and, in June, played three sold-out shows at Michigan's Pine Knob Theatre. Immediately following the third show, on 12 June, Geils made their way to Bookie's Club 870 (a former disco and drag bar) in Detroit and performed a secret gig as 'Jimmy and the Juke Joints.' Admission was $2.00. The tour wrapped up on 4 July 1979 with a set at 'Day On The Green', a three-day outdoor festival in Oakland, California, where at the start of the show, Wolf rode to the front of the stage in the sidecar of a motorcycle.

In February 1979, *Sanctuary* was certified gold in the US for sales of 500,000 (with awards presented at the 10 February show in Boston). Japan was the first country to issue *Sanctuary* on CD in the late 1980s/early 1990s, with the UK releasing the CD on BGO Records not long after. When US record label Razor & Tie licensed the music and issued *Sanctuary* on CD in 1998, it included as bonus tracks the two live singles from *Showtime!*: 'I Do' and 'Land Of A Thousand Dances.'

'I Could Hurt You' (Wolf, Justman) (3:49)
The mid-tempo 'I Could Hurt You' opens with hard-hitting guitar and piano before drums and bass enter. The propulsive music underscores the attitude in Wolf's lyrics about a man being mistreated and cheated on by his girlfriend. She's had her last chance with him, but rather than give her the same treatment, he's merely going to send her walking. The threat implied in the song's title is emotional. He could cheat on her, jerk her around, break her heart, but in the end, he's the better of the two and will simply push her out of his life because he's through with her: 'Now let me show you where the front door is.'

The break has an edge to it. First comes Jay's brief but biting guitar, anchored by Bladd's heavy drumming, Klein's fat bass, and Justman's low piano notes. Dick follows with an extended, fiery harmonica bit before the next chorus. The song ends with Wolf repeating, 'I'm through with ya', as the backing vocals repeat, 'yeah, yeah, yeah, yeah, yeah.' It's an excellent opener for the album with its passionate performance.

'One Last Kiss' (Wolf, Justman) (4:22)
Highest chart place: US: 35, CA: 58, UK: 74
The piercing guitar that opens the song is instantly recognizable. At its core, 'One Last Kiss' is a brutally honest breakup song: 'I never promised you the

things you promised me.' The lyrics are from the perspective of a broken-hearted man with bittersweet memories: 'The good times are the best times, the bad times fade away' but 'the last time is today.' The chorus comes with beautiful harmony vocals from Bladd and Justman. After all is said and done, in the end, 'the feeling's gone.' Just prior to the song's midpoint, Jay offers up some tight guitar work; then Dick arrives with a longer harp piece. After the next chorus, Jay carries the song to the finish. His stunning solo has melancholy overtones yet carries a sting.

The US single was issued in a black and white picture sleeve featuring the palmprint logo on one side and a photo of the band standing near a rowboat on the other. The photo was taken on the property of Long View Farm, where the band recorded the album. The German picture sleeve has a colour photo from the same session, with the band in the rowboat in the fog. The single's B-side was the non-album cut 'Revenge.' The song reached the top 40 in the US and charted in both Canada and the UK, the first time Geils appeared on any UK chart.

'Take It Back' (Wolf, Justman) (3:20)
Highest chart place: US: 67, CA: 94, UK: –
'Take It Back' is the second single from *Sanctuary*. Musically, it's an upbeat tune that sounds like it was influenced by Major Lance's 'The Monkey Time' (written by Curtis Mayfield), yet lyrically, it's another breakup number. Bright harmonica and melodic bass lift the r&b-styled track while Wolf assumes the posture of a burned lover who 'can't stand this pain no more' and sings, 'now the tables are turned and you're gonna get it.' In some ways, it's the antithesis of 1974's lustful 'Give It To Me', this time insisting, 'Take it back, take back your love.' Bladd and Justman provide harmony and backing vocals, Justman's piano fills highlight the lines of each verse, and Dick's harp solo adds sweet wistfulness to the song. Justman briefly adds organ in the final verse, 'after all that we've been through...' Although they lip-synced their performance of the song on Dutch television's *TopPop*, the band members looked effortlessly cool and at the top of their game and their appearance provided an excellent visual of the band in 1979.

'Sanctuary' (Wolf, Justman) (3:52)
Drums, piano, and harmonica launch 'Sanctuary' with an insistent punch. The harp evokes an emergency siren, adding darkness and urgency. Wolf announces, 'Times are tough' and rattles off a catalogue of situations and grievances that require sanctuary, from frustration and temptation to stagnation and desperation, all entwined by driving harp. The chorus consists of nothing more than an uncluttered plea of 'Sanctuary' repeated four times.

Following the first verse and chorus, Dick shines with a harp solo. Another verse and chorus bring a longer instrumental break. Dick returns, taking the harp higher before turning it over to Jay for some biting guitar work. The song turns darker when Wolf sings over Justman's low piano notes about 'When I was young…' and cries, 'There's no escape, there's no salvation, it's much too dark for revelation.' Guitar, bass, piano, harp, and drums vie for attention as 'Sanctuary' is repeated through the fadeout. The song was released as a single in Spain.

'Teresa' (Wolf, Justman) (3:48)
Side one closes with the stark, beautiful 'Teresa', about self-doubt, loss, and helplessness. It's almost a self-elegy, the lyrics lamenting the singer's situation. It's unclear whether that situation is failed love, with the singer trying to make his way back to the titular Teresa, or if it's about being lost in life in general, as the singer begs a friend to help him find peace and direction. Rather than use the full band, this is a stripped-down number with forceful piano, strong yet vulnerable lead vocals, and rich harmony and backing vocals.

Each word and note radiates grief and confusion. 'What should I do next, Teresa?' sings Wolf. 'Where did I go wrong?' Unlike 'I'm Falling', from *Monkey Island*, there is no sense of resolution and hope, no soaring, uplifting comfort at the end. 'Teresa' is more a prayer for help: 'Please help me but don't wait too long.'

'Wild Man' (Wolf, Justman) (5:21)
After the brooding 'Teresa', 'Wild Man' crashes in on piano, bass, and drums. Justman climbs up and down the keyboards, often with a jazz influence. Wolf takes the role of a howling wild man: 'I look out, you look in. You can't lose, I can't win.' Dick delivers the first solo with a snarl in his harp. After another verse and chorus, Justman gets in a few licks on piano and clavinet before Jay enters with stinging guitar. Under all of it, Klein has been moving the rhythm along on bass with thick, popping notes. Then, it's his turn for a brief, funky run before the extended outro. Klein explained, 'I could never learn slap bass' and instead would just 'pluck 'em (the bass strings) in my own inimitable style.'

Edited to 4:00, the single was issued in a picture sleeve (with Wolf half-crouched, holding a microphone stand) showing 'Wildman' as one word, though the centre label on the vinyl 7-inch still displayed the two-word 'Wild Man.' It's a different mix, with some of the drumming more upfront, the piano a bit brighter, and handclaps keeping time. Dick's harmonica break and a verse and chorus in the middle section of the song are completely excised; instead, the song moves straight to the guitar and bass solos. The single did not chart. The single edit was later included on a limited-edition reissue of the *Sanctuary* CD in Japan in 2022.

'I Can't Believe You' (Wolf Justman) (4:13)
In the r&b-rooted 'I Can't Believe You', a dejected Wolf looks back at a crumbling relationship after being betrayed. There's a reluctance to end the

affair, but it's reached a point where there's no alternative, even as she begs for forgiveness. So Wolf sings, 'It's just so hard for me to say that it's over, but now I've got to pass you by.' Justman's work on organ feeds the heartbreak, adding to the nostalgic feeling of what should've been. Jay delivers a brief guitar solo with a bittersweet tone.

Just past the midpoint, the track settles and begins to simmer, carried at first on Klein's bass lines. Wolf sings, 'You know I can't believe you, oh, no.' He's answered by Bladd with the same line. Wolf and Bladd continue their call-and-response as the song surges, with bass, organ, and drums growing louder. Jay then attacks with fierce guitar, carrying the song's tension and emotion through to the finish. 'I Can't Believe You' was the B-side to 'Take It Back.'

'I Don't Hang Around Much Anymore' (Wolf, Justman) (4:19)
A sense of weariness and resignation permeates 'I Don't Hang Around Much Anymore.' Similar in thought to *Monkey Island*'s 'I'm Falling', Wolf sings about the emptiness of the rock star life ('The lights are glarin', the people starin', and now I don't hang around much anymore'). But the lyrics are about love and failed relationships as well ('And I saw her yesterday and I thought that I would die'). Bladd's drums pack a punch, while Jay brings low key, lilting guitar to the verses and chorus, underscoring pain and disillusionment. Klein's bass notes are doubled with Justman's low-end piano notes for a deeper, richer sound.

Wolf initially sings from a place of detachment, standing on the outside of what his life used to be, but with each verse and chorus, he digs a little deeper, projecting louder, even adding an edge of anger. Over the swelling music and Jay's solo, Wolf repeats the 'I don't hang around much anymore' line, talking about 'the same old faces and the same old places', until he belts out, 'I just can't take it any*mooooore*', holding that last note nearly ten seconds.

'Jus' Can't Stop Me' (Wolf, Justman) (3:37)
At the end of an album of songs of love, pain, loss, and more comes a pure celebration track. It fades in on incessant stomping and barely heard shouts of 'hey, hey, hey, hey' before Jay rips into the song with raunchy guitar. Justman joins the party on organ, Klein and Bladd burst in on bass and drums, and Dick blasts away on harmonica. For Wolf, it's about blowing his savings on a good time in the city: 'I ain't lookin' for trouble, I just want a good time.' As he sings, 'Let this poor boy riiiiiide', the musical tension swells and he introduces the instrumental break with, 'Magic Dick, talk to me!' and Dick lets loose.

Dick's solo ends as the band stomp, clap, and chant another round of, 'hey, hey, hey, hey.' Wolf returns with, 'People sometimes ask me why I scream and I shout. I just say it's in me and it's got to come out.' That line is a direct nod to one of the band's early influences, John Lee Hooker, and his song

'Boogie Chillen" (sometimes 'Boogie Chillun"), in which Hooker sings, 'Let that boy boogie woogie 'cause it's in him and it's got to come out.' There's an unrestrained energy on the Geils track, which is why it made such a great opener for their live shows. 'Jus' Can't Stop Me' served as the B-side to 'Wild Man.'

Related Tracks
'Revenge' (Wolf, Justman) (1:45) (1978)
The flipside to the 'One Last Kiss' single, 'Revenge' had never appeared on any album until a limited-edition CD of *Sanctuary* was issued in Japan in 2022. It's a short, lumbering track, opening with swirling organ as someone counts off, 'One, two!' The band tumble in and shout, 'Revenge!' Wolf's vocals are often deep and muddy, but he sings of 'that time that we were torn apart, I had this feeling deep in my heart.' The sound of a sharp, metallic hammer paints an image of forced labour and confinement. Two ferocious solos carry the second half of the song. First is Jay on guitar, then Dick on harp. 'Revenge' is one of Geils' heavier, more menacing tracks.

House Party Live In Germany (1979)
Personnel:
Peter Wolf: vocals
Seth Justman: keyboards, vocals
Magic Dick: harp
J. Geils: guitar
Danny Klein: bass
Stephen Bladd: drums, vocals
Record label: Eagle Vision/Universal
Recorded: 21 April 1979
Released: 2014 (Europe), February 2015 (US)
Running time (CD): 58:23
Running time (DVD): 67:30
Highest chart place: US: –, CA: –, UK: –
Tracklisting: 'Jus' Can't Stop Me', 'I Could Hurt You', 'Sanctuary', 'One Last Kiss', 'Teresa', 'Nightmares', 'Wild Man', 'Looking For A Love', 'Give It To Me', 'Whammer Jammer', 'Ain't Nothing But A House Party', 'Where Did Our Love Go', 'Pack Fair And Square', 'First I Look At The Purse'

While undertaking the European leg of their *Sanctuary* tour, the band appeared at the fourth *Rockpalast Nacht* (Rock Palace Night) at Grugahalle Essen, Germany, on a bill with Patti Smith and headliner Johnny Winter. Following a full rehearsal on 20 April 1979, Geils' performance in front of more than 9,000 rowdy ticket holders on 21 April was broadcast live on German television's popular *Rockpalast* program. Not part of the Atlantic and EMI America catalogue, *House Party* wasn't released in the UK until 2014 and in the US until 2015. This 14-song package consists of an audio CD and a video DVD. Though it didn't make *Billboard*'s Top Albums chart, the release made it to number five on the music video sales chart upon its 2015 release, proving there was still a demand for Geils music.

The DVD was a welcome addition, providing professional video footage, something lacking from the band's history. The DVD is about nine minutes longer than the CD but doesn't offer any additional music. Instead, it provides extra non-musical footage, including some between-song patter. It opens with the German announcer introducing Geils. Baton twirlers and a marching band (around 30 members in all) make their way to the stage, playing for about a minute. Before the marching band is completely off the stage, Geils are announced again. It's a treat to see Bladd hammering away behind the drums, Klein prowling near the drumkit with his bass, a longhaired, thin-as-a-rail Justman pounding the keyboards, Dick strutting around as master of the harp, Jay showing just how great a guitar player he was, and Wolf leaping, twisting, shimmying, dancing, and working the crowd.

The fiery show opens with five tracks from *Sanctuary* and features six in all from the new album. On the CD, there's little rapping or patter from Wolf.

Instead, the band race through their set, including two encores, packing in as much music as possible.

The set launches with 'Jus' Can't Stop Me.' Instead of the 'The sky's the limit, so let this poor boy ride' line, Wolf calls to the crowd, 'Come on, Europe, let this poor boy ride.' Dick gets no introduction the way he does on the studio track but blasts away on harp just the same. Wolf works the crowd with the 'hey, hey, hey, hey' chant and throws in a few ad-libbed lines like, 'Shakin' my booty from Monday to Tuesday' and 'Give me that backbeat.' The music surges faster and faster to the ending, followed immediately by the piano- and harp-driven 'I Could Hurt You.' Wolf again tosses in some revised lyrics, with lines like 'aw, you jerked me off, darlin', too many times' rather than 'you jerked me around just too many times.' Klein's funky bass licks announce the instrumental break and usher in Justman's keyboards and Dick's harp. After 'I Could Hurt You', the DVD features a short rap from Wolf that's not on the CD. With a cry of 'Sanctuary', the band dive into a scalding version of the tune. Jay has switched to his Flying V guitar, Justman and Bladd add their vocals to the chorus, and Dick again shines on harmonica. 'One Last Kiss' follows. Dick takes the first break on harp. By the mid-point, the song settles into a sublime groove, with Jay and Dick playing in tandem before taking flight and winging over and under each other to the finish.

As the crowd chant, things quiet down with 'Teresa.' Not on the CD but on the DVD, Wolf is adjusting his microphone stand as he introduces it by saying, 'This next song was written in captive – captivity. It was written under great stress. It means a lot to us. It's called 'Teresa'.' Justman and Wolf are spotlighted, alone on stage, Justman handling piano and harmony vocals. Wolf turns in a heartfelt vocal and despite the raucous audience, he and Justman maintain the song's sincerity. The band pull out 'Nightmares' next and the party resumes. Bladd attacks the drums, Klein and Jay work percussion, Dick is on tambourine, and Justman plays the ominous organ parts while Wolf shouts those lines about 'a wild man runs away with your shoes' and 'when burning blood is dripping from your face.' The song intensifies and segues into 'Wild Man.' The band members charge into it, everyone playing hard. Dick and Wolf share a microphone as the song reaches its 'yeah, yeah, yeah' groove.

Then, it's time for some older numbers. First is a super-charged 'Looking For A Love.' Guitar and harp trade licks, and soon Klein, Dick, Jay, and Wolf are down on their knees at the front of the stage as Wolf, Justman, and Bladd chant, 'I'm lookin', I'm lookin', I'm lookin', I'm lookin'.' Next comes 'Give It To Me' with bright harp and piano, funky bass, and wailing guitar. Immediately following, Wolf tells the crowd, 'On the licking stick, the incomparable, the incredible Mister Magic Dick. 'Whammer Jammer', let me hear ya.' Though Geils had yet to crack the German music charts, it's clear the audience were familiar with 'Whammer Jammer' and had been waiting to hear it, chanting along with the opening notes. Over Bladd's drumming at the start of 'Ain't

Nothing But A House Party', Wolf shouts, 'We are gonna blow your face out!' At the chorus, he sings, 'Ain't nothin' but a Grugahalle house party.'

Wolf closes the set by thanking the audience and giving them 'a little bit of old rock and roll' with 'Where Did Our Love Go.' Geils play it nice and loose, with some honkytonk piano thrown in. Even those in the crowd who weren't familiar with The J. Geils Band likely knew the song, with the Supremes' version making it to number 16 on the German singles chart in 1964. The first encore finds Wolf talking to the crowd before singing, 'Wellllll.' The crowd answer with the same and the band tear into 'Pack Fair And Square.' The second and final encore brings a high-octane 'First I Look At The Purse' with some funky bass work. While the band keep the rhythm moving, Wolf playfully introduces the band, including 'on guee-tar, Jay Jerome Junior Geils' and mentions Pittsfield Slim when introducing Magic Dick. All too soon, the show is over and the band, drenched in sweat, depart the stage.

Though not included on the DVD (there are no extras), after the show, *Rockpalast*'s Alan Bangs conducted a short interview with the band. Bangs asked about Wolf's days as a radio disc jockey; Dick played and sang Sonny Boy Williamson's 'Peach Tree' with the others clapping along, providing the beat; Wolf thanked everyone involved with the show and the band signed the WDR *Rockpalast* board.

There are some surprises here. First is that 'Nightmares' appears in the setlist, providing the perfect lead-in to 'Wild Man.' Second, *Rockpalast* has been using 'Believe In Me' from 1975's *Hotline* as the show's instrumental opening theme music since 1976. 'Believe In Me' wasn't in the band's setlist in 1979, but it would've been worth rehearsing to perform it on the show. It's also odd that 'Must Of Got Lost' wasn't somehow squeezed into the setlist. *House Party* presents the full show from that April 1979 night, but had Geils been the headliner, there would've been at least another hour of music recorded. Four nights after filming *Rockpalast*, Geils appeared on The Netherlands *TopPop* television program with 'Wild Man' and 'Take It Back.' Despite the songs being lip-synced, the band performed with just as much energy as their live set on *Rockpalast*.

While not directly related to *House Party*, it's worth mentioning that among non-German speaking fans, there is sometimes a belief that 'Geils' means 'horny' in the German language. Sort of. The German word 'geil' (without the *s*) can sometimes mean horny but requires context to be understood as such. More commonly, 'geil' is used to mean excellent or awesome or to refer to a person as 'hot.'

Love Stinks (1980)

Personnel:
Peter Wolf: vocals
Seth Justman: keyboards, vocals
Magic Dick: harmonicas
J. Geils: guitars
Danny Klein: bass
Stephen Jo Bladd: drums, vocals
Producer: Seth Justman
Engineer: Dave Thoener
Record label: EMI America
Released: 28 January 1980
Running time: 37:27
Highest chart place: US: 18, CA: 4, UK: –

The band's ninth studio album continued *Sanctuary*'s upward trajectory. *Love Stinks* spawned three hit singles, two of which cracked the US top 40 and became the band's second-highest charting album after 1973's *Bloodshot*. Like its predecessor, the album was recorded at Long View Farm in Massachusetts, with Justman handling production, creating a cleaner sound without becoming clinical. It's a transitional album, the music shifting toward new wave, synthesizers added to the mix but without detaching from the band's r&b roots. Justman has joked in several interviews that the reason he didn't use synthesizers previously was because he couldn't afford them.

David Thoener, who had worked on *Hotline*, *Monkey Island* and *Sanctuary*, served as engineer. 'We started the *Love Stinks* album with drums and keyboards as the basic track', he said, 'and they were recorded in the milk barn. (It was) a first and new approach involving miking the ceiling and room, which was a medium size wood room, so I could get the sound heard on the drums. The house recording studio was dead (as recounted in the *Sanctuary* chapter), but the milk barn was very 'live' and gave the record and the following record, *Freeze Frame*, the drum sound that many have admired.' Thoener continued, 'We recorded the guitars in the horse barn, and several times would have to punch in to redo a spot because one or several of the horses would neigh – loud enough to get my attention, wind the tape back, and punch back in the recording. Suffice it to say that every aspect of *Love Stinks* was a new and different way to approach recording. We would have a cable stretching from the control room to the barn so Jay could stand in the control room listening with me to the studio monitors while he was recording guitars and the speaker stack was in the barn. In the morning it was a funny sight to see birds perching on the cable by the dozens. It (*Love Stinks*) was pretty quick compared to previous albums. I think we spent about three months (on it), including the two weeks of mixing at Record Plant New York.' Thoener added that after his success with *Love Stinks*, his career took off, 'and the opportunity to work with different genres became a reality, which was a wonderful experience.'

The album's cover was designed by Carin Goldberg, who had designed the previous year's *Best Of* on Atlantic Records, which depicted a bowling ball striking pins. She would later design the covers for 1982's *Showtime!* and Peter Wolf's *Lights Out* in 1984. The *Love Stinks* cover image was taken from a 1951 issue of *My Romance*, a US confession-style magazine geared toward women in their 20s and 30s. The tawdry headlines, story excerpts, and racy images on the inner sleeve are also from issues of *My Romance*. The back cover features photographs of the band members as children, which might've been Justman's idea. Klein joked about the photos, 'I wanted the one of me pissing, but they didn't do that.' Below the photos and song titles was a small version of the palmprint logo that had been used on *Sanctuary*. The palmprint was also found at the top of the LP's centre label. Similar to *Sanctuary*, no lyrics were included.

The promotion included a stop on the US television program *Saturday Night Live* on 8 March. The band performed 'Love Stinks' and 'Sanctuary', with Jay on his Flying V guitar and Magic Dick handling the deep-voiced 'love stinks' response. In addition to their scheduled tour stops, in March, the band performed a surprise set at Madame Wong's, a restaurant and live venue in Chinatown, Los Angeles, with a capacity of about 350. The 22 March show at Oakland Coliseum in California was recorded for US radio's *King Biscuit Flower Hour*. April meant another three nights at Cobo Arena in Detroit and shows at Boston Garden in Massachusetts. On 27 April, under the billing of Juke Joint Jimmy & His House Party Rockers, the band performed a sold-out 'secret' show at The Great Gildersleeves in New York, with attendance above the club's official capacity. The set, which lasted over two and a half hours, included new songs 'Love Stinks', 'Night Time', 'Just Can't Wait' and 'Till The Walls Come Tumblin' Down.' Magic Dick took lead vocals on Sonny Boy Williamson's 'Nine Below Zero', and both Wolf and Dick handled vocals on 'Be Careful (What You Do).'

Geils appeared at Pinkpop Festival in Geleen, Netherlands, on 26 May, where they were introduced by four cheerleaders calling out, 'Gimmie a J! Gimmie a G!' until they spelt out J. Geils, then yelled, 'Whatta ya got? J. Geils! J. Geils! J. Geils!' The 11-song set included three from the new record: 'Just Can't Wait', 'Come Back' and 'Love Stinks', with Wolf demolishing a bouquet of roses during the latter. Magic Dick sang 'Peach Tree', explaining that Sonny Boy Williamson 'taught it to me.' Photos and video from the concert show Wolf with a black eye from an incident at a London pub days prior. It happened when Wolf was on his way to see friends Nick Lowe and Elvis Costello in a recording studio. Wolf asked his driver to stop in a questionable neighbourhood so he could get some 'English beer' before the pubs closed. Several locals at the pub started to harass Wolf. It spilt outside, where Wolf found a constable and asked for help, and soon, all of them were running down the street past a police undercover operation. The detectives in charge of the undercover operation saw several people being chased by a constable and not knowing what was happening, jumped in to assist, resulting in Wolf's black eye. It's not clear if Wolf ever got his pint.

May and June also included stops in France, the UK, Switzerland, Germany, and Sweden. Their time in Germany included mimed performances of 'Come Back' and 'Love Stinks' on the television program *RockPop* on 20 June. A string of five shows in Japan followed. At one of the soundchecks there, a mild earthquake struck but caused no damage. The following month, on 16 July, Geils opened for The Who at Toronto's Canadian National Exhibition (CNE) stadium. Footage from that set appeared on *The New Music Show* and included the band being presented with gold awards (Canada sales of 50,000 units prior to 1 May 2008) for *Love Stinks*, which reached number four in Canada. July tour dates included three nights at Pine Knob Theatre near Detroit, Michigan, and three nights at Cape Cod Coliseum, about 75 miles southeast of Boston.

Love Stinks was one of J. Geils' biggest albums. In addition to reaching the top five in Canada, it graced the Australia album chart, hitting 43, their highest to date. In America, it was certified gold on 22 April 1980, three months after its release, and attained platinum status in Canada (100,000 units prior to 1 May 2008) on 1 December 1980. Nautilus Recordings issued a half-speed master of the LP in 1981. As the back cover of the album says, 'Play it loud!'

'Just Can't Wait' (Wolf, Justman) (3:24)
Highest chart place: US: 78, CA: –, UK: –
The band pounce on 'Just Can't Wait', living up to the song's title. Jay's guitar announces the up-tempo track before drums, bass, and harp join in. It's a hard rock track for the first measures, then Justman's brilliant keyboards give it a push towards new wave. Wolf's lyrics are from the perspective of someone impatient to get together with his girlfriend, not caring 'if your daddy says it's wrong. I just can't stand to be away from you too long.'

Handclaps drive the song through the choruses. The break shows off Jay's guitar, keeping that rock edge before Wolf is back for another verse as Justman stabs the keys in staccato fashion underneath. The last notes of the track crossfade into 'Come Back', forever linking the two cuts. 'Just Can't Wait' serves up the textures and edgy sound that would be further explored on the next studio album. This was the third single from *Love Stinks* and one of three Geils songs in Adam Sandler's 2010 film *Grown Ups*.

'Come Back' (Wolf, Justman) (5:09)
Highest chart place: US: 32, CA: 19, UK: –
'Come Back' crossfades in from 'Just Can't Wait' on crisp synth and drums. The song ventures even further into new wave territory than the previous

track – and approaches disco – but still carries a hard edge. Guitar and keyboard riffs, riding atop Klein's driving bass, create an irresistible dance beat at odds with the desperation of the lyrics. Wolf sings from the perspective of a man whose girlfriend walked out on him. He's still in love and is begging her to return. Jay leads the lengthy instrumental break with a blistering solo. As his guitar notes echo and fade, keyboards, drums, and bass come to the front, pounding away. Wolf returns, asking, 'Tell me, tell me, what you gonna do, tell me, pretty baby 'cause I'm still in love with you.' After a chorus, Justman's synthesizer drives the track for the last 90 seconds to the end.

'Come Back' was the first single from the album. It was edited to 3:32, omitting about 40 seconds from the first instrumental break and nearly a minute from the break at the song's end. The single made the top 40 in the US and Canada and became the second Geils single to chart in Australia (after 1974's 'Must Of Got Lost') at number 31. 'Come Back' was another Geils song featured in the 2010 film *Grown Ups*.

'Takin' You Down' (Wolf, Justman) (4:06)
Piano starts the track, bass enters like a heartbeat, and soon the rest of the band dive in. After the new wave synth sounds of the first two tracks, this one emphasises guitar, harp, and piano. 'Takin' You Down' has sinister undertones, reminiscent of 'Somebody' from *Monkey Island*, with a bit of paranoia and unknown fate threatening the singer. Wolf sings, 'They're dealin' out your fate' and 'they say they know your price.'

Just past the mid-point, Wolf shouts, 'Blow!' and Dick takes over with harp. His solo is followed by another verse and final chorus, with guitar climbing around Wolf's vocals. The track fades out over piano and bass, mimicking the heartbeat intro. 'Takin' You Down' was the flipside to the 'Come Back' single.

'Night Time' (Bob Feldman, Gerald Goldstein, Richard Gottehrer) (4:29)
The songwriting team of Feldman, Goldstein, and Gottehrer had earlier hits with 'My Boyfriend's Back' by The Angels and 'I Want Candy' for their own group, The Strangeloves. As the Strangeloves, they also wrote and released 'Night Time' in 1965 (shown as the hyphenated 'Night-Time' on their LP but 'Night Time' on their single), taking it to number 30 in the US.

Geils stay mostly true to The Strangeloves' version, with a slightly faster tempo and a few lyric changes. The track, about working hard during the day and living it up at night, stomps along on piano, bass, and drums. Wolf ushers in the first break with, 'Wooo! Alright, get ready boys, get ready. Hit me!' After some heavy pounding, Dick takes flight on harmonica. Then it's Jay on guitar. Like the Strangeloves' version, around the midpoint, Wolf says, 'Come here, baby' and 'turn your radio up.' The final minute of the song belongs to Jay, scratching it out on guitar, and Justman, with a smoking organ solo. 'Night Time' was featured in the 2013 film *Grown Ups 2*.

'No Anchovies, Please' (Wolf, Justman) (2:39)

Every Geils fan is familiar with the strange, surreal 'No Anchovies, Please.' Parts of the track feel like a spoken word freeform jazz piece and the opening notes are like something out of a horror film or a television soap opera. Bladd voices the various characters and Dick handles saxophone, which is carried along on a *duh-duh, duh-duh, duh-duh-dah-duh, duh-dah* undercurrent, and begins with Wolf intoning, 'This is the story of a young couple from Portland, Maine.' It tells of a woman who finds a note with a telephone number at the bottom of a can of anchovies. Soon, she's abducted and betrayed and 'finds herself in a strange, foreign-speaking nation.' At this point, the band used a back-masked recording to create unintelligible, foreign language babblings in the background. As Klein explained, it's a recording played in reverse, which actually says, 'It doesn't take a genius to know the difference between chicken shit and chicken salad.' As the tension builds toward an explanation, Wolf declares, 'For the first time, a human being is transformed into a–' but is quickly shushed with 'Shhhh. Keep a secret.'

Dick returns on sax and Wolf quietly says, 'Meanwhile, back in Portland, Maine...' The woman's husband, Don, is now at a local bar 'chain-smoking 40 packs of cigarettes a day.' The bar's television is tuned to *Bowling For Dollars*. The sound of a bowling ball crashing into pins is courtesy of Patricia Glennon and Jesse Henderson from Long View Farm, who were sent off to a candle pin (a New England twist on ten pin) bowling alley in nearby Worcester to get the authentic recording. Crazy Al points out something on the TV screen and Don recognises, 'That bowling ball – it's my wife!' To wrap up the tale, Wolf reminds the listener there's a lesson here: 'Next time you place your order, don't forget to say, 'No anchovies, please" (with echo on those last words). The song was the B-side to 'Just Can't Wait.'

'Love Stinks' (Wolf, Justman) (3:45)

Highest chart place: US: 38, CA: 15, UK: –

While most other bands were cranking out radio-friendly love songs, Geils released one of the greatest anti-love pop songs of all time. Wolf was divorcing actress Faye Dunaway during the making of the *Love Stinks* album but has said many times that the album's title song had nothing to do with his relationship. In a 17 April 1980 *Boston Globe* article, Justman stated the song 'came about from a conversation I had with my brother on the telephone. We were talking about love troubles and all that, and he just said something like, 'Aw, (bleep), love stinks.' And we sat down with that and wrote a song.'

The track carries an attitude from the first note. It begins with Bladd slamming the drums and Jay churning out a gritty guitar riff. Wolf's opening sums it up: 'You love her, but she loves him, and he loves somebody else. You just can't win.' The band again successfully marry rock and new wave, meshing guitar and harp with synthesizer to create a top 40 track. This was the second single from the album and Geils' highest-charting track in

Canada to date. When Music Television (MTV) debuted on US television on 1 August 1981, just over 200 videos were presented in the first 24 hours of programming. 'Love Stinks', which includes images of a bride and groom in gas masks to emphasise the point, made the cut, being the 85th video to be aired that first day. Despite the song's cynicism, it's proved to have an enduring quality. The 1996 film *Mr. Wrong* featured a cover of the song by Joan Jett. Adam Sandler performed it in *The Wedding Singer* in 1998. The 1999 movie *Love Stinks* was named after the song. In April 2007, the US television show *The Simpsons* revamped the song as 'Bart Stinks.' One of the more bizarre appearances of the song came in 2009 when the Geils recording was used in an American TV advertisement for Swiffer Wet Jet mop. 'Love Stinks' was made available for the video game *Rock Band 4* in 2016.

'Tryin' Not To Think About It' (Wolf, Justman) (6:19)
Jay's gritty, scraping guitar riffing over the top of Justman's synthesizer opens 'Tryin' Not To Think About It', one of the heavier and darker tunes on the album. From start to finish, the lyrics are sinister but nebulous. 'Three years in the ice box': has the song's narrator been in prison, trapped in a bad relationship, in hiding, or something else? Even if the meaning isn't straightforward, the grim essence of the song comes through. At the instrumental break, guitar and harp play in tandem, with Klein's bass pushing underneath. Bladd's funky drum fill then gives way to Dick's soaring harp before Wolf returns with, 'The sniper will grin as he slowly takes aim, why didn't they tell me the rules of the game?' The final break brings a smouldering keyboard-bass groove. Guitar and harp return through the song's ending.

'Desire (Please Don't Turn Away)' (Wolf, Justman) (3:35)
The keyboard introduction sets the tone for 'Desire', a mournful number about times and loves lost. Wolf gives a strong performance, an ache in his voice as he sings, 'Time will pass as it must, dreams explode into dust.' There are only two short verses with an equally short chorus that's repeated three times during the track.

The break brings a backwards guitar solo. To accomplish it, Thoener used the existing multitrack recording, marking the beginning and end of the break, and played it in reverse while Jay recorded within that allocated space as normal. Then, Jay's solo was reversed and slotted into the original forward-playing multitrack for the desired result. 'When recording backwards, I'd minimise what was playing back', Thoener said. 'For example, I'd play just a kick and snare for time and maybe a keyboard for chords.' The effect is ethereal.

'Till The Walls Come Tumblin' Down' (Wolf, Justman) (4:01)
In an inspired opening, Bladd strikes the drumkit once, hits hard several more times, and Justman descends across the piano to create a sense of

everything tumbling down. Dick's harp and Klein's bass give it a brash jazzy feel and Jay draws out those initial notes before Wolf comes in for that first line: 'Smashed a hole through my TV screen, too much too soon if you know what I mean.' 'Till The Walls Come Tumblin' Down' is the type of party tune that the band does so well and makes a perfect closing number, similar to 'Jus' Can't Stop Me' wrapping up *Sanctuary*.

The track is about living it up to the end. As Wolf says, 'You gotta rock, rock, rock it (*oooh yeah!*) till the walls come tumblin' down.' The rhythm section chugs beneath as Dick's harp blares through the first break. Jay answers with an equally raucous guitar solo. At the bridge, Wolf prowls in over some funky bass: 'Mash those potatoes and don't be shy' (a reference to the dance known as the mashed potato). The band continue to strut and Wolf soon declares, 'You gotta brush your teeth with... *rock and roll!*' The tune gets rowdier and rowdier, drums and bass thundering, Justman hammering away on the keys, guitar and harp jamming through the fadeout. The track was the B-side to 'Love Stinks.'

Related Tracks
'Love Stinks' (Live) (Wolf, Justman) (1980) (4:05) [Promotional Release]
In late April 1980, Geils played a secret set at The Great Gildersleeves in New York, billed as Juke Joint Jimmy & His House Party Rockers. The recording of 'Love Stinks' from that show was pressed on vinyl and distributed solely to radio stations. It begins with the club's answering machine message: 'This is the Great Gildersleeves... appearing tonight, Sunday April 27, Juke Joint Jimmy and His House Party Rockers. This show is completely sold out. For those of you who have tickets, doors open up at 8:30 and showtime is 9 pm. Once again, this show is completely sold out...'

The song blasts off with Bladd's drums and Jay's raw guitar. Dick provides the low growl 'love stinks' and the crowd nearly drown out the band while shouting the 'love stinks' chorus. Nothing else from that show has been released.

Freeze-Frame (1981)

Personnel:
Peter Wolf: vocals
Seth Justman: keyboards, vocals
Magic Dick: harmonica, sax
J. Geils: guitars
Danny Klein: bass, flex bass
Stephen Jo Bladd: drums, vocals
Luther Van Dross, Fonzi Thornton, Cissy Houston, Tawatha Agee, Kenny Williams: backing vocals
Randy Brecker, Ronnie Cuber, Lou Marini, Tom Melone, Alan Rubin, George Young: horns
Producer: Seth Justman
Engineer: Dave Thoener
Record label: EMI America
Released: 26 October 1981
Running time: 40:56
Highest chart place: US: 1, CA: 1, UK: 12

After more than a decade of recording and relentless touring, The J. Geils Band hit the top with *Freeze-Frame*. It took about a year, working on and off at Long View Farm Studios, to put the album together. Jim Mazza, president of EMI America, wasn't too concerned about the lengthy time in the studio. 'We had a gold album and a platinum album already under our belts', said Mazza, 'so whatever time it took for (*Freeze-Frame*), we knew that creatively, it's going to be growing and moving forward and a step up. The forecasts were pretty bold. There was a sense of anticipation for that record from an audience point and the live shows were starting to kick-in in a big way. So I felt pretty confident about the financial aspects of that.' Though it wasn't evident to fans, creative tensions were starting to surface as work progressed – not unusual for any band putting together a new record, but now the conflicts were greater than usual and not as easily resolved. The album contained nine original tunes, although, for the first time, Justman was credited as the sole songwriter on five. *Freeze-Frame* continued the push into new wave and experimental – at times *avant-garde* – music. The result was a globally successful monster that spawned three hit singles.

As with 1980's *Love Stinks*, Justman handled arrangements and production. David Thoener again served as engineer. Work started in September 1980 and stretched to the American Thanksgiving holiday at the end of November, when the band took a two-week break to do some writing. The two weeks, however, turned into several months. Thoener was kept on standby for the band's return and, during his time off, turned down several other big engineering gigs, including what would become Hall & Oates' *Private Eyes*. Geils finally resumed work in the studio in February 1981. Promised that

Freeze-Frame would be wrapped up in time, Thoener accepted an offer in May from Robert 'Mutt' Lange to work on AC/DC's *For Those About To Rock*, requiring Thoener to be in Paris and London starting in August. That almost didn't happen. Thoener explained, 'The Geils band and I mixed *Freeze-Frame* for the month of July and when we were done, we had a playback party, where the band and invited guests would come and listen to the final album. After the party, Seth came in to talk to me. He said, 'Dave, I want to re-mix a few songs.' This was a Saturday and I had a flight to Paris Monday morning.' For Thoener, the additional work wouldn't be possible, and multiple alternate mixes were already available for each of the songs. In the end, Thoener said, 'I left as scheduled and Seth sat with my assistant Steve Marcantonio (who would return for the band's final studio album) for a week or so going through all the takes that we mixed, and no songs were remixed.'

The front cover of the album displayed the band's name across the top (some of the earliest printings showed it as The J. Geils Band, without a period after the *J*) and 'Freeze-Frame' in cursive at the bottom. The album was almost named *Insane Again* after the 'Insane, Insane Again' track, but *Freeze-Frame* won out. The focus of the album cover was the bold, surreal work of artist and musician Georganne (misspelt 'Georgann' on the credits) Deen. Her illustration depicted a creature with a large, bespectacled head – something between an asteroid and a metallic potato – taking musical notes and analyzing a flat, three-eyed creature gazing at a freeze-frame of a video. The art reflects the often experimental, new wave-styled music within. The inner sleeve featured lyrics and a palmprint on one side, with credits and a photo on the reverse. Listed in the 'Thanks to' section is Seth Justman's brother Paul, who directed two music videos for the album. The LP centre label carried the palmprint above the band name, album title, and track listing.

The photos for the back cover and inner sleeve were courtesy of Thomas Weschler and were done under a strict timeline. Earlier photos, taken three days prior in New York with a different photographer, were not a problem, but due to circumstances afterwards, those photos were scrapped, creating an emergency. As Weschler explained, 'I was at my studio (Woodward Studio) in Birmingham, Michigan, and went out to get lunch. As I stepped into the street a Thunderbird sped to me and stopped with the door flying open. In movies, it would have looked like a mafia hit. The driver was EMI promotion man Howard Lesnick, who yelled: 'Get in!' I got in and Pete Wolf was in the back seat. He asked me if I could set up an emergency photo shoot for that night; they had to get the back cover art to the label the next day. I told him I could for sure. He told me what they had in mind.'

Weschler continued, 'They were playing Pine Knob (near Detroit) that night. I suggested we shoot it at their hotel, The Northfield Hilton. Omar Newman (my studio partner) and I set up in the catering hallway of the hotel. At 4:30 in the morning, we finished; I rushed the film to our lab and got it to Pete by noon. He had the label guy expedite it to LA.' The photos showed the band wearing painters' clothes, covered in bright paint. For the back cover, the band are standing, facing the camera. On the inner sleeve, they're in their pyramid pose.

The band hit the road around September 1981, starting in the US. October found them opening for The Rolling Stones (who had rehearsed at Long View Farm) for several shows on the US West Coast before headlining across the States with support acts like Boston's Jon Butcher Axis and Irish rockers U2. Along the way, Geils played the final show at Chicago's Uptown Theater on 19 November 1981 before it closed, and on Christmas Day 1981, they played two shows for inmates at a prison near Boston. Three sold-out nights at Boston Garden in February 1982 set an attendance record. Other promotion included The Joe Franklin Show in New York, one day before their sold-out Madison Square Garden gig on 20 February 1982 (Jay's birthday). Manager Bob Hinkle said that because Franklin's show was taped in midtown New York, 'Everybody in the whole music world was there' in the studio to watch. Wolf and Franklin co-hosted, with the rest of the band sitting in through the entire program. Mario Medious, who spotted Geils in the late 1960s at the Boston Tea Party and was instrumental in getting them signed to Atlantic Records, was a guest on the program. The band presented Franklin the 'J. Geils King of Television Award' for promoting music acts, Magic Dick played Sonny Boy Williamson's 'Peach Tree' and the entire band performed 'Freeze-Frame.' For 'Freeze-Frame', the musicians had paint poured over them, similar to the music video, but there was a problem. Hinkle explained, 'Before the show, Joe talked to them in the dressing room and said, 'I'll send my guy out to get paint; you don't have to worry about it.' The guy bought oil-based paint. After the pyramid, the guys suddenly realised they couldn't get the paint off. Took 'em weeks.' To make up for it, Franklin 'did the only thing Joe knew how to do: he came into the dressing room and handed out coupons for sandwiches.' The band couldn't help but track the paint into their limousine after the show and into their hotel, leaving a mess along the way.

By May, Geils were in Canada, then Europe in June and July, where they opened for The Rolling Stones again. Doug Slade, Wolf and Bladd's bandmate from their days in The Hallucinations, was not travelling with the band but could often be found backstage. In London in late July, Wolf, Jay, and Justman joined Keith Richards, Ron Wood, and Bobby Keys and assembled a band dubbed The (Original) Carltones (after the Carlton Hotel where they were staying) for a brief jam on Mick Jagger's birthday, though nothing came of it.

August 1982 found Geils back in America. The September concerts at Pine Knob Theatre in Michigan would be recorded for the live *Showtime!* A date in Toronto, Canada, followed in October before shows in New England in December. The last concerts performed by the original band occurred on 31 December 1982 and 1-2 January 1983 in Worcester, Massachusetts. At the 31 December show, Mayor Sara Robertson presented the band with the Key to the City.

Freeze-Frame entered *Billboard*'s album chart at 39, reaching number one eleven weeks later on 6 February 1982 and spending 19 weeks total in the US top ten. It hit number one in Canada and provided the band with its only charting album in the UK, at number 12, and made it to 21 in Australia. The album was certified gold in the US on 30 December 1981 and platinum in early January 1982. In Canada, it achieved triple platinum certification on 1 May 1982.

'Freeze-Frame' (Wolf, Justman) (3:57)
Highest chart place: US: 4, CA: 2, UK: 27

The album opens with a shout of 'Freeze-Frame!' and the clicking and whirring of a camera shutter before Justman's keyboard leaps in. The song originated with Justman working out a riff on organ. Once the freeze-frame term was used, Wolf started tossing out photography expressions: 'rough cut', 'snapshot image', 'zoom lens.' The song is about realizing an instant in time, a moment where things become crystal clear, be it love at first sight or the feeling of pure joy. Bright horns and crisp keys play over the drum and thick bass rhythm section, creating an upbeat party track. The band brought in six outside horn players, including Randy Brecker and Ronnie Cuber, who contributed to 1977's *Monkey Island*.

Seth Justman's brother Paul directed the song's video, his second for the band after 'Centerfold.' In the video, band members perform in a room padded with white parachute material while images of old movies and album cover art come and go. Two-thirds through, the artwork becomes animated. The next clips show the band in white painters' attire. Red handprints are stamped on white steps and soon, the band members are doused in colourful paint, complementing Thomas Weschler's album back cover and inner sleeve photos. The video ends with the band's pyramid, Justman's red-painted palm facing the camera.

Released while 'Centerfold' was still on the Hot 100 chart in the US, 'Freeze-Frame' was the second single from the album, becoming the band's second-highest charting in the US and Canada, earning gold certification in both countries. In addition to a picture sleeve, the single was issued as a novelty disc shaped like the album cover's potato head image. 'Freeze-Frame' has been heard in films like 2006's *10th & Wolf* and television programmes such as season one of *Wicked City* (2015) and season 16 (2005) and 18 (2007) of *The Simpsons*. The instrumental introduction was used in St. Louis, Missouri, weekend children's TV quiz show *D.B.'s Delight* over the opening and closing credits from 1984-1988. 'Freeze-Frame' became available for *Rock Band 4* in 2011.

Wolf has joined Little Steven and the Disciples of Soul on stage for 'Freeze-Frame' multiple times, with one performance captured on Little Steven's 2018 *Soulfire Live!* and another on Little Steven's 2021 *Summer Of Sorcery Live!*

'Rage In The Cage' (Wolf, Justman) (4:57)

Dick's harmonica riffs brashly announce 'Rage In The Cage', a number about revolt and escape from norms and restrictions, with music as salvation. The song's protagonist conveys the no-one-understands-me attitude after being 'laid off (made redundant) since last summer', claiming 'this town is like a prison', and being told his girlfriend's father doesn't want him around. Rage and frustration grow and he proclaims, 'My transistor's 'bout the only antidote to keep my temperature from running wild. Let me hear that radio!' The band reflect the simmering rage in the way they attack their instruments. The bass has a fat sound, the drums hit rapid and heavy, the harp is almost a siren, and keyboards stab in and out.

Altogether, it's a frantic burst of energy, with the band repeating, 'There's a rage in the cage!' Leading into the break, Wolf sings, 'I've gotta get me on that rocket ship to outta here. Watch out.' First, Dick's harp, then Jay's guitar, play out over equally frantic bass and drum. It tumbles into a middle four with metallic hammering conveying drudgery and sweaty labour. Wolf returns with fast-paced lyrics before it melts into a sense of mind control with the deep, slowed-down lines, 'They don't want me paralyzed, they just want me neutralised.' The band return, shouting, 'There's a rage in the cage' over more frenzied playing through the fade. 'Rage In The Cage' was the B-side to 'Centerfold.'

'Centerfold' (Justman) (3:35)

Highest chart place: US: 1, CA: 1, UK: 3

Rosalie Trombley served as music director at CKLW, a Canadian radio station across the border from Detroit, Michigan. Trombley, immortalised in Bob Seger's song 'Rosalie' ('She knows music'), was hugely influential in the US Midwest and Canada when it came to picking hit singles. The band and the record company originally planned to make 'Angel In Blue' the lead single, but Trombley knew better.

Geils were already filming a video for 'Angel In Blue' when EMI America President Jim Mazza received a call from Trombley. She told Mazza that Wolf had sent her a cassette of the new album and she wanted to know what the single would be. Mazza said, 'I told her ('Angel In Blue') and she said, 'That's not it. Tomorrow morning at 8:00 on CKLW, I've added 'Centerfold' in heavy rotation' and I said, 'That's the single'.' Mazza's rationale was solid: CKLW is part of the North American RKO radio network, Trombley knew her stuff, and once she put the song in heavy rotation, other big markets like Boston and Los Angeles would pick it up as well.

After talking with Trombley, Mazza called Wolf and asked, 'Did you send a cassette to Rosalie Trombley?' Mazza relayed the conversation with Trombley, then told Wolf to stop making the 'Angel In Blue' video and immediately start one for 'Centerfold.' The video, directed by Seth Justman's brother Paul, featuring models bouncing through a school classroom and showing Bladd hitting a snare drum filled with milk, was soon in heavy rotation on MTV. Although Paul had worked on other film ventures, 'Centerfold' was his first music video. He would go on to direct other projects, including videos for The Cars and Rick Springfield and the 2002 documentary *Standing In The Shadows Of Motown*.

The song is straightforward – the narrator had a crush on an innocent girl 'in soft, fuzzy sweaters' back in high school, and years later, he's shocked when he's 'looking through a girlie magazine, and there's my homeroom angel on the pages in between.' There are differing stories as to the origin of the song. One version has it that one of Bladd's friends spotted an old high school girlfriend in a pornographic magazine, and when Bladd mentioned it to Justman, Justman wrote the song. Another story is based on a model whom Wolf briefly dated, who then later turned up in *Playboy*.

Patricia Glennon, who tended horses (among other duties) at Long View, said, 'You would never meet a more down-to-earth bunch of guys', echoing the words of others who loved working with Geils. She recalled being 'inside the barn loading ramp to do background vocals' (with John Farrell, Jemima James and likely Geoff Myers and others) for 'Centerfold' and possibly 'Freeze-Frame.'

The band's biggest hit, 'Centerfold' hit number one in the US, Australia, and Canada and made it into the top five in at least five other countries. Jay mentioned on the Groton, Massachusetts, program *Around Town With Jane Bouvier* that he was more impressed with the number one single than the number one album, and 'Centerfold' was one of the few gold records hanging in his house. The song spent six weeks at number one in the US. After Jay's unfortunate passing in 2017, 'Centerfold' made it to number 21 – with 3,000 downloads sold – on *Billboard*'s Hot Rock Songs, a chart which did not exist when 'Centerfold' was released in 1981. It's the only J. Geils song to be nominated for a Grammy award. It was in the category of 'Best Rock Performance for a Duo or Group' but lost to Survivor's 'Eye Of The Tiger.'

Of all the songs from the Geils catalogue, this has been used in more films and TV shows than any other. It's appeared in everything from movies like *Charlie's Angels: Full Throttle* (2003) and *Grown Ups 2* (2013) to TV's *The King Of Queens* (2000), *The Office* (US) (2008) and *Glee* (2013). It's also possibly the most covered song from Geils. In 1995, comedy metal band J.B.O. (James Blast Orchester) released a German parody ('Mei Alde Is Im Playboy Drin'). Status Quo recorded a straight-up version in 2003. As part of their *Sunday Lunch* YouTube series, in 2023, Robert Fripp and Toyah Willcox performed a short, quirky version of it, with Willcox spotting her angel (Fripp) in *Prog* magazine. The Geils version of 'Centerfold' was made available for the video game *Rock Band 3* in 2010.

'Do You Remember When' (Wolf, Justman) (4:45)
Wolf's wistful lyrics in 'Do You Remember When' are simultaneously looking back at a failed relationship, at simpler times, and at lost youth. Time

hasn't erased the memories like it should have. Jay's biting five-note guitar incantation introduces the track, with bass, drums, organ, and strings easing in. 'I overheard someone mention your name', sings Wolf, 'I overheard, now my heart feels the pain.' As the background singers vocalise the 'tick tock, tick tock' of a clock, Wolf tells how time and life move slowly now that he's on his own. There's no inner strength to try to put things back the way they were, just a feeling of emptiness, though maybe not total regret.

The opening guitar riff re-emerges on and off through the song, with strings adding the right amount of heartbreak at the right times. At the break, Jay milks the notes on his guitar, building the nostalgic mood. Another chorus follows, with the final falsetto 'You're *gooonne*' drawing out over ten seconds. Strings and drums guide the track to the finish, with Jay's backwards guitar (recorded similar to *Love Stinks*' 'Desire') closing the fadeout to evoke disappearing memories.

'Insane, Insane Again' (Justman) (4:44)
The manic, rapid-fire 'Insane, Insane Again' closes side one. Thick synthesizer, rapid keys, harsh guitar, drums, and bass create the madhouse framework for the lyrics: 'panic rules the moment with no mercy or desire.' It's a bad dream or a life out of control. Vocals urge, 'relax, relax', in a frantic manner, which is intentionally anything but soothing. The harmonica break adds to the chaos, with Dick even throwing in several measures of the nursery rhyme/folk song 'Row, Row, Row Your Boat.' Justman comes in, assaulting the piano keys as Bladd adds madcap percussion. Clipped, staccato piano follows while someone vocalises over the disjointed melody. Some of the instruments were recorded at half speed, then played back normally for a more intense effect.

Wolf returns, repeating, 'I need some breathing room' before spitting out brisk stream-of-consciousness lines: 'open fire – shell shock', 'mind bend – echo send.' The claustrophobia builds until Wolf cries, 'Mama! Won't you tell me, please, please, what is going on?' At the end of the verse, the song is suspended for a moment as a synthesizer note swirls and descends before the band crash back in. The track finishes like an out-of-control engine finally losing steam, some lost harp notes adding to the collapse.

'Flamethrower' (Justman) (4:59)
The opening cut on side two is one of the band's funkiest, most infectious dance tunes. 'Flamethrower' stomps in on Bladd's drumkit. Klein's bass connects and the two settle in with Dick's harp riffs bounding on top. The track tells of a woman working a soul-numbing job, trying to make it through her days so she can unleash herself at night and feed her spirit to return to work the next day. She's controlling her life however she can, finding inner strength, pushing through life. Even if she's not much to notice at work, 'she carries a burning torch inside' and at night, 'the headlines flash in neon that the girl has taken flight.' Under the verses, Jay and Klein propel a boogie beat with jangly guitar and climbing and descending bass.

The instrumental break brings a superb harp solo. Drums grab the spotlight for a few measures, followed by synthesizer and piano – the band are clearly in the pocket. Two more rounds of chorus follow, with 'red-hot' playing, pushing the song to the end. Backing vocalists include Cissy Houston and Luther Vandross (credited here as Luther Van Dross), who also assisted on 1977's *Monkey Island*.

'Flamethrower' was the B-side to 'Freeze-Frame' (in the UK, the B-side to 'Centerfold') but was never released on its own as a pop single. It did, however, receive considerable airplay in the US and proved hugely popular in clubs, reaching number 12 on the Hot Dance Club Play chart and number 25 on *Billboard*'s Hot Black/Soul Singles chart. The song appeared in the American television show *Freaks And Geeks* in 2000.

'River Blindness' (Justman) (6:06)
The album's longest track opens with a foreboding atmosphere to set the scene, like the soundtrack to a murder mystery noir film. River blindness is an actual disease, spread via bites from parasite-infected black flies, which breed near rivers. The infection causes rashes, skin lesions, and potentially permanent blindness. The song is one of the darker Geils numbers and might be about a loss of faith in humanity, with talk of angels crying and the 'cessation of life expectancy.' After the opening measures, harp riffs and upfront bass create a hypnotic rhythm. Background vocals chant: 'Human kindness, river blindness.'

Near the song's midpoint, things quiet briefly while Bladd keeps the beat. Klein's bass work is the star for the first 50 seconds. He begins with one thick pluck before he's manoeuvring up and down the frets, alternating between chunky and clipped notes, wringing the neck of his custom bass. When the song was played live, a cart machine – an analogue, continuous loop cartridge tape player used by radio stations for background music, station identification, or similar – was used to hold down some of the percussive beat. Klein said he had to start his solo at exactly the right moment and end it at exactly the right place, 'or the (cart) music would stop and you'd still be playing.' He laughed, 'I was very happy when that thing broke.' Klein also said every time he played 'River Blindness', his bass 'would go out of tune as soon as I did my solo.'

As Klein steps back from his solo, Dick returns, riffing on harp. The chant of 'human kindness, river blindness' builds. Jay's guitar pierces through, scrabbling and churning for over a minute and destroying everything in its path. The background singers from 'Flamethrower' return for 'River Blindness.' The track was the B-side to 'Angel In Blue.'

'Angel In Blue' (Justman) (4:51)
Highest chart place: US: 40, CA: 39, UK: 55

'Angel In Blue' brings a melancholy mood swing and was intended as the first single from *Freeze-Frame*. Jim Mazza, president of EMI America, said prior to the album's release, the band and record label 'pulled a meeting together (at Long View, where the album was recorded) for everyone involved with Geils – concert promoters, booking agents, record label people, and more. The purpose was to establish the first single and after four days, a consensus was agreed upon.' All agreed 'Angel In Blue' would be the first release from *Freeze-Frame*. The following Monday, as the band were filming a video for 'Angel In Blue', Mazza received a call from Rosalie Trombley at radio station CKLW. As recounted above with 'Centerfold', Trombley had a 'golden ear' and knew 'Centerfold' should be the lead single over 'Angel In Blue.'

In some ways, the song is a dark counter piece to 'Centerfold.' Instead of that song's fantasy and fun, 'Angel In Blue' presents harsh reality and despondency. It's a reflection of an exotic dancer – the kind who 'would smile on cue' – who has mostly given up on life, having been used and tossed aside by everyone she ever trusted or loved. Even when someone new tries to love her, 'she just said, baby, don't even bother to try.' Jay strums his guitar to start this slower tempo, doo-wop-influenced track. Organ settles in, and Wolf begins: 'We met in a bar, out on Chesapeake Bay.' The ache in Wolf's voice conveys as much sadness as the lyrics themselves. There are no big solos. The backing vocalists from 'Flame Thrower' and 'River Blindness' assist again, and the horn section from 'Freeze-Frame' returns. Together, horns and backing vocals create an outro requiem for this Angel who 'never had dreams, so they never came true.'

Similar to the novelty disc for 'Freeze-Frame', a limited-edition 'Angel In Blue' was issued on a picture disc shaped like Georganne Deen's potato head-style album artwork.

'Piss On The Wall' (Wolf, Justman) (3:02)
The closing track brings some boogie rock and roll. When everything's going wrong in the world, sometimes it's best to ignore it and do whatever brings relief. It's also a reminder that Geils are going to do whatever they want. 'Politics – schmolitics', a cynical Wolf declares as he searches for his own thrills in life. 'Piss On The Wall' chugs along over a chant of 'bauw bauw-bauw ba-bauw bauw ba-bauw' and handclaps, with everyone living it up, bringing a raucous attitude to the track.

Jay opens with some Duane Eddy-style twang guitar, and the break brings more thick, twangy playing over sharp Little Richard-influenced piano from Justman. It segues into Dick's harp riffs as the band shout in the background. Another verse follows, then Wolf proclaims, 'I'm just tryin' to hold it steady while I piss on the wall.' Guitar, piano, harp, and honkin' sax push the track forward. As the ending draws near, the music stops and the song finishes with a hearty, 'Piss on the wall!'

Showtime! (1982)

Personnel:
Seth Justman: keyboards, vocals
Peter Wolf: vocals
Magic Dick: harmonica, sax
Stephen Jo Bladd: drums, vocals
J. Geils: guitars
Danny Klein: bass
Uptown Horns (Arno Hecht, Crispin Cioe, 'Hollywood' Paul Litteral): saxophone, trumpet
Producer: Seth Justman
Engineer: John Mathias
Record label: EMI America
Recorded: Pine Knob Music Theater, Detroit (Clarkstown), Michigan, September 1982
Released: 12 November 1982
Running time: 47:37
Highest chart place: US: 23, CA: 21, UK: –
Tracklisting: 'Jus' Can't Stop Me', 'Just Can't Wait', 'Walls Come Tumblin' Down', 'Sanctuary', 'I'm Falling', 'Love Rap', 'Love Stinks', 'Stoop Down #39', 'I Do', 'Centerfold', 'Land Of A Thousand Dances'

Recorded over multiple dates at a Detroit outdoor amphitheatre in September 1982 and in the shops a short two months later, the manic *Showtime!* was the band's third live album (*House Party Live In Germany* wasn't released until 2014/2015) and provided a souvenir of the *Freeze-Frame* tour, which hadn't wrapped up yet. Three tunes are pulled from the band's Atlantic years, six from the EMI releases, with one new song in the mix. Production and arrangements are again handled by Justman and pre-mixing work was done at Longview (listed as Long View on previous albums) Farm. Film from the Pine Knob shows allegedly exists but, aside from snippets used in videos for 'I Do' and 'Land Of A Thousand Dances', has never been released.

The album's cover graphics faithfully replicate a 1954 *MusiQuiz* album cover, from the orange and black colours and nearly identical fonts to the stereo speaker illustration on the left producing wavy bars of music to the musicians' heads sketched over those bars of music. In place of the *MusiQuiz* Period Records logo in the lower right corner is the band's now famous palmprint. The cover was designed by Carin Goldberg, who had designed the *Love Stinks* cover but the actual artwork was created by Zavier Leslie Cabarga, a New York illustrator, cartoonist, and author. The back cover shows the track listing with star-shaped headshots of the band members in columns down the sides. One side of the record's inner sleeve displays black and white shots of the band along with a photo of The Uptown Horns, who were guests on tour. The reverse side of the sleeve lists album credits and ends with a note stating,

'(And special thanks to all our fans in Detroit for their many years of loyal support.)' The centre labels on the LP feature the palmprint above the track listing, with THEESELBEE etched into the runout groove on side one and PUDAKRADUP on side two.

The Uptown Horns (Arno Hecht, Crispin Cioe, 'Hollywood' Paul Litteral) came to join the *Freeze-Frame* tour through a serendipitous phone call between manager Bob Hinkle and saxophonist Cioe. Detroit native Cioe had been part of a duo when he'd moved to New York in the mid to late 1970s, with bookings handled by Hinkle. Eventually, Cioe met Arno Hecht and Paul Litteral and formed The Uptown Horns, playing once a week at Tramps nightclub, with trombonist Bob Funk joining soon after. 'We called it the Uptown Horns Party', said Cioe. At Tramps, everyone from Tom Waits to Solomon Burke would sit in with the band. It was sometime in 1982 when Cioe and Hinkle talked on the phone and were getting caught up in each other's lives. 'Hinkle said he was managing The J. Geils Band with Jeb Hart', explained Cioe, 'and asked what I was up to.' Cioe told him about The Uptown Horns. Hinkle paused and said to Cioe, 'That's interesting because Geils is in Europe right now opening for the Stones. They're looking for either a horn section or female backup singers.'

Hinkle soon visited Tramps, liked what he heard and saw, then called Justman when Geils returned from Europe and told Justman about The Uptown Horns. 'Seth came down to New York on a Tuesday night', said Cioe, 'and was there for the whole (show). Seth liked what he heard and we talked for a while.' The next day, Justman and Cioe talked on the phone; Justman talked to the rest of Geils, and 'within a day or two, they asked if we wanted to come up to Boston.' The Uptown Horns were soon at Geils 'secret' rehearsal space (inside the 'Jim Did It Sign Co' building, at the entrance with the 'T&A Research' brass plaque), where they spent a day playing together. 'They asked if we wanted to go on the road with them and literally a week later, I think, we were on the road with them.' It was a perfect match. 'We all loved the same kind of music', said Cioe, 'blues, r&b, and we listened to the same kind of records. Their commitment to performing was just so intense. That was easy for us to get behind. It was just a thrill to play with them.' Cioe was equally impressed with Geils' fans, who were 'true fanatics. It was like a religious experience. I never saw fans like that again. We also felt that as a lead singer/frontman, Peter Wolf was on a level with James Brown and Mick Jagger – and we've worked with both of them. Wolf has that same kind of near-magical, compelling energy and drive onstage with an audience.'

Not surprisingly, the album opens with the track the band had been using as a show-opener for several tours already. As Bladd's drums pound through the speakers, the announcer shouts, 'Are you ready? It's showtime! Please welcome to the stage The J. Geils Baaaaaand!' and 'Jus' Can't Stop Me' explodes. When Wolf sings, 'And I feel so good, Detroit, are you gonna rock me?' the crowd responds with an energy that pushes the band higher. Dick's harp solo takes the audience right into the 'hey, hey, hey, hey' audience part. The track is three minutes of pure adrenaline. Before anyone can recover, Wolf says, 'No sense wastin' any time. Lemme hear ya, Jay!' and Jay starts the riff for 'Just Can't Wait.' Justman's keyboards propel the track. At the break, Jay tears into a raunchy solo before it's back to the next verse. The band and the crowd react to Wolf's call of 'Just can't wait' with the expected response of 'bop bop ba-dah dah' before the track finishes.

Next is 'Walls Come Tumblin' Down' (titled 'Till The Walls Come Tumblin' Down' on the LP centre label and on *Love Stinks*). Wolf introduces it, saying, 'Now this next song, this next song is a drinking song' and he dedicates it 'to the beer drinkers out there.' He begins with a call-and-response of 'Ooh yeah!' before shouting, 'Till the Walls Come Tumblin' Down.' Harp and bass set the groove in time for the first verse and the track motors along with some lively piano. When Wolf calls, 'Blow some blues!' Dick delivers hot licks on harp, followed by Jay on guitar. The song downshifts as Wolf sings, 'mash those potatoes and don't be shy.' Immediately after the track winds down, Wolf announces the next song with a cry of 'Sanctuary!' and the band tear into it. Klein's heavy bass is more prominent and the track is pushed along a little faster than the studio version.

Slowing things, 'I'm Falling' comes next. Wolf says, 'This is a song, uh, that was written in one of those kind of periods where no matter what you're doin', everything just seems to keep on falling, falling, falling, falling.' Even in the live setting, the track retains its heartbreak. Two-thirds through, The Uptown Horns get to strut their stuff, elevating the track, and when Wolf yells, 'Blow your horn', Cioe executes a brilliant solo to carry the song through to the end.

'Love Rap' (titled 'Love Rap (Rap)' on the LP centre label) is one of Wolf's spoken jive introductions but gets its own track listing. Strangely, the writing credit lists both Wolf and Justman. Wolf uses the time to expound on when love trouble first began, giving mention to Raputa the Beauta from *Blow Your Face Out* and 'No Anchovies, Please' from *Love Stinks*. The big flaw in the rap is that as it's building toward the song 'Love Stinks', it abruptly ends with Wolf saying, 'Let me tell you, Angel, love ...' Then the listener has to turn over the record or tape to hear '... stinks!' The audience is primed and 'Love Stinks' gets a roar of approval. When Wolf sings, 'One thing for sure', the crowd needs no encouragement and shouts out the 'love stinks' response along with Dick.

'Stoop Down #39', an unexpected gift from *Nightmares*, follows. Dick launches into his wild harp intro, working the audience. The Uptown Horns return, giving the tune a bit more funk than the studio version. The Uptown Horns also perform on 'I Do', originally a non-charting single off 1977's *Monkey Island*. The album would not be complete without the global hit 'Centerfold.' The band stretch out the song a little, first winding it down when it gets close to the 3:00 mark, then Wolf gets the crowd singing along with the 'na, na, na-na na-na' chorus. The album closes with a new track, a cover of 'Land Of A Thousand Dances', prominently featuring The Uptown Horns.

As grateful as fans were to have another live album, there were some flaws with *Showtime!* First, it was a single LP. Every concert on the tour was long enough for a double (or triple) LP, even if some songs from the earlier live albums might have been repeated. Nothing else from those Pine Knob shows has been released. Second, the 'Love Rap' cutting off at the end of side one and finishing at the start of side two proved irritating (resolved with the CD release). Third, the top 40 hits 'One Last Kiss', 'Angel In Blue' and 'Come Back' would've been fitting for the record but were omitted, likely due to the time constraints of the single album.

Showtime! was certified gold in the US in January 1983 and gold in Canada in February 1983, just months after its release. In 2005, *Showtime!* was re-released as part of EMI Special Markets/Madacy Entertainment's budget-priced *Rock On Breakout Years: 1982* CD series. The entire recording was identical, but the packaging and album title (simply *J. Geils Band* on this release) were changed.

'I Do' (Johnny Paden, Frank Paden, Jesse Smith, Willie Stephenson, Melvin Mason) (3:00)
Highest chart place: US: 24, CA: 30, UK: –
The first single from *Showtime!*, 'I Do' hit the top 40 in the US and Canada. The Uptown Horns add to the party vibe of the song, which remains faithful to Geils' studio version. An accompanying video consists of clips of the band on stage, including Dick on sax. 'I Do' was issued in a picture sleeve about two weeks before the album. The artwork on the sleeve said, 'From the historic live album *Showtime*', but the centre label of the single stated, 'From the forthcoming LP *It's Showtime.*' The live 'Sanctuary' was the B-side.

The New Song
'Land Of A Thousand Dances' (C. Kenner, A. Domino) (5:06)
Highest chart place: US: 60, CA: –, UK: –
'Land Of A Thousand Dances' has been covered by many acts (typically as 'Land Of 1000 Dances') but is most associated with Cannibal and the Headhunters and later Wilson Pickett (as well as Three Midniters in Canada) in the mid-1960s. Geils' version is modelled after Pickett's, from the intro of 'one, two, three… one, two, three' to the blazing horns to Wolf's grunting. Like most versions since Chris Kenner's original recording, Geils omit the intro lines of 'Children, go where I send you (*where will you send me?*), I'm gonna send you to that land, the land of a thousand dances' but includes the 'naaah, na na na na, na na na na, nanna na nanna na' vocables added by Cannibal Garcia.

The Geils track kicks off with, 'One, two three!' and a blast from the band, then another 'one, two, three', and a second blast. Several dances from the 1950s and 1960s are name-checked ('do the Watusi', 'do the Alligator, do the Mashed Potato') and Wolf tosses in a 'yeah, yeah, yeah, yeah' line from

'Detroit Breakdown.' The first break brings a harmonica solo. Wolf then tells the crowd how to strut before calling, 'Uptown Horns, let me hear ya.' Arno Hecht delivers a sax solo, and Cioe said, 'As a surprise for the Pine Knob shows, the band had made a cape with a big 'A' on it, which they draped around Arno's shoulders, James Brown-style, during his solo feature.' It was reflective of Geils' collective personality, 'blending showmanship and a reverence for rock/r&b history with a little bit of humour – that was their trademark as a performing band.' After the solo, Wolf starts a call and response with the band: 'Let me hear it one time' (*bam!*), 'Let me hear it two times' (*bam! bam!*), up to four times. It's a throwback to Geils' 1968 radio recording from The New Penelope Club when the band performed 'Funky Broadway.' In 'Funky Broadway', Wolf briefly riffed on 'naaah, na na na na' and called to the band, 'let me hear one' (*bam!*), 'two' (*bam! bam!*), and on.

'Land Of A Thousand Dances', edited to 3:15, was the second single released from *Showtime!*, charting only in the US. Its B-side was 'Jus' Can't Stop Me.'

You're Gettin' Even While I'm Gettin' Odd (1984)

Personnel:
Seth Justman: keyboards, lead and background vocals
Magic Dick: harmonicas, sax, background vocals
Stephen Jo Bladd: drums, lead and background vocals
J. Geils: guitars
Danny Klein: bass, flex bass
Uptown Horns (Arno Hecht, Crispin Cioe, 'Hollywood' Paul Litteral): saxophone, trumpet
Phoebe Snow, Cookie Watkins, Fonda Rae, Judith Spears, Jim Donnelly, Institutional Radio Choir: background vocals
Producer: Seth Justman
Engineer: Steve Marcantonio
Record label: EMI America
Released: 5 October 1984
Running time: 43:58
Highest chart place: US: 80, CA: 84, UK: –

Work on *You're Gettin' Even While I'm Gettin' Odd* began around February 1983, less than two months after the *Freeze-Frame/Showtime!* Tour at Long View Farm, where the band had previously conceived three highly successful studio albums and did pre-mix work on *Showtime!* From an outside perspective, a new hit album was guaranteed. That turned out not to be the case. According to a January 1985 Associated Press article by Mary Campbell, Justman, Bladd, Jay, Klein, and Dick had been working on the music and arrangements of seven songs that extended the band's evolution from *Monkey Island* through *Freeze-Frame*, preparing for Wolf's inputs. When Wolf arrived to work out his parts, he brought in five or six of his own songs – nearly complete – that he'd been working on with outside musicians, a first for any member of the band. In a 28 April 1994 *Los Angeles Times* article, Wolf said, 'It started deteriorating and getting more difficult. I think it was all based on the music, with maybe subliminal aspects' of personal conflicts. He added, 'It's a tragic tale and it disturbs me, and I think it was quite wasteful.' Wolf later stated in a 1 June 2016 *Atlanta Journal-Constitution* interview that rather than continue the trajectory of *Freeze-Frame*, he felt the band needed to return to their roots. They had capitalised on the exposure provided by MTV, but he felt 'there was an aspect of our roots that we needed to re-establish' and 'they (the other band members) wanted to continue in a pop-techno way. It wasn't my thing.'

Differing opinions on songwriting credits and the direction of the music created friction, with little give and take. Bob Hinkle, who managed the band with Jeb Hart, said, 'It was one of the most difficult periods of my life. Jeb and I spent a lot of time on the Eastern Airlines shuttle between New York and Boston, meeting with the band to try to get them to come to their senses. We couldn't do it. We finally had to realise it was not meant to be. It wasn't a surprise, just sad because they were poised (for still bigger things).' Even the president of their record label, EMI America, tried to help the band work out their differences. 'I went to Boston', said Jim Mazza, 'and spent a whole week trying to convince them to repair the damage and difficulties that they were experiencing', but with no luck.

As late as July 1983, the band were still appearing publicly as the six-man original team, taking part in a 'Good Words for Boston' tourism campaign filmed at Hatch Memorial Shell, but around September 1983, the members made the decision to split. With Wolf leaving, the band needed a new lead singer. They briefly considered outside vocalists, including a couple of female singers (Joan Jett's name was mentioned though never pursued) but ultimately kept the work in-house, with Justman handling the bulk of the new tracks, Bladd singing on two, and Justman and Bladd sharing vocal duties on another. Justman and Bladd had been working background vocals since the band's early days, so it was no surprise to use them, yet it's disappointing Dick didn't get lead vocals at least once. The musical style continued in the adventurous *Freeze-Frame* vein without completely losing its r&b and soul roots, and outside singers were used for some backing vocals. The Uptown Horns returned after being part of 1982's *Showtime!* In rock and pop music, horns are too often an afterthought, being wedged into spaces after songs are recorded, but with Geils, the songs were crafted with horns in mind. 'We went up to Long View', said Crispin Cioe, 'and spent almost a week up there' working out ideas for the songs with Justman and the other band members. There was no drama, just a focus on making the best music possible. Shortly after completing their work on *You're Gettin' Even*, The Uptown Horns were on the road with Robert Plant's Honeydrippers.

Including the downtime trying to work out the band's differences plus time in the studio, the project lasted about 18 months. During that period, Wolf was forging his own album, with *Lights Out* released about three months before *You're Gettin' Even*. Although Wolf's later solo records did harken back to his blues, r&b, country, and rock roots, on the surface, *Lights Out*, with its techno-funk, wasn't a complete divergence from the music of *You're Gettin' Even*, so from an outside perspective it may have been hard to comprehend what musical differences drove the band apart.

With David Thoener busy on other projects, Steve Marcantonio, who had worked as a mixing assistant on *Freeze-Frame* and *Showtime!* handled engineering duties. The LP cover was designed by Bladd and Justman, a quirky image that appeared to be a photo negative of a sketch with the album title across the top and down the right side, and the band's name scrawled at the bottom. The back cover showed five band members and stated, 'Music written by Seth Justman. Lyrics written by Seth Justman and Paul Justman.' Paul Justman had worked with Geils as far back as the *Ladies Invited* tour documentary, contributed photos to *Blow Your Face Out*, and filmed videos for some *Freeze-Frame* singles, so he was familiar to the fans but not as a lyric writer. The album's inner sleeve featured lyrics in various styles of handwriting on one side, with album credits and a collage of black and white photo negatives on the reverse. The record's centre label included a stylised palm print above the band name and song titles.

There was talk of a tour to support the new music, but the only performance from the five-piece band seems to have been a few months before the release of the album, in August 1984, in Ohio. The final record had a different sound due to the departure of Wolf but still contained great music. In addition to the LP and cassette, *You're Gettin' Even* was later released on CD in Japan for a very limited time.

'Concealed Weapons' (Justman, Paul Justman) (3:30)
Highest chart place: US: 63, CA –, UK: –
The album's first cut might be considered a continuation of 1981's 'Centerfold', with the same playful sexuality. 'Concealed Weapons' features plenty of not-so-subtle double-entendres, the lyrics simultaneously about a woman enforcing the law while also about using her 'concealed weapons' to get what she wants, but only when she wants it. Justman sings lead, delivering lines like, 'she can change hands – turn around, and take a fancy shot if you can put the bullet into her cartridge slot.'

The track combines 1950s surf-rock guitar riffs with 1980s pop, furthering the duality found in the lyrics. After the second chorus, Dick steps forward with a harp solo reminiscent of his work on *Freeze-Frame*'s 'Rage In The Cage' over handclaps and 'bah-bah-bah-bah-bah bah-dah-dah' background vocals. Horns accent the outro. 'Concealed Weapons' was the first single released from the album. It charted only in the US.

'Heavy Petting' (Justman, Paul Justman) (4:16)
The track opens with a fat, funky, very 1980s synthesizer, followed by horns. Unlike 'Concealed Weapons', there's no double (or subtle) meaning behind the lyrics. Bladd handles lead vocals on this song about teenage lust, telling of making out in places like a movie theatre, an alley, on the beach, in the car, with 'overwhelming sensations wherever we are.' Synth and bass push the track, with saxophone blasting away on the first instrumental break.

After the break, there's a cheerleader-style chant with female singers – 'stop it, stop it, stop-it-stop-it-stop-it' – before they have a change of mind with, 'owwww, we love it, uh-huh, we love it, uh-huh.' Background singers Cookie Watkins, Fonda Rae, and Judith Spears appear on the track. Justman was clearly happy with them, using the singers again, as well as The Uptown Horns, on Debbie Harry's 1986 *Rockbird* album, which Justman produced.

'Wasted Youth' (Justman, Paul Justman) (4:30)
Justman returns on lead vocals for this nostalgic number about 'cherry' cars, teen sex, leather jackets, guitars, and more. The song looks back at those

teenage years with fondness: 'love was eternal, and no one could die.' Guitar and organ play out under the verses. The first break begins with Jay's guitar, followed by keyboards.

There's no regret in the lyrics. The chorus sums it up plainly, proclaiming, 'I love my wasted youth, I was shy but so uncouth, some were lies and some's the truth.' The track finishes with some beautiful gospel harmonies, drawing out the last word ('yooouuth') for 15 seconds.

'Eenie Meenie Minie Moe' (Justman, Paul Justman) (3:54)
On the rollicking 'Eenie Meenie Minie Moe', lead vocals are shared by Bladd and Justman, backed again by Watkins, Rae, and Spears. The song's title and chorus are from the nursery rhyme for counting out and choosing or eliminating a person or thing. In this case, it's about trying to pick from among all the beautiful women available. There's no reason to hesitate, 'You got to take your chances.'

Guitar, prominent bass, and horns fill the break. Mid-song, the chorus shifts momentarily and creates the impression of a toy carousel going 'round. After another chorus, Phoebe Snow ('Poetry Man', 'Games') comes in with her distinctive voice for some lead vocals. The song's outro features climbing and descending Beatle-esque horn work courtesy of The Uptown Horns. 'Eenie Meenie Minie Moe' was the second single from the album, but it did not chart.

'Tell 'Em, Jonesy' (Justman, Paul Justman) (4:46)
With a sci-fi synth opening, Justman narrates the setting of the side one closing track: 'Two a.m. in the all-night market, pushing an empty cart...' It's a quirky setup, but the song transitions to a hard riff under the chant of 'Tell 'em Jonesy' as it sketches the story of a woman (Jonesy) overwhelmed by life and possibly on the verge of a breakdown. She's lost her son, 'and now there's Jonesy kneeling, telling what she's feeling.' There's a surprising sensitivity in the vocals, relating the scene without condescension or disdain.

The chorus urges, 'Tell 'em, Jonesy, tell 'em 'bout your son... now he's never coming home.' The final chorus leads into layered synthesizers, building on the surreal atmosphere. This song was the B-side to 'Concealed Weapons.'

'You're Gettin' Even While I'm Gettin' Odd' (Justman, Paul Justman) (6:56)
Side two opens with some harsh plucking on piano wires. Horns, bass, and synths join the chaos, creating the most experimental song on the album. The lyrics come from the viewpoint of someone cheating on his girlfriend after being 'smitten with a kitten from the Kit-Kat Club.' When he got caught and his girlfriend left him, 'I got creamed in the face with a reality pie.' Watkins, Rae, and Spears return on backing vocals.

The instrumental break brings horns and harp. Another verse and chorus follow. Jay opens the second break with a few measures of guitar before turning it over to Klein for some heavy bass. Another chorus follows. The backing singers join in, declaring, 'He never meant to hurt you.' The final instrumental break builds on synths, horns, and plucked piano wires until the final moments, with backing vocals caught like a stuck record as the song fades out.

'The Bite From Inside' (Justman, Paul Justman) (5:50)
The track sidles in with an easy feeling on doo-wop vocals: 'doomp-doomp-doomp, doomp, doomp-doomp-doomp-doomp.' But soon there's a jolt – not only musically but also in attitude – as the full band joins, chanting over the music, 'It's all so sick.' Justman takes lead vocals and sets the tone: 'What kind of soap is used in a bloodbath? What kind of darkness brings a killer sleep?' Anger and disgust permeate the lyrics. The world is burning and those who should be helping are simply making things worse. For them, it's about power ('with every dirty deed, the jaw grows stronger'), politics ('briefcases drawn and loaded, these men travel halls in packs'), and money ('just for good old moo la la').

Raunchy saxophone and stomping bass underscore the verses and each chorus is shouted more than sung. An extended break starts with slick keyboards before harp enters. Bass, guitar, and horns take over, borrowing some riffs from *Freeze-Frame*'s 'River Blindness.' Jay wraps it up with a sharp guitar solo before the final choruses, his guitar continuing through the fadeout.

'Californicatin'' (Justman, Paul Justman) (4:07)
Not to be confused with Red Hot Chili Peppers' 1999 song 'Californication', the tempo and tumultuous style of 'Californicatin'' harken back to *Freeze-Frame*'s 'Insane, Insane Again.' Opening the track is a burst of rapid-fire drumming, interrupted by a clip of conversation: 'Not only that.' A second blast of drums and another snippet of conversation follow: '... the weather's great out there.' Horns and bass drive everything at a frantic tempo. Justman cynically sings about ignoring the ugly things in life and instead focusing on the superficial, from hot tubs and sports cars to nitrous oxide and swimming pools. There's no need to burden oneself with contemplating society's ills. It's better to exist in ignorance, living the good life and 'Californicatin'.'

There's no true chorus, but background singers add to the frenzied feeling with their, 'dit dit dit dit dit dit dit, zoom, zoom, zoom, zoom, ma ma ma ma ma ma ma, bah bah bah bah' repeated under the line 'Ca-li-forniaaa, Ca-li-forniaaa.' One-third through the song comes a short harp break and a few more verses follow before Justman tosses out the line, 'California, here I come', from the 1920s song of the same name. Toward the end of the tune, Dick throws in a few riffs of 'When You Wish Upon A Star' from the 1940 film *Pinocchio*, which is also the Walt Disney Company theme song, fitting for a track about Hollywood and all things make-believe. Dick finishes with harp work inspired by Charlie Parker's 1951 'Blues For Alice', with bebop language and attitude.

'I Will Carry You Home' (Justman, Paul Justman) (6:09)
Bladd returns on vocals for the closing cut, leading 'I Will Carry You Home' with a gospel introduction, accompanied by Brooklyn, New York's Institutional Radio Choir under director Carl Williams, Jr. Watkins, Rae, and Spears return to assist with vocals as well. For more than a minute and a half, the intro builds, then builds again for another half minute, with Justman's church organ and the choir creating tension and the promise of something big. The song shifts into full gear as Bladd sings, 'But it won't matter to me what you become, 'cause I will come find you, I will find you, and I will carry you home.' In contrast to *Sanctuary*'s 'Teresa', with its plea for help and guidance, 'I Will Carry You Home' is about unconditional support, a promise to provide direction and light in even the darkest of times.

Handclaps, horns, organ, piano, and choir bring a jubilant, revivalist tone. The song is lifted higher in the final minute. Bladd and the choir sing and shout, repeating *'whoooooah*, I'll be there' and 'don't you worry.' The song provides an uplifting ending to a difficult album and a reassurance that whatever's wrong can be fixed. Perhaps the song was a message to the fans and the band members themselves, but *You're Gettin' Even* ended up being the final studio album from The J. Geils Band. 'I Will Carry You Home' was the B-side to 'Eenie Meenie Minie Moe.'

Related Tracks
'Fright Night' (J. Lamont) (3:45) (1985)
Highest chart place: US: 91, CA: –, UK: –
The last studio release from Geils turned out to be 'Fright Night', from the 1985 vampire horror/comedy film of the same name. Written by Australian Joe Lamont, the Geils recording starts with chants of 'Fright, fright, fright, fright' and 'Night, night, night, night' followed by a call of 'Wooo!' With a definite 1980s pop sound, the song sums up the movie plotline. The title character (Charley) discovers his neighbour is a vampire, yet no one believes Charley ('People say I'm crazy and I make no sense'), so he sets out to resolve the issue himself ('I've got to drive a stake right through his heart').

A video was made for the song, using movie clips interspersed with band members on stage and in the house used in the film's set. Released in a picture sleeve featuring the same image as the movie poster, 'Fright Night' made it onto the US charts but nowhere else. The single's B-side was 'Boppin' Tonight' by Fabulous Fontaines.

Start All Over Again – Latter Days

Since the band splintered in the 1980s, there have been no new J. Geils Band studio records, no expanded editions of their catalogue and no box sets unleashing previously unheard tracks. There have, however, been Geils reunions, Geils benefit/charity shows, live performances outside of Geils, records outside of Geils, awards, production work, appearances in documentaries and movies, business ventures, culinary work, a patent and more.

After spending well over a decade together on stage or in the studio, a break might've been welcome, but not under the circumstances that happened in 1983 and 1984. It would've been a jolt. Band members filled the void in their own ways. Jay played very little guitar between the mid-1980s and the early 1990s. Instead, he started a vintage automobile business, working on (and racing) Maseratis, Ferraris, and the like. He sold the business in 1996 but continued working there at times. Jay began to play again in late 1991 when he started sitting in with and mentoring The Blood Street Band, a Boston-area blues band, who played some Geils songs. Soon, Jay devoted more and more time to jazz, performing and recording. On 1 December 2009, the city of Groton, Massachusetts, where Jay had been a resident since 1982, declared 'J. Geils Day.' By the early 2010s, he was occasionally performing with his Jay Geils Jazz and Blues Revue. In 2015, he returned to his high school in Bernardsville, New Jersey, where he was inducted into the school's Wall of Honor.

Danny Klein stopped playing music for about a decade and used the downtime to fulfil a lifelong interest and attend culinary school. He became part-owner of a restaurant and served as its pastry chef, later selling the business. When he had the itch to play music again, he started working with friends in the punk band Soma Crush, but nothing came of it, and eventually, he found himself working with blues artist Debbie Davies before forming his own band, Stonecrazy. Klein was later part of *Rockphoria*, a classic rock multimedia event, but performed only one show as far as he can recall. In early 2011, Klein and Magic Dick toured as members of The Boston Legends, performing across New England with musicians like Skunk Baxter (Steely Dan, Doobie Brothers), Elliot Easton and Greg Hawkes (The Cars), Jon Butcher, Barry Goudreau (Boston), and The Uptown Horns. In June 2017, Klein played some shows with The Classic Rock Experience. He's been regularly performing (often for charity gigs) with his Full House band since the mid-2000s (first as Dennis Montgomery and Friends, then Danny Klein and Friends, then as Danny Klein's Full House), doing it for the pleasure of playing live.

Magic Dick spent those early days after the breakup riding motorcycles, logging plenty of miles. He played little music until receiving a call from Mick Jagger to be part of Jagger's 1988 Australia tour. Occasionally, Dick would sit in with jazz fusion band Pieces of a Dream and with the Cambridge Harmonica Orchestra under the direction of Pierre Beauregard. On 12 April

1989, Dick performed with jazz group Full Circle at the Boston Music Awards. In 1992, Dick was invited to perform at a festival in Holland, playing harmonica and singing with a band. Returning to the States, he found himself sitting in with Jay and The Blood Street Band for a benefit show, and the seeds for Dick and Jay's Bluestime project were planted. He also spent time working with Pierre Beauregard from the Harmonica Orchestra engineering a different, more dynamic harmonica, for which the two would receive a US patent in 1992. Dick's been performing on stage with harp player Mark Hummel since about 2006, often as part of Hummel's *Blues Harmonica Blowout* shows. Along with everything else, Dick often teaches harp.

Seth Justman did some production work and has popped up as a guest on other bands' albums but has been relatively quiet for someone with his songwriting, arranging, playing, and singing skills. In a 1988 interview, Justman mentioned a possible new Geils album for 1989, though nothing came of it. A decade later, during a 1999 interview on radio station WPYX in Albany, New York, Justman said he was recording with a band, but nothing further has been mentioned. In 2006, Justman wrote the music score for the Public Broadcasting Service three-part documentary *Country Boys*, with Jay contributing guitar and Dick harmonica. It's rumoured Justman recorded a solo album along the way with a female lead singer, but it's never surfaced.

Stephen Jo Bladd has made occasional public appearances with the band but has been little involved in the music industry since the mid-1980s.

Peter Wolf has been most visible of all members since the mid-1980s, and not just for his eight solo albums and occasional tours. Though Geils still isn't in the Rock And Roll Hall Of Fame, Wolf had the honour of inducting Jackie Wilson into the Hall in 1987 and later inducted The Paul Butterfield Blues Band in 2015. When songwriter Jesse Stone was inducted in 2010, Wolf performed Stone's song 'Money Honey', originally a hit for The Drifters, at the ceremony. In 1993, Wolf, with Robert Greenfield, read for the audiobook of the late Bill Graham's autobiography *Bill Graham Presents: My Life Inside Rock And Roll*. Graham had been one of Geils' early champions. In 2008, Wolf narrated the documentary *America's Lost Band: The Story Of The Remains*, which told the story of friend Barry Tashian and his band The Remains. Wolf also appeared in 2016's *Boys From Nowhere: The Story Of Boston's Garage Punk Uprising*. On 14 April 2016, the City of Boston proclaimed 'Peter Wolf Day.' Wolf was featured in the 2019 *Creem: America's Only Rock 'N' Roll Magazine* documentary and was interviewed for the 2022 documentary *Heaven Stood Still: The Incarnations Of Willy Deville* (Wolf, a fan of Deville, was brought into the project by Crispin Cioe of The Uptown Horns, who co-produced the film). Wolf also had a part in *Space Baby*, a 2023 comedy science fiction film which just happened to use a celestial image of the Geils palmprint as part of the plot. He was featured in HBO's 2024 documentary *Stevie Van Zandt: Disciple*. Additionally, Wolf's been working on his memoir, something he's mentioned at least as far back as 1997 when he told *Entertainment*

Weekly the title would be *Further Tales From The Vinyl Jungle*. Retitled *Waiting On The Moon*, it is set for a 2025 release (at the time of writing).

Over the years, band members have occasionally been back together. Carter Alan wrote in his 2013 book *Radio Free Boston, The Rise And Fall Of WBCN* that at the 25th-anniversary celebration of WBCN, held at Boston's Hard Rock Café on 28 February 1993, The J. Geils Band performed an a cappella rendition of 'Looking For A Love.' It's not clear how many band members were present, and Danny Klein has no recollection of the event. Two years later, when Boston Garden (where much of *Blow Your Face Out* was recorded and where Geils set a three-night attendance record in 1982) was slated for closing in 1995, there were talks of the band reuniting for the Garden's closing show. That never happened, but Wolf did perform with his own band, The Houseparty 5.

The first J. Geils official reunion came in 1999. Drummer Stephen Jo Bladd was the only member to sit out 'The Great American Houseparty Tour', with Sim Cain (Rollins Band) filling in. Announced in April 1999, the first public performance came as the band played 'Looking For A Love' and 'Centerfold' on an 'All Boston Episode' of US television's *Late Show With David Letterman* on 21 May 1999 (with Klein on a five-string bass). A month later, on 18 June, the band made a second US TV appearance, this time with The Uptown Horns, on *The Today Show*. The following night, under the name Juke Joint Jimmy and His House Party Rockers, the band played Boston's Paradise Club. The setlist was over 20 songs, with every studio album represented except *Ladies Invited* and *You're Gettin' Even*. The tour began on 23 June in Boston. Earlier that same day, Boston's mayor declared 'J. Geils Band Day' and the band received its star on the Tower Records Walk of Fame in Boston. The entire band, including Bladd, was in attendance.

Following the 1999 tour, the band laid low for a while, with nothing until a charity show in February 2005. The biggest surprise came on 22 May 2006 when Klein's then-wife Valerie brought together the entire band (including Bladd) at Scullers Jazz Club in Boston, Massachusetts, to play for Klein's birthday. Klein had been told he would be playing a charity gig and had no clue what was happening until he entered the club. It was the first time all six members had played on stage together in about 23 years. Since then, there have been short tours, one-off shows, and charity concerts, like the 2013 'Boston Strong' benefit for the victims of the Boston Marathon bombings the month prior.

A low point came in 2012 when Jay filed a lawsuit against Dick, Justman, Klein, and Wolf over their use of The J. Geils Band name on a pending tour that would not include Jay (Duke Levine and Kevin Barry would handle guitar). Francesca Records, co-owned by Jay, had registered the trademark name to the band in 2009, allegedly without the other members' knowledge. The lawsuit was eventually resolved and dropped, with all parties claiming satisfaction. The band's final show was in September 2015. Sadly, Jay passed away on 11 April 2017.

On 10 January 1994, The J. Geils Band was inducted into the Boston Garden Hall of Fame. A point of contention for fans is that Geils have been nominated for the US Rock And Roll Hall Of Fame no fewer than five times – in 2005, 2006, 2011, 2017, and 2018 – but so far have not been inducted. What follows is a rundown of projects since the mid-1980s.

Lights Out – Peter Wolf (EMI America) (1984)
Released shortly before The J. Geils Band's final album, *Lights Out* featured some songs Wolf had brought to the band for *You're Gettin' Even*. Wolf recorded *Lights Out* with co-producer Michael Jonzun (from funk hip-hop group Jonzun Crew). It's a slick, pop/funk/hip-hop record and not as different from *You're Gettin' Even* as might be expected, since musical direction was the main reason for Wolf leaving Geils. Guest artists on *Lights Out* include Adrian Belew, Elliot Easton (The Cars), and Mick Jagger. The 11 tracks include the singles 'Lights Out' (written by Wolf and Don Covay, who had been a co-writer on 'The Usual Place', which Geils covered on *The Morning After*), 'I Need You Tonight' and 'Oo-Ee-Diddley-Bop!' Promotion included an October appearance on US television's *Saturday Night Live*. Wolf, whose band for the show included Elliot Easton and Michael Jonzun, performed 'Lights Out' and 'I Need You Tonight.' *Lights Out* was certified gold in Canada in November 1984.

'Push' – Aretha Franklin With Peter Wolf (Jeffrey E. Cohen, Narada Michael Walden) (Arista) (1985)
Wolf duetted with Aretha Franklin on this r&b dance track from her *Who's Zoomin' Who?* album. In a November 1989 *Rolling Stone* article, producer Narada Walden stated, 'a lot of (male singers) were frightened to death to sing with (Franklin)' but Wolf didn't hesitate. The 1980s synth/layered keyboard sound gives 'Push' a dated feel. The track features Carlos Santana on guitar.

'Sun City' – Artists United Against Apartheid (Stephen Van Zandt) (Manhatten) (1985)
In October 1985, Wolf was part of Steven Van Zandt's Artists United Against Apartheid, with Bono, Keith Richards, Ringo Starr, Jimmy Cliff and Bruce Springsteen. The rock/hip-hop single was a criticism and protest against South Africa's apartheid policy, and, together with the album of the same name, raised over one million dollars for anti-apartheid programs. A live version with Wolf is included on Little Steven's 2021 *Summer Of Sorcery Live!*

Rockbird – Debbie Harry (Geffen Records/Chrysalis) (1986)
Debbie Harry's (Blondie) *Rockbird* was produced and arranged by Seth Justman. Justman also co-wrote three songs and played keyboards and provided bass and drum programming for the album. Magic Dick played harp on 'I Want You', some or all of The Uptown Horns performed on four tracks, and Justman used some of the same backing singers he'd employed

on *You're Gettin' Even*. When 'In Love With Love' was issued in the UK, the team of Mike Stock, Matt Aitken, and Pete Waterman were used as additional producers, though there is little difference between the US and UK singles. Justman was part of Harry's band when she performed 'French Kissin' In The USA' and 'In Love With Love' on US TV's *Saturday Night Live* on 24 January 1987. *Rockbird* was certified gold in the UK in January 1987.

Come As You Are – Peter Wolf (EMI America) (1987)
Wolf's second solo album was more rock-oriented than *Lights Out* and notable for having five of its songs, including the hit 'Can't Get Started', written solely by Wolf. Michael Jonzun, from *Lights Out*, shares a co-write on one track and playwright/lyricist Tim Mayer co-wrote five. Arno Hecht, from The Uptown Horns, performed on the album. The song 'Come As You Are' was one of Wolf's biggest singles, reaching number 15 in the US and 29 in Canada. Bizarrely, when Facebook debuted in 2004 (as 'thefacebook'), a cropped headshot of Wolf from the back cover of *Come As You Are* was used in the web page's banner.

'Give It Time' – Patty Smyth (Rob Hyman, David Kagan) (Columbia) (1987)
Patty Smyth's (Scandal) first solo album, *Never Enough*, contained 'Give It Time', with Magic Dick. Dick comes in about two-thirds through the up-tempo rock track with, at first, fat and then sweet-sounding harp, riding over organ during the break. By the end of the solo, it's obvious it's Dick.

Smoking In The Fields – The Del Fuegos (RCA) (1989)
Smoking In The Fields, by Boston-based garage rockers The Del Fuegos, has multiple links to Geils. The album was partially recorded at Long View Farm, where Geils did most of their work for the EMI America label. Dave Thoener, who had worked with Geils from 1975's *Hotline* through 1981's *Freeze-Frame*, produced, recorded, and mixed *Smoking In The Fields*. Guest appearances include Justman on piano and organ and Dick on harmonica. One or both can be heard on much of the album, including 'Move With Me, Sister', 'I'm Inside You', 'Headlights', 'Breakaway', 'Part Of This Earth' and 'Lost Weekend.'

'Southern Crossing' – Full Circle (Columbia) (1989)
Magic Dick guests on Boston-based jazz-fusion band Full Circle's 'Southern Crossing' from the album *Myth America*. The gospel-tinged track is, at turns, wistful and uplifting. Dick weaves blues harp through piano, flute, and acoustic bass, creating a sound that wraps around the listener. In April 1989, Dick performed with Full Circle at the Boston Music Awards.

Up To No Good! – Peter Wolf (MCA) (1990)
Wolf found himself on a new record label for *Up To No Good!* In addition to vocals, Wolf played harmonica (also on harmonica was Terry McMillan).

Guests include Arno Hecht from The Uptown Horns and Barry Tashian, friend of Wolf since the late 1960s, on guitar. In the liner notes, Wolf stated the song 'Never Let It Go' is about his high school sweetheart, who later died in a car accident. This is likely the same friend who inspired Geils' 'Must Of Got Lost.' The cut '99 Worlds' was Wolf's last single to chart, reaching 77 in the US and 56 in Canada.

'Are You A Boy Or Are You A Girl' – Peter Wolf (Doug Morris, Ron Morris) (MCA) (1990)

This non-album track was the B-side to '99 Worlds.' Recorded in 1965 by The Barbarians, a Massachusetts rock band, the song was a novelty number poking fun at people questioning the trend toward long hair and tight pants in bands like The Rolling Stones. The guitars and organ in Wolf's version remain true to the original and give the song a vibe from the British Invasion of the 1960s.

'Rap The World' – Ryuichi Sakamoto (Ryuichi Sakamoto, Jungle DJ Towa Towa, Super DJ Dmitry) (Virgin Records) (1991)

Ryuichi Sakamoto might be best known as a member of Yellow Magic Orchestra, but he also released two dozen solo albums and worked on nearly 50 film soundtracks. Magic Dick plays harmonica on this electronic hip-hop number – which includes a rap in Russian – from Sakamoto's *Heartbeat* album. Dick's harp provides texture and contrast to the tune's edgy electronica.

'Rooster Blues' – Peter Wolf With Ronnie Earl And The Broadcasters (Jerry West) (1992)

'Rooster Blues' was released as a single by Lightnin' Slim in 1959. Wolf, with blues guitarist Ronnie Earl and his band The Broadcasters, recorded the track for the soundtrack to the 1991 film *Fried Green Tomatoes*. It has an early rock and roll/rockabilly revved-up attitude, with piano, harp, and guitar all getting time in the spotlight as Wolf sings, 'We've gotta rock the night, baby.'

Loose Tonight – Debbie Davies (Blind Pig Records) (1994)

Danny Klein handles bass on nine of the 11 tracks on singer and blues guitarist Debbie Davies' *Loose Tonight*. Davies, who was part of blues legend Albert Collins' band for three years starting in the late 1980s, serves up a set of contemporary blues of mostly originals with some covers added in. Klein, who also toured with Davies, is never showy and stays in the background as part of the solid rhythm section with drummer Don Castagno. Ken Pino, who introduced Klein to Davies, later formed Stonecrazy with Klein.

Bluestime – Magic Dick & Jay Geils (Rounder Records) (1994)

Though the record's title is *Bluestime,* the band that Magic Dick and Jay put together came to be known as Bluestime, with Michael 'Mudcat' Ward on bass,

Jerry Miller on guitar, and Steve Ramsay on drums. The album's Chicago blues most closely resembles the Geils's 1971 debut album but displays greater swing and jazz influences, with Jay's admiration for guitarist Charlie Christian shining through. The album was produced by Jay and Dick. Among covers of blues numbers by Little Walter, Sonny Boy Williamson, Muddy Waters, and B.B. King are two originals: 'Full Court Press' and '(I'm The) Coolest Cat In This Car.' Dick handles lead vocals, and on the instrumental 'Full Court Press', he uses the Magic Harmonicas he and Pierre Beauregard engineered and patented. Under 'Special Thanks' in the liner notes is 'The J. Geils Band.'

'Nine Below Zero' – Magic Dick & Jay Geils (Sonny Boy Williamson II) (KBCO 97.3 FM) (1995)
When the Bluestime band stopped at KBCO in Boulder, Colorado, in August 1994 while promoting their *Bluestime* album, they performed for the radio station's *Studio C* program, with this swinging blues number later appearing on *KBCO Studio C Volume 5*. Similar to their 'Whammer Jammer' performance for the show (released in 2008), 'Nine Below Zero' features jazz guitar work from Jay along with Dick's intense harp.

'You're Breakin' My Heart' – Peter Wolf And The Houseparty 5 (Harry Nilsson) (Music Masters) (1995)
Shortly after Harry Nilsson's ('Everybody's Talkin", 'Without You') passing in 1994, the two-CD *For The Love Of Harry – Everybody Sings Nilsson* was assembled, with various musicians recording their favourite Nilsson tracks. Wolf, who had known Nilsson since those *Brandy Bunch* drunken sessions with John Lennon in 1974, if not earlier, contributed the glib 'You're Breakin' My Heart', originally on Nilsson's 1972 *Son Of Schmilsson*. The brief number stomps along, with Wolf enjoying the lyrics and ad-libbing some comments along the way. The track finishes with an unequivocal 'f– you!'

Long Line – Peter Wolf (Reprise) (1996)
After some legal issues with MCA, who had issued his previous album, Wolf signed with Reprise Records. The 'Long Line' title track refers to Wolf giving himself to rock and roll for his entire life ('I've been tossed around and twisted up, I'm on the outside looking in'). The album continues the shift started with *Up To No Good!*, demonstrating a more mature rock and blues sound, but still reflects hip-hop influences on tracks like 'Romeo Is Dead.' Wolf worked with some of the same songwriters from his previous album but also wrote two tracks with Aimee Mann ('Til Tuesday), and three tracks are credited solely to Wolf. He again plays harmonica on several numbers. Brad Delp from the band Boston is among those providing backing vocals. The track 'Long Line' was issued as a single but did not chart. In 2007, *Long Line* was reissued on American Beat Records. It was reissued a second time in 2016 on Wounded Bird Records.

Little Car Blues – Magic Dick & Jay Geils (Rounder Records) (1996)
Two years after *Bluestime*, the same group of musicians (Jay, Dick, Jerry Miller, Steve Ramsay, Michael Ward) released *Little Car Blues*, another collection of blues with a jazz and swing sensibility. Dick again handles lead vocals. Along with covers of tunes by Little Walter, Charlie Parker, Willie Dixon, and Junior Wells is the original 'Bluestime Theme', written by bassist Ward, in which Dick proclaims, 'Hey, brother, we're Bluestime and it's blues time now.' The CD radiates an energy that sounds like the band had a great time recording it.

'The Last Detail' – Meliah Rage (Backstreet Records) (1996)
From Boston-based thrash metal band Meliah Rage's *Death Valley Dream* album (shown as *Death Valley Dreams* on the CD itself) comes the track 'The Last Detail.' Although it's mostly instrumental, the song features Stephen Jo Bladd on backing/harmony vocals. Bladd can be heard adding subtle 'ooh, ooh, ooooh, ooooh' vocals.

Blues Guitar Improvisation – Jay Geils (VHS) (Hot Licks Productions, Inc) (1996), rereleased (DVD) (Music Sales Corporation) (2009)
From the *Hot Licks* series comes this instructional *Blues Guitar Improvisation*. In the nearly 80-minute video, Jay explains bebop, swing, open tunings, slide guitar and more, exploring the styles of guitarists like Chuck Berry and Charlie Christian. Bluestime bandmates Michael Ward, Steve Ramsay, and Jerry Miller assist.

Fool's Parade – Peter Wolf (Mercury Records) (1998)
One of his best, Wolf's fifth solo album is another stellar effort of soul, Memphis-style rock and roll, r&b, and blues tunes, but the disc suffered from lack of promotion when Mercury Records parent company PolyGram was purchased by Seagram beverage company and then shunted to Universal Music Group.

Fool's Parade was recorded live in a small studio using analogue equipment. The disc includes nine tracks with Duke Levine on guitar, later part of The J. Geils Band tour in 2012, and three tracks featuring The Uptown Horns.

'Rollin & Tumblin' – Peter Wolf (McKinley Morganfield aka Muddy Waters) (Hybrid Recordings) (1999)
This number was recorded live at the Kennedy Center in Washington, DC, on 11 October 1997 as a tribute to Muddy Waters. The CD, titled *Tribute To Muddy Waters – King Of The Blues*, consists of Waters' songs performed by acts like Buddy Guy, John Hiatt, and Phoebe Snow. Wolf turns in a performance of 'Rollin & Tumblin', with Charlie Musselwhite on harmonica and G.E. Smith on guitar. Wolf also wrote the CD liner notes.

Standing In The Shadows Of Motown Soundtrack (Hip-O/Motown) (2002)

Seth Justman's brother Paul had worked with J. Geils as far back as 1973's *Ladies Invited*. Paul's multi-award-winning documentary *Standing In The Shadows Of Motown* tells the story of The Funk Brothers, the house band who performed on most Motown hits from 1959 through the early 1970s. The Grammy Award-winning soundtrack, consisting of contemporary takes on Motown classics, credits Seth Justman with 'handclaps' and for the 'arrangement of the breakdown section' of 'What Becomes Of The Brokenhearted', performed by Joan Osborne ('One Of Us') and The Funk Brothers.

Sleepless – Peter Wolf (Artemis) (2002)

Sleepless is 12 tracks of soul, blues, country, and rock and proves to be another high point in Wolf's solo career. Magic Dick and Keith Richards help out on Sonny Boy Williamson's 'Too Close Together', and Mick Jagger plays harp and harmonises with Wolf on the country-tinged 'Nothing But The Wheel' (a hit for Patty Loveless in 1993). Steve Earle ('Copperhead Road') duets on 'Some Things You Don't Want To Know' and The Uptown Horns perform on the title track. *Sleepless* contains a reworking of 'Run Silent, Run Deep', originally on Wolf's 1987 *Come As You Are*, this time with a harsher attitude. Another restyled tune is Otis Rush's 'Homework', which Geils covered for their 1970 debut album. Here, it's a low-key, stripped-down number with Wolf growling the lyrics. Somewhat belatedly, Wolf appeared on US television's PBS *Soundstage* in July 2004. Among the ten numbers Wolf performed on the 55-minute program were three Geils tracks ('Homework', 'Believe In Me', 'Cry One More Time') and three tracks from *Sleepless* ('Growin' Pain', 'Nothing But The Wheel', 'Sleepless').

New Guitar Summit – Jay Geils, Duke Robillard, Gerry Beaudoin (Stoney Plain Records) (2004)

Jay stated many times that jazz was one of his first loves, but he never had the time to learn it properly until the 1990s. With *New Guitar Summit*, Jay, Duke Robillard, and Gerry Beaudoin put together an album of swing jazz tunes with a blues influence, weaving their guitar parts over, under and around each other. John Turner on bass and Gordon Grottenthaler on drums complete the band. It's a mostly instrumental CD, with vocals on two songs by Robillard and one by Beaudoin. The 11 tracks include covers of songs by jazz greats like Benny Goodman and the Gershwin brothers but also feature three numbers written by Beaudoin.

New Guitar Summit Live At The Stoneham Theatre (DVD) – Jay Geils, Duke Robillard, Gerry Beaudoin (Stoney Plain Records) (2004)

Showcasing the same musicians and brilliant playing as the *New Guitar Summit* CD, this DVD consists of seven tracks. Four of those appeared on the band's studio record and three ('Broadway', 'Lonely Boy Blues', 'Flying Home') are new. There's no wild stage show, just a chance to see these musicians showing their stuff. The set runs about an hour, with another 20 minutes of interviews.

Jay Geils Plays Jazz! – Jay Geils With Scott Hamilton Et Al. (Stony Plain Records) 2004
Jay dedicated this album to his father, 'who took me to see Louis Armstrong and the All-Stars when I was 12 years old, for which I am eternally grateful.' In addition to Jay's core band (Al Wilson, with Gordon Grottenthaler and John Turner from New Guitar Summit), numerous guests appear, including Crispin Cioe (The Uptown Horns), Jerry Miller (Bluestime), and Gerry Beaudoin (New Guitar Summit). Jay worked in the style of the earliest jazz recordings, putting the musicians in the same room at the same time, using just a few microphones. *Jay Geils Plays Jazz!* was recorded live with minimal overdubs, save for Crispin Cioe's layered horns on 'L.B. Blues.' With these tracks, Jay pays tribute to big names like Duke Ellington, Roland Kirk, and Benny Goodman and spotlights lesser-knowns like Dickie Thompson.

Nail It! – The Installers (Francesca Records) (2004)
Released on the record label co-owned by Jay Geils, blues-rock band The Installers' *Nail It!* was also produced and co-engineered by Jay. Even before recording The Installers, Jay occasionally sat in with the band at some of their shows. On *Nail It!*, he's featured on seven tracks, playing slide guitar, rhythm guitar, guitar solos on three cuts, and synth horns (providing the horn arrangement as well) on the closing number.

Stonecrazy – Stonecrazy (Black Rose Records) (2005)
Danny Klein's blues band (with Babe Pino, Ken Pino, and Mark Hylander) spent about three years putting together *Stonecrazy*, recording ten covers – by artists like Johnny Copeland and Joe 'Guitar' Hughes – and four originals. Ken Pino had played in Johnny Copeland's band, and Ken was the one who introduced Klein to blues guitarist Debbie Davies in the early 1990s when Klein was getting back into music. The CD was produced by Jay, who also plays on three cuts, handling rhythm guitar on one, rhythm and a solo on another, and a solo on Otis Rush's 'Homework', which The J. Geils Band had recorded for their own debut album. Seth Justman is also present, contributing keyboards on four songs. Though the band was named after Buddy Guy's song 'Stonecrazy', that tune is not covered here.

Learn Chicago Blues Guitar With 6 Great Masters! (DVD) (Music Sales Corporation) (2005)
Part of the *Hot Licks Style Series*, this short DVD features a chapter with Jay providing lessons on Chicago blues. He demonstrates playing 'B.B. King

Style', 'Vibrato' and 'Blues Styling.' Others providing lessons on the disc include Buddy Guy and Otis Rush.

The Kings Of Strings – Jay Geils And Gerry Beaudoin Featuring Aaron Weinstein (Arbors Records) (2006)

Similar to *New Guitar Summit*, Gerry Beaudoin and Jay return as The Kings of Strings, playing swing jazz and Tin Pan Alley tunes, this time adding Aaron Weinstein on violin and mandolin. Weinstein was one of the musicians, with Jay, Seth Justman, and Magic Dick, who contributed to the PBS 2006 documentary *Country Boys*. Along with a couple of Beaudoin originals, Jay, Beaudoin, and Weinstein cover tunes like 'Take The A Train', 'Minor Swing' and 'Sweet Georgia Brown.'

'Gyro Ball' – Danny Bernini (Danny Bernini, Loren Harriet) (EMI Music Special Markets) (2007)

The somewhat mythical gyroball pitch is used by baseball players in Japan and came to be known in the US through Daisuke 'Dice-K' Matsuzaka. Taken from *Music From The Mound*, released around the time the Boston Red Sox signed Daisuke, 'Gyro Ball' features Magic Dick on harp and Nuno Bettencourt (Extreme) on guitar. The CD consists of songs Daisuke listened to before games, along with one of his 'walk-up' songs that was played as he approached home plate to bat. 'Gyro Ball' is the sole track specifically recorded with Daisuke in mind. It's a hypnotic hip-hop number with a chaotic montage of sounds, including a baseball announcer proclaiming Daisuke's gyroball 'was everywhere, it was nowhere.' Dick's harmonica riff plays over most of the track. A percentage of sales from the CD went to the Red Sox charity foundation.

Jazz Thing II – Randy Bachman & New Guitar Summit (Ranbach Music) (2007)

Recorded 'one afternoon in the spring of '06 in Vancouver', this disc brings together Duke Robillard, Gerry Beaudoin, and Jay (with John Turner on bass and Gordon Grottenthaler on drums) from *New Guitar Summit* with Randy Bachman (Guess Who, Bachman Turner Overdrive, solo). The guitarists work out seven jazz/blues tunes, including a couple of Mose Allison numbers, Del Shannon's 'Runaway', and three Bachman songs, including 'Takin' Care Of Business.' The four guitarists play without stepping on each other, putting the music first. Bachman handles vocals on all tracks.

Command Performance – The Legendary Rhythm & Blues Revue (Delta Groove Music) (2008)

Soul-blues guitarist and singer Tommy Castro brought together Ronnie Baker Brooks, Deanna Bogart, and Magic Dick for this 13-song live CD recorded in October 2007. Dick performs on six tracks, including 'Whammer Jammer' and

'Looking For A Love.' Dick has been part of Castro's Rhythm & Blues Revue (often performing on the Blues Cruise) on and off through 2022.

Shivers – New Guitar Summit (Stoney Plain) (2008)
New Guitar Summit (Jay, Duke Robillard, and Gerry Beaudoin) return with another disc of swing jazz/blues. Two of the tracks ('Everybody's Cryin' Mercy', 'Your Mind Is On Vacation') feature Randy Bachman and are taken from 2007's *Jazz Thing II*. *Shivers* includes several original songs in addition to jazz standards.

Toe Tappin' Jazz – Jay Geils (North Star Music) (2009)
Recorded similarly to 2004's *Jay Geils Plays Jazz!* but allowing for more overdubs and separation of the instruments in the process, *Toe Tappin' Jazz* is 12 tracks of loose, easy-flowing music. With Jay are Gordon Grottenthaler, John Turner and Gerry Beaudoin from New Guitar Summit. Horns and piano are more prominent on this CD, but Jay's playing (on vibraphone as well as guitar) remains the centrepiece.

Midnight Souvenirs – Peter Wolf (Verve) (2010)
Wolf's seventh solo LP showcases soul, rock, country, and other styles, featuring plenty of guest performers. The album begins with 'Tragedy', a duet with singer-songwriter Shelby Lynne. Neko Case (New Pornographers) joins Wolf on 'The Green Fields Of Summer', and Crispin Cioe and Arno Hecht from The Uptown Horns assist on three cuts. Country music legend Merle Haggard duets on the gentle lament 'It's Too Late For Me.' 'Thick As Thieves', from 1987's *Come As You Are*, has been reworked with a more organic feel. As part of the record's promotion, Wolf and Shelby Lynne performed 'Tragedy' on US TV's *Late Night With Jimmy Fallon* in April 2010. Two months later, Wolf appeared on *Late Show With David Letterman*, performing 'I Don't Wanna Know', playing harmonica in addition to singing. The tracks 'Overnight Lows' and 'Always Asking For You' appeared in the 2011 film *Hall Pass*. In addition to being issued on CD, *Midnight Souvenirs* was released as a double LP. *Midnight Souvenirs* was awarded the 2010 *Album Of The Year* at the Boston Music Awards.

'(Your Love Keeps Lifting Me) Higher And Higher' (A Tribute To Jackie Wilson) – Bruce Springsteen Et Al. (Gary Jackson, Raynard Miner, Carl Smith) (Time Life) (2010)
To celebrate 25 years of the Rock And Roll Hall Of Fame, two nights of concerts were held at New York's Madison Square Garden in October 2009. Closing the first night was this performance of '(Your Love Keeps Lifting Me) Higher And Higher', made famous by Jackie Wilson and issued on *The 25th Anniversary Rock & Roll Hall Of Fame Concerts*. Bruce Springsteen leads the E Street Band along with John Fogerty, Darlene Love, Billy Joel, and Sam

Moore. Although not seen in the video until near the very end of the song and not truly heard on the CD, Wolf assists with backing vocals. It's a full circle moment for Wolf, who can be heard injecting some lines from 'Higher And Higher' in 'Musta Got Lost' off 1976's *Blow Your Face Out*.

'Meet Me At Mary's Place' – Seth Justman And Peter Gammons (Sam Cooke) (ABKCO) (2012)

To celebrate a century of Boston's Fenway Park (home of the Red Sox baseball team), *Fenway Park Greatest Hits: 100 Year Anniversary Of Fenway Park*, a CD of baseball and Boston-related tracks, was released in January 2012. Seth Justman worked with sportswriter and television sports analyst Peter Gammons on the soulful, blues-influenced 'Meet Me At Mary's Place.' Written by Sam Cooke and based on Cooke's own 'Meet Me At The Twisting Place', the song proclaims 'there's gonna be a party goin' on' and 'we're gonna have us a ball today.' Two-thirds through the song, the chorus is revised to 'Why don't you meet me at Fenway Park.' Justman handles organ and piano and the song rocks along at an easy pace. A percentage of sales from the CD went to the Red Sox charity foundation.

American Girl – Jeff Pitchell And Jay Geils (Vizztone Label Group) (2012)

Jay shifted back towards blues on this disc with Blues Hall of Famer Jeff Pitchell. The songs are a mix of smouldering blues, some r&b, and a little soul. Jay, who had sat in with Pitchell on stage a few times over the previous year, helped produce the album and plays slide guitar on 'Prisoner Of Love' and lead on 'T-Bone Shuffle.' Jay also plays lead on two tracks representing his earlier days: 'Homework' and 'Hard Drivin' Man.' Gerry Beaudoin, from New Guitar Summit, takes a lead on 'T-Bone Shuffle.'

'Two Steps Forward' – Tommy Castro & The Painkillers (Tommy Castro) (Alligator Records) (2014)

Magic Dick features prominently on this fast-rocking, gritty blues number with Tommy Castro from Castro's *The Devil You Know* album. Dick has worked with Castro in The Legendary Rhythm & Blues Revue since at least 2007, so the pairing is a natural. The track powers along and at the break, Dick turns in a rapid-fire solo, sounding at times like an organ and pushing like a locomotive.

A Cure For Loneliness – Peter Wolf (Concord) (2016)

Wolf's eighth solo album is another strong disc of blues, r&b, country, and rock. He stated in multiple interviews that he structured the album with a beginning, middle, and end, the way albums were made in his early days in music. Wolf performs harp on six of the tracks and the opening track, 'Rolling On', is a statement similar to 1996's 'Long Line' – that Wolf is still here, still making his way through life. Wolf wrote 'It's Raining' with Don Covay, his co-writer for 1984's 'Lights Out', and who co-wrote 'The Usual Place', which Geils covered on 1971's *The Morning After*. Wolf begins 'It's Raining' by stating, 'I wrote this song with the great Don Covay and I'd like to dedicate it to the one and only Bobby Womack.' The tune was intended to be a duet with Womack (who had a hit with 'Lookin' For A Love' in 1962 when he was in The Valentinos, almost a decade before Geils scored big with the song), but Womack passed away before they had a chance to record together.

Although the album contains a cut titled 'Tragedy', it's not the same-named song from 2010's *Midnight Souvenirs*. This 'Tragedy' is a cover of the 1959 hit by Thomas Wayne and The DeLons. Also on the album are two live tracks: 'Wastin' Time' and 'Love Stinks.' The reworked 'Love Stinks' is done Bill Monroe bluegrass-style, with Duke Levine on mandolin. Wolf begins the track with, 'Let's take 'em to the Appalachian Hills, come on.' *A Cure For Loneliness* was also issued on vinyl.

About Time – Magic Dick And Shun Ng (MDSN Records) (2016)
Recorded live with no overdubs, *About Time* is a six-song EP from the duo of Magic Dick on harp and some vocals and Shun Ng on acoustic guitar (fingerstyle) and most vocals. After meeting through Dick's friend Ralph Jaccodine, Dick and Ng started working together in 2013, creating their unique sound. *About Time* features three cover tunes (the jump blues 'Let The Good Times Roll', Jimi Hendrix's 'Fire', James Brown's 'Papa's Got A Brand New Bag'), two originals (the locomotive instrumental 'Dixiology', the bluesy 'Space') and a powerful, stripped down take on 'Whammer Jammer.' Five tracks were recorded in a studio, with 'Dixiology' captured in front of an audience at the Fallout Shelter in Norwood, Massachusetts.

Official Compilations

With any legacy act, there are innumerable overlapping retrospectives, often created with no input from band members. Because Geils' career spanned two record labels, most collections consist of tracks exclusively from one or the other. These are some of the more notable compilations. Still not on any album is 'Magic's Mood' (B-side to 'Peanut Butter', 1976).

Best Of The J. Geils Band (Atlantic) (1979)

With a cover depicting a bowling ball delivering a ten pin strike, this was Geils' first compilation. After the success of *Sanctuary* on EMI America, Atlantic Records released *Best Of*, consisting of nine tracks from five albums. It's a solid collection for anyone interested in learning about the earlier years of the band, but nothing from the first two studio albums is included, nor are the *Ladies Invited* and *Hotline* releases represented. 'Whammer Jammer' and 'Looking For A Love' are sourced from *Full House*. *Bloodshot* provides 'Southside Shuffle', 'Give It To Me' and '(Ain't Nothing But A) House Party.' From *Nightmares* are 'Detroit Breakdown' and 'Must Of Got Lost' (listed here as 'Musta Got Lost'). 'Where Did Our Love Go' is not the studio single but comes from *Blow Your Face Out*, and 'I Do' is the studio cut from *Monkey Island*. The back cover photo of the band is by David Gahr, who handled the photos on *Bloodshot*. Gahr took this photo in New York on 12 June 1974, five years before it was used on *Best Of*.

Best Of The J. Geils Band Two (Atlantic) (1980)

Following the even greater success of *Love Stinks* on EMI America, Atlantic issued *Best Of Two*, another nine-track collection, using Lou Brooks' artwork from the back of *Hotline* for the front cover here. This is the only album to include 'Trying To Live My Life Without You', the 1977 B-side recorded during the *Monkey Island* sessions but not included on that album. Although this collection, like the first *Best Of*, overlooks the debut album, it does contain one track from *The Morning After* ('Cry One More Time'), one from *Ladies Invited* ('The Lady Makes Demands'), and two from *Hotline* ('Love-Itis', 'Mean Love'). It also pulls from *Full House*, *Nightmares*, and *Monkey Island*. Together, *Best Of* and *Best Of Two* make a respectable retrospective of the Atlantic years. *Best Of Two* has never been issued on CD.

Flashback – The Best Of The J. Geils Band (EMI America (1985)

A ten-song collection from the EMI America albums, *Flashback* covers *Sanctuary* through *Showtime!* (and ignores *You're Gettin' Even*). This album has the big hits and best-known tracks from the latter-day Geils. 'Centerfold', 'Freeze-Frame', 'Flamethrower', 'Love Stinks', 'Come Back', 'One Last Kiss' and 'I Do (Live)' are all here, alongside 'Just Can't Wait', 'Wild Man' and 'Land Of A Thousand Dances (Live).' The record cover has a very 1980s look with florescent colours and video stills. The sole complaint is that several of the songs are the single edits rather than the longer album tracks.

Anthology – Houseparty (Rhino) (1993)
Anthology is the best, most encompassing Geils retrospective. As is nearly always the case with Rhino Records, this is an excellent compilation and covers much of Geils' music from both of its record labels. Two CDs and 38 tracks, *Anthology* includes the singles 'Dead Presidents', 'Peanut Butter' and the studio version of 'Where Did Our Love Go', which have never appeared on any other album (the cassette features 32 tracks and excludes 'Peanut Butter'). Three songs are single edits. The tracks are presented mostly in chronological order, the exception being that all live tracks are placed on the first half of the second disc for a concert flow. *Anthology* does not include anything from *Ladies Invited* or *You're Gettin' Even*.

Champions Of Rock (Disky) (1996) Europe Only
From the EMI years, notable for being probably the only compilation that features tracks from *You're Gettin' Even* ('You're Gettin' Even While I'm Gettin' Odd', 'Concealed Weapons'). It's also unusual for its inclusion of 'No Anchovies, Please' from *Love Stinks*.

Best Of The J. Geils Band (Capitol) (2006)
A single CD with 18 tracks, *Best Of The J. Geils Band* leans heavily toward the EMI America years but does include five songs from the Atlantic catalogue. The Atlantic tracks are from *Full House* and *Blow Your Face Out*, along with the single edit of 'Give It To Me.' The EMI selections include all the big hits, from 'Centerfold' and 'Freeze-Frame' to 'Love Stinks' and 'I Do (Live).'

Covered By Geils (Rhino) (2006)
Rhino Records highlights 12 songs from the Atlantic years, all written by and initially recorded by other artists and later covered by Geils. There are no rarities or previously unreleased tracks. *Covered* includes such cuts as 'First I Look At The Purse', 'Looking For A Love', 'Love-Itis' and 'Serves You Right To Suffer.'

Original Album Series (Atlantic Rhino) (2009)
In 2009, Atlantic/Rhino released a five-CD budget package of the first five Geils albums: *The J. Geils Band*, *The Morning After*, *'Live' Full House*, *Bloodshot*, and *Ladies Invited*.

Each disc is housed in a slipcase replica of the original album cover, although *The Morning After* backside omits the track listing, likely due to lack of legibility on the small cover. No bonus tracks and no liner notes are included. Still, it provides an easy way to collect those early albums on the cheap.

Original Album Series Vol 2 (Atlantic Warner) (2014)
Five years after the first *Original Album Series*, Atlantic/Warner returned with a second five-CD budget packet for the next five J. Geils albums: *Nightmares ...And Other Tales From The Vinyl Jungle, Hotline, Live – Blow Your Face Out, Monkey Island* and *Best Of*. Like the first *Album Series*, all five CDs are housed in slipcase replicas of the original album covers, and there are no bonus tracks or liner notes. With all the original albums presented in the two volumes of this series, *Best Of* is redundant here.

Bibliography

References
Billboard magazine – billboard.com
British Phonographic Industry – bpi.co.uk
Discogs Marketplace – discogs.com
Funky Judge Fan Site – jgeilsband.wordpress.com
Music Canada – musiccanada.com
Music Museum of New England – mmone.org
Nelson, Steve, *Gettin' Home: An Odyssey Through The '60s* – gettinhome.com
Recording Industry Association of America – riaa.com
Wolfgang's Archives – wolfgangs.com
Danny Klein – dannykleinsfullhouse.com
Magic Dick – magicdick.com
Peter Wolf – peterwolf.com

Interviews
Crispin Cioe (phone) 20 Dec 2023, (email) Jan, Feb 2024
Corriston, Peter (phone) 20 Nov 2023
Cullen, Susan (email, phone) Nov, Dec 2023
Glennon, Patricia (messenger) Nov, Dec 2023, Jul 2024
Hinkle, Bob (phone) 16 Nov 2023
Klein, Daniel (phone) 10 Nov 2023
Lanning, Paul (email) Jan 2024
MacWeeney, Alen (phone) 16 Nov 2023
Mazza, Jim (phone) 3 Jun 2023
Medious, Mario (phone) 15 Nov 2023
Nelson, Steve (email) May, Dec 2023
Paley, Stephen (phone) 21 Jun 2023
Paret, Raymond (phone) 13 Nov 2023
Robinson, Francis (email) Nov, Dec 2023
Salwitz, Richard (messenger video) 4 Jun 2023
Shapiro, Paul (phone) 3 May 2023, (email) May, Dec 2023
Szymczyk, Bill (phone) 8 Apr 2024, (email) Apr, Jun 2024
Thoener, David (email) Nov, Dec 2023
Weschler, Thomas (email) 22 May 2023

Also available from Sonicbond

On Track Series
Allman Brothers Band – Andrew Wild 978-1-78952-252-5
Tori Amos – Lisa Torem 978-1-78952-142-9
Aphex Twin – Beau Waddell 978-1-78952-267-9
Asia – Peter Braidis 978-1-78952-099-6
Badfinger – Robert Day-Webb 978-1-878952-176-4
Barclay James Harvest – Keith And Monica Domone 978-1-78952-067-5
Beck – Arthur Lizie 978-1-78952-258-7
The Beatles – Andrew Wild 978-1-78952-009-5
The Beatles Solo 1969-1980 – Andrew Wild 978-1-78952-030-9
Blue Oyster Cult – Jacob Holm-Lupo 978-1-78952-007-1
Blur – Matt Bishop 978-178952-164-1
Marc Bolan And T.rex – Peter Gallagher 978-1-78952-124-5
Kate Bush – Bill Thomas 978-1-78952-097-2
Camel – Hamish Kuzminski 978-1-78952-040-8
Captain Beefheart – Opher Goodwin 978-1-78952-235-8
Caravan – Andy Boot 978-1-78952-127-6
Cardiacs – Eric Benac 978-1-78952-131-3
Nick Cave And The Bad Seeds – Dominic Sanderson 978-1-78952-240-2
Eric Clapton Solo – Andrew Wild 978-1-78952-141-2
The Clash – Nick Assirati 978-1-78952-077-4
Elvis Costello And The Attractions – Georg Purvis 978-1-78952-129-0
Crosby, Stills & Nash – Andrew Wild 978-1-78952-039-2
Creedence Clearwater Revival – Tony Thompson 978-178952-237-2
The Damned – Morgan Brown 978-1-78952-136-8
Deep Purple And Rainbow 1968-79 – Steve Pilkington 978-1-78952-002-6
Dire Straits – Andrew Wild 978-1-78952-044-6
The Doors – Tony Thompson 978-1-78952-137-5
Dream Theater – Jordan Blum 978-1-78952-050-7
Eagles – John Van Der Kiste 978-1-78952-260-0
Earth, Wind And Fire – Bud Wilkins 978-1-78952-272-3
Electric Light Orchestra – Barry Delve 978-1-78952-152-8
Emerson Lake And Palmer – Mike Goode 978-1-78952-000-2
Fairport Convention – Kevan Furbank 978-1-78952-051-4
Peter Gabriel – Graeme Scarfe 978-1-78952-138-2
Genesis – Stuart Macfarlane 978-1-78952-005-7
Gentle Giant – Gary Steel 978-1-78952-058-3
Gong – Kevan Furbank 978-1-78952-082-8
Green Day – William E. Spevack 978-1-78952-261-7
Hall And Oates – Ian Abrahams 978-1-78952-167-2
Hawkwind – Duncan Harris 978-1-78952-052-1
Peter Hammill – Richard Rees Jones 978-1-78952-163-4
Roy Harper – Opher Goodwin 978-1-78952-130-6
Jimi Hendrix – Emma Stott 978-1-78952-175-7
The Hollies – Andrew Darlington 978-1-78952-159-7
Horslips – Richard James 978-1-78952-263-1
The Human League And The Sheffield Scene – Andrew Darlington 978-1-78952-186-3
The Incredible String Band – Tim Moon 978-1-78952-107-8

Also available from Sonicbond

Iron Maiden – Steve Pilkington 978-1-78952-061-3
Joe Jackson – Richard James 978-1-78952-189-4
Jefferson Airplane – Richard Butterworth 978-1-78952-143-6
Jethro Tull – Jordan Blum 978-1-78952-016-3
Elton John In The 1970s – Peter Kearns 978-1-78952-034-7
Billy Joel – Lisa Torem 978-1-78952-183-2
Judas Priest – John Tucker 978-1-78952-018-7
Kansas – Kevin Cummings 978-1-78952-057-6
The Kinks – Martin Hutchinson 978-1-78952-172-6
Korn – Matt Karpe 978-1-78952-153-5
Led Zeppelin – Steve Pilkington 978-1-78952-151-1
Level 42 – Matt Philips 978-1-78952-102-3
Little Feat – Georg Purvis - 978-1-78952-168-9
Aimee Mann – Jez Rowden 978-1-78952-036-1
Joni Mitchell – Peter Kearns 978-1-78952-081-1
The Moody Blues – Geoffrey Feakes 978-1-78952-042-2
Motorhead – Duncan Harris 978-1-78952-173-3
Nektar – Scott Meze – 978-1-78952-257-0
New Order – Dennis Remmer – 978-1-78952-249-5
Nightwish – Simon Mcmurdo – 978-1-78952-270-9
Laura Nyro – Philip Ward 978-1-78952-182-5
Mike Oldfield – Ryan Yard 978-1-78952-060-6
Opeth – Jordan Blum 978-1-78-952-166-5
Pearl Jam – Ben L. Connor 978-1-78952-188-7
Tom Petty – Richard James 978-1-78952-128-3
Pink Floyd – Richard Butterworth 978-1-78952-242-6
The Police – Pete Braidis 978-1-78952-158-0
Porcupine Tree – Nick Holmes 978-1-78952-144-3
Queen – Andrew Wild 978-1-78952-003-3
Radiohead – William Allen 978-1-78952-149-8
Rancid – Paul Matts 989-1-78952-187-0
Renaissance – David Detmer 978-1-78952-062-0
Reo Speedwagon – Jim Romag 978-1-78952-262-4
The Rolling Stones 1963-80 – Steve Pilkington 978-1-78952-017-0
The Smiths And Morrissey – Tommy Gunnarsson 978-1-78952-140-5
Spirit – Rev. Keith A. Gordon – 978-1-78952- 248-8
Stackridge – Alan Draper 978-1-78952-232-7
Status Quo The Frantic Four Years – Richard James 978-1-78952-160-3
Steely Dan – Jez Rowden 978-1-78952-043-9
Steve Hackett – Geoffrey Feakes 978-1-78952-098-9
Tears For Fears – Paul Clark - 978-178952-238-9
Thin Lizzy – Graeme Stroud 978-1-78952-064-4
Tool – Matt Karpe 978-1-78952-234-1
Toto – Jacob Holm-Lupo 978-1-78952-019-4
U2 – Eoghan Lyng 978-1-78952-078-1
Ufo – Richard James 978-1-78952-073-6
Van Der Graaf Generator – Dan Coffey 978-1-78952-031-6
Van Halen – Morgan Brown – 9781-78952-256-3
The Who – Geoffrey Feakes 978-1-78952-076-7

Also available from Sonicbond

Roy Wood And The Move – James R Turner 978-1-78952-008-8
Yes – Stephen Lambe 978-1-78952-001-9
Frank Zappa 1966 To 1979 – Eric Benac 978-1-78952-033-0
Warren Zevon – Peter Gallagher 978-1-78952-170-2
10cc – Peter Kearns 978-1-78952-054-5

Decades Series
The Bee Gees In The 1960s – Andrew Mon Hughes Et Al 978-1-78952-148-1
The Bee Gees In The 1970s – Andrew Mon Hughes Et Al 978-1-78952-179-5
Black Sabbath In The 1970s – Chris Sutton 978-1-78952-171-9
Britpop – Peter Richard Adams And Matt Pooler 978-1-78952-169-6
Phil Collins In The 1980s – Andrew Wild 978-1-78952-185-6
Alice Cooper In The 1970s – Chris Sutton 978-1-78952-104-7
Alice Cooper In The 1980s – Chris Sutton 978-1-78952-259-4
Curved Air In The 1970s – Laura Shenton 978-1-78952-069-9
Donovan In The 1960s – Jeff Fitzgerald 978-1-78952-233-4
Bob Dylan In The 1980s – Don Klees 978-1-78952-157-3
Brian Eno In The 1970s – Gary Parsons 978-1-78952-239-6
Faith No More In The 1990s – Matt Karpe 978-1-78952-250-1
Fleetwood Mac In The 1970s – Andrew Wild 978-1-78952-105-4
Fleetwood Mac In The 1980s – Don Klees 978-178952-254-9
Focus In The 1970s – Stephen Lambe 978-1-78952-079-8
Free And Bad Company In The 1970s – John Van Der Kiste 978-1-78952-178-8
Genesis In The 1970s – Bill Thomas 978178952-146-7
George Harrison In The 1970s – Eoghan Lyng 978-1-78952-174-0
Kiss In The 1970s – Peter Gallagher 978-1-78952-246-4
Manfred Mann's Earth Band In The 1970s – John Van Der Kiste 978178952-243-3
Marillion In The 1980s – Nathaniel Webb 978-1-78952-065-1
Van Morrison In The 1970s – Peter Childs - 978-1-78952-241-9
Mott The Hoople And Ian Hunter In The 1970s – John Van Der Kiste 978-1-78-952-162-7
Pink Floyd In The 1970s – Georg Purvis 978-1-78952-072-9
Suzi Quatro In The 1970s – Darren Johnson 978-1-78952-236-5
Queen In The 1970s – James Griffiths 978-1-78952-265-5
Roxy Music In The 1970s – Dave Thompson 978-1-78952-180-1
Slade In The 1970s – Darren Johnson 978-1-78952-268-6
Status Quo In The 1980s – Greg Harper 978-1-78952-244-0
Tangerine Dream In The 1970s – Stephen Palmer 978-1-78952-161-0
The Sweet In The 1970s – Darren Johnson 978-1-78952-139-9
Uriah Heep In The 1970s – Steve Pilkington 978-1-78952-103-0
Van Der Graaf Generator In The 1970s – Steve Pilkington 978-1-78952-245-7
Rick Wakeman In The 1970s – Geoffrey Feakes 978-1-78952-264-8
Yes In The 1980s – Stephen Lambe With David Watkinson 978-1-78952-125-8

On Screen Series
Carry On… – Stephen Lambe 978-1-78952-004-0
David Cronenberg – Patrick Chapman 978-1-78952-071-2
Doctor Who: The David Tennant Years – Jamie Hailstone 978-1-78952-066-8
James Bond – Andrew Wild 978-1-78952-010-1
Monty Python – Steve Pilkington 978-1-78952-047-7

Also available from Sonicbond

Seinfeld Seasons 1 To 5 – Stephen Lambe 978-1-78952-012-5

Other Books
1967: A Year In Psychedelic Rock 978-1-78952-155-9
1970: A Year In Rock – John Van Der Kiste 978-1-78952-147-4
1973: The Golden Year Of Progressive Rock 978-1-78952-165-8
Babysitting A Band On The Rocks – G.d. Praetorius 978-1-78952-106-1
Eric Clapton Sessions – Andrew Wild 978-1-78952-177-1
Derek Taylor: For Your Radioactive Children –
Andrew Darlington 978-1-78952-038-5
The Golden Road: The Recording History Of The Grateful Dead –
John Kilbride 978-1-78952-156-6
Iggy And The Stooges On Stage 1967-1974 – Per Nilsen 978-1-78952-101-6
Jon Anderson And The Warriors – The Road To Yes –
David Watkinson 978-1-78952-059-0
Magic: The David Paton Story – David Paton 978-1-78952-266-2
Misty: The Music Of Johnny Mathis – Jakob Baekgaard 978-1-78952-247-1
Nu Metal: A Definitive Guide – Matt Karpe 978-1-78952-063-7
Tommy Bolin: In And Out Of Deep Purple – Laura Shenton 978-1-78952-070-5
Maximum Darkness – Deke Leonard 978-1-78952-048-4
The Twang Dynasty – Deke Leonard 978-1-78952-049-1

And Many More To Come!

www.ingramcontent.com/pod-product-compliance
Lightning Source LLC
Chambersburg PA
CBHW052143070526
44585CB00017B/1952